READING MACHIAVELLI

Reading Machiavelli

SCANDALOUS BOOKS, SUSPECT ENGAGEMENTS, AND THE VIRTUE OF POPULIST POLITICS

JOHN P. McCORMICK

PRINCETON UNIVERSITY PRESS
PRINCETON & OXFORD

Published by Princeton University Press
41 William Street, Princeton, New Jersey 08540
6 Oxford Street, Woodstock, Oxfordshire OX20 1TR

press.princeton.edu

Library of Congress Control Number 2018935644
ISBN 978-0-691-18350-3

British Library Cataloging-in-Publication Data is available

Editorial: Rob Tempio and Matt Rohal
Production Editorial: Jill Harris
Jacket Design: Pamela Schnitter
Jacket Credit: Stefano Ussi, "Niccolò Machiavelli in his study," 1894.
Production: Jacqueline Poirier
Copyeditor: Lynn Worth

This book has been composed in Arno

Printed on acid-free paper. ∞

Printed in the United States of America

10 9 8 7 6 5 4 3 2 1

For Alyssa

I will say something that will seem crazy to you; I am going to propose a plan that will seem to you either foolhardy or ridiculous. Nevertheless, the times require audacious deliberations, unusual, and strange. You and everyone else who know how to reason over things of this world know that the people are varying and foolish. Nevertheless, however much they are, very often they say precisely what should be done.

—LETTER FROM NICCOLÒ MACHIAVELLI TO
MESSER FRANCESCO GUICCIARDINI
15 MARCH 1526, FLORENCE

CONTENTS

ABBREVIATIONS FOR
MACHIAVELLI'S WRITINGS

P   *The Prince,* or *On Principalities* (composed 1513, published
    1532). Niccolò Machiavelli, *Il Principe.* In *Opere I: I Primi
    Scritti Politici.* Edited by Corrado Vivanti (Turin:
    Einaudi-Gallimard, 1997), 114–192.

D   *Discourses on Titus Livy's First Ten Books* (composed c.
    1513–1518, published 1531). Niccolò Machiavelli,
    Discorsi sopra la prima deca di Tito Livio. In
    Opere I, 193–525.

FH *Florentine Histories* (composed c. 1520–25, published 1532).
    Niccolò Machiavelli, *Istorie Fiorentine.* Edited by Franco
    Gaeta (Milan: Feltrinelli, 1962), 68–577

READING MACHIAVELLI

Vulgarity and Virtuosity

MACHIAVELLI'S ELUSIVE "EFFECTUAL TRUTH"

NICCOLÒ MACHIAVELLI would have undoubtedly secured enduring fame for any one of the roles he so adeptly performed during his life in and out of Renaissance Florence: diplomat, military strategist, civil servant, poet, playwright. However, it was in his capacity as political philosopher that Machiavelli earned eternal renown by sparking several of the most intense scholarly controversies and by inspiring some of the most profound political changes in Western history. Not without reason, many commentators consider Machiavelli the father of modern political thought or modern political science— some even ordain him the founder of "modernity" itself. Yet the specific meaning and precise objectives of his political writings remain elusive. Was Machiavelli an amoral proponent of tyranny or a stalwart partisan of liberty? A neutral technician of power politics or a devout Italian patriot? An anticlerical reviver of pagan virtue or a devious initiator of modern nihilism? Most simply, to what extent was Machiavelli a "Machiavellian"? These questions, among countless others concerning the fundamental core of the Florentine's thought, will continue to generate contentious debates for as long as people reflect seriously on political affairs.

In this spirit, I intend the present study to serve as an endeavor in interpretation and counterinterpretation. The book offers original readings of crucial themes within Machiavelli's three major—each, in its own way, scandalous—political writings: *The Prince*, the *Discourses* and the *Florentine Histories*.[1] Moreover, this text challenges what I consider to be misguided interpretive efforts offered by three illustrious, widely influential appraisals of the Florentine's work. Building upon and elaborating arguments that I previously developed in the book *Machiavellian Democracy*,[2] here I further substantiate Machiavelli's consistent advocacy for a new form of muscular, populist politics conveyed across his three greatest works; and I show in detail how and why major interpretive schools of Machiavelli's political thought have either missed or deliberately obscured the radical extent of the Florentine's decidedly democratic form of republicanism. In particular, I confront suspect engagements with Machiavelli's political thought undertaken by Jean-Jacques Rousseau, Leo Strauss, and scholars affiliated with the Cambridge School, especially John Pocock and Quentin Skinner.

This reconstructive cum critical engagement with Machiavelli's political thought and its reception explores the following themes: it demonstrates how Machiavelli conceives of the common people as an audience amenable or susceptible to persuasion, manipulation, and edification by "appearances and outcomes" (P 15); and, consequently, how he advises princes or republics to motivate and enlist the people to act as a formidable, historically novel, political force. The book likewise elaborates the Florentine's ideas concerning the advantages and limits of intense social conflict between common citizens and elites within the domestic politics of democratic republics, especially over the question of economic redistribution. Indeed, I analyze in considerable depth Machiavelli's diagnosis of how increasing socioeconomic inequality invariably generates political corruption in all republics—especially those that pursue empire. I further accentuate the institutional arrangements and constitutional forms discussed in *Machiavellian Democracy*—specifically, plebeian tribunates, legislative plebiscites, and popularly judged political trials—that Machiavelli thought most conducive to well-ordered popular government. Perhaps surprisingly, this book investigates the proper role that our notoriously impious author seemingly insists religious symbolism must play in every politics—princely or republican—that extensively enlists the power of the people.

My overriding intention is to explore and expound upon the explicit if still elusive goal of Machiavelli's major writings: specifically, what the Florentine identifies as the "effectual truth" of politics, and the nature of the peculiar affinity that Machiavelli establishes between, on the one hand, this more accurate and efficacious form of truth, and, on the other, the judgment of the common people, explicitly, "the vulgar" (P 15). Machiavelli's pursuit of the effectual truth, he declares, entails an orientation toward the world as it actually "is," rather than—in a way that bedeviled previous writers—how it "ought" to be. Machiavelli professes that his orientation toward the *is* of politics is motivated by a desire to provide something useful to his readers; that is, a motivation to provide advice for how political actors *should* behave having received and reflected upon the Florentine's unprecedentedly wise, if audacious and often outrageous, advice. Hence, Machiavelli's political thought does not simply supplant an idealist *ought* with a more realistic *is*; rather, it elaborates an entirely new ought for political thinking and practice—an ought in which the vulgar assume an unprecedented prominent role. Therefore, despite appropriating resources from ancient political practice, in which peoples played a vital civic and military function (if not necessarily from ancient political theory, in which, comparatively, they did not), Machiavelli's political thought represents nothing less than an entirely innovative vision for how politics and popular empowerment *should* be conceptualized and practiced in the future.

Yet, notwithstanding the infinite parchment, feather and ink devoted to commentaries on Machiavelli's writings, neither the descriptive nor the normative aspect of Machiavelli's populist political agenda has proven as easily ascertainable as the Florentine implies them to be.[3] The readings and counterreadings presented in the six chapters that constitute this book (any of which, I concede, may be deemed a "suspect engagement") are intended to clarify Machiavelli's effectual conceptualization of the new "ought" of democratic politics. At the center of this novel conceptualization, analyzed in Part I, is the appropriate role that the people—the plebs, the many, the multitude, again, the vulgar—should play in the political world. I will argue that Machiavelli promotes the people as agents who must be empowered to act in the following politically salutary ways: the people, in both principalities and republics, should serve as the ultimate arbiters of good and evil, the final judges of outcomes and appearances (chapter 1); the people of republics ought to relate to each other as free and equal citizens—not only politically equal but socioeconomically as well (chapter 2); the people must assert their necessary, salutary role as the guardian of liberty against predatory oligarchs and tyrants (chapter 3); and the people should be civically and militarily enabled by well-ordered laws and institutions to act in politically virtuous ways (chapters 1–3).

If Machiavelli himself serves as my interlocutor in Part I, major representatives of the interpretive tradition assume the role of intellectual adversaries in Part II. Here I focus on widely influential misapprehensions of Machiavelli's intentions regarding the people's proper role in a democratic republic (a *governo popolare* or *governo largo*): I demonstrate that Rousseau deliberately repudiates Machiavelli's democratic reconstruction of the Roman Republic as an emulable model for future large-scale republics; and that the Genevan replaces it with a constitutional model that both empowers wealthy citizens to outvote poorer ones and neutralizes the populist institution of the plebeian tribunate (chapter 4); I delineate the subtle and often blatant distortions of Machiavelli's texts perpetrated by Leo Strauss in his efforts to undermine Machiavelli's explicit arguments in favor of the people and to convert the Florentine into an advocate of enlightened oligarchic rule (chapter 5); and finally, I suggest that Cambridge scholars such as Skinner and Pocock attempt to shoehorn Machiavelli's politics into a Ciceronian model of a harmonious mixed regime; one in which, contrary to Machiavelli's intentions, class conflict is minimized and the people, whose motivations these scholars deem just as dangerous to liberty as those of the nobles, are subordinated to elite domination (chapter 6).[4]

In short, Part I explicitly demonstrates that a fierce populism seeded all of Machiavelli's political writings, one that manifested itself in radically democratic institutional prescriptions, while Part II uncovers, through my interrogations of Rousseau, Strauss, Pocock, and Skinner, a common agenda running throughout Machiavelli's largely republican reception, one that approximates an aristocratic conspiracy to repress and obscure his emphatically democratic politics.[5]

Reading Machiavelli

The chapters that make up Part I accentuate Machiavelli's substantive political lessons, and they further serve as models for how to engage his texts—literally (or literarily), how to *read* them. In this sense, this book is not only an exercise in reading Machiavelli for political wisdom (although it certainly is that), but just as importantly, it is an exhibition of how to read Machiavelli as a practice, how to experience and reflect upon his mode of writing. Despite appearances to the contrary—appearances that the Florentine went to great lengths to conjure by writing deceptively accessible "how to" books—Machiavelli is not exclusively or perhaps even primarily a didactic thinker; he does not merely provide easily applied maxims for what to do in the political world, even if that is first and foremost what conventional wisdom attributes to him. Rather, Machiavelli offers multiple avenues for pursuing the effectual truth of politics—ways that accentuate if not the utter ineffability of effectual truth, then certainly its easily overlooked, concealed, obscured, elusory qualities.

The many difficulties that Machiavelli's texts pose to interpreters—which, of course, account for the myriad interpretations generated over the centuries—emulate the challenges presented by politics' effectual truth. Both the textual and secular realities central to Machiavelli's concerns can only be apprehended through acts of spotting, pursuing, penetrating, and digesting the following elements of his writings: confusing, jarring twists and turns in otherwise straightforward narratives; biblical, classical and contemporary allusions, sometimes implicit and sometimes explicit; surprising, often ear-splitting silences; individual actors who transmute from positive to negative political examples and then back again; violent imagery meant to immediately shock readers, and subtle misdirection that readers only recognize as such long after the fact; historical events, great and small, directly invoked or silently implied—I could, of course, go on and on. For all the editorializing and explication concerning his own intentions and lessons that famously characterize Machiavelli's writings, our author, by and large, leaves the literary techniques just mentioned, and the pedagogical objectives for which they are employed, for readers themselves to ponder and interpret with no commentary supplied by the Florentine himself. Allow me to provide a sense of how I employ this hermeneutic approach to Machiavelli's writing in subsequent chapters. As I illustrate in chapter 1, once the reader detects that Machiavelli's narrative of Cesare Borgia's career—to which he devotes more space than any other in *The Prince*—is presented as a story in which a holy father sends his son to redeem, to bring peace to, his people, then chapter 7 begins to open up in new, exciting, even titillating respects. All of a sudden, religious tropes or images jump out and impose themselves on the reader in potentially subversive ways: one begins to discern within the chapter's confines the presence of the crucifixion, the transfiguration, a circumcision, a bloody sacrifice that atones for political sins, an empty tomb, even St. Paul—all of which signify Machiavelli's beliefs concerning the appropriate covenants that should characterize prince-people relationships.

Moreover, as I indicate in chapter 2, when one realizes that Machiavelli presents the Gracchi's career in the *Discourses* in such a way that that he may be read as both endorsing and criticizing the ill-fated Roman tribunes' redistributive agenda, the reader is compelled to doggedly pursue what Machiavelli actually means when he repeatedly declares that republics must keep the public rich but the citizens poor. At the end of this interpretive expedition, one discovers a radical answer to perhaps the most controversial question within the Roman-Florentine republican tradition: political liberty requires genuine economic equality. Furthermore, as I suggest in chapter 3, once readers appreciate that one of the most frequently quoted passages in the entire *Florentine Histories* (concerning the Florentine people's unwillingness to share offices with the nobles) occurs just a mere few paragraphs after Machiavelli has demonstrated this to be a deeply inaccurate assessment of events, they are encouraged to begin rethinking the entire relationship of words and deeds in that book—a reconsideration which reveals that Machiavelli, perhaps more often than not, seems to undermine his own expressly declared evaluative judgments throughout the entire *Histories*.

Through such readings, I endeavor to show how playfully and seductively Machiavelli goes about educating his readers; I attempt to show how pleasurable, perplexing, and beguiling the careful reading of Machiavelli's political writings can be; how he so often leaves us satisfied and stupefied—but, since human edification is his ultimate goal, never permanently so (P 15; D I preface). Machiavelli does not encourage play for the sake of play—reading Machiavelli is certainly fun, but it stands as no less a gravely serious endeavor for that fact. Indeed, reading Machiavelli is all the more serious—often deathly serious—since the pleasure of reading him animates within his interpreters the desire to further, and ever further, pursue the substantive truth of political outcomes and ends.

Learning how to read Machiavelli appropriately serves as an education in how to act effectively in the political realm—this applies not only to leaders or prospective leaders, but also to peoples, who in well-ordered republics, Machiavelli declares to be "princes" (D I.58). Machiavelli's writings encourage the people to further sharpen the inclination, which he already attributes to them, to judge phenomena by their "appearances and outcomes" (P 15); specifically, he encourages people to enhance this judgment by better apprehending the essential nature of the outcomes and to avoid being deceived by the glamour of the appearances. Therefore, by writing in the manner described above, Machiavelli, I would suggest, trains his readers in the practice of Machiavellian *virtù*. It would not be entirely far-fetched to venture that the qualities of a virtuous reader mirror the Florentine's descriptions of the *virtuoso* political actor.[6]

Readers, peoples, and princes must first examine apparent and surface statements or states of affairs in Machiavelli's writings, then drill down into the deeper truth of his lessons, without being distracted, let alone shamed, by the judgment of previous writers or "the few." This mode of learning especially entails appreciating lessons concerning the art of reversal, of adaptation to context, which, without much exaggeration, largely characterize the very essence of Machiavellian *virtù*.[7] Readers must examine concrete events and individual exemplars when reflecting upon Machiavelli's rules or maxims in order to consider the effectually true status of such circumstances and the actual success or failures of his figures rather than merely accept his overt evaluations of them; they must constantly return to Machiavelli's previously invoked examples and to his historical sources to comprehend what he may be including, excluding, amplifying, or distorting, and, most importantly, why.

In what follows, I demonstrate how Machiavelli encourages readers to engage his texts in the ways that he enjoins people to interrogate political phenomena; Machiavelli bids readers, subjects and citizens to engage with all of the aesthetic elements of effectual truth. His mode of writing creates an environment in which readers participate in the vibrant intellectual-sensory habitus of his books, in much the same way as he encourages the citizens of republics, and even the subjects of principalities, to do; thus, adding new dimensions to thinking about and to acting within the world as it "is" as opposed to, in a traditional sense, how it "ought to be."

I generally call the kind of writing performed by Machiavelli "literary-rhetorical" in character, and I rather steadfastly resist the term "esoteric writing." Leo Strauss is, of course, the interpreter most lauded and reviled for reading Machiavelli as an esoteric writer; conversely, the Cambridge School is perhaps not unfairly accused of exhibiting a certain tone-deafness when evaluating the full political ramifications of his literary, allegorical, allusory form of writing.[8] In chapter 5, I show how Strauss does not, as he professes, employ esoteric reading to understand Machiavelli "as he understands himself," but rather to exploit apparent ambiguities within the Florentine's texts in the service of a pre-determined ideological agenda. On the basis of questionable evidence, Strauss asserts that Machiavelli, contrary to his own declarations, ultimately refused to depart from the "aristocratic or oligarchic republicanism of the classical tradition."[9] Cambridge scholars, whom I discuss in chapter 6, refer to historical context to more or less affirm Machiavelli's maxims as he states them, encouraging readers to take them at face value or as largely consonant with established intellectual-philosophical traditions. These scholars seldom persevere in efforts to understand how Machiavelli's literary allusions and concrete examples consistently undermine these precepts and further upset their relationship with extant traditions; how thereby the Florentine often engenders radically qualified, and indeed more effectually truthful, reformulations of those seemingly simple maxims.

Rousseau, for his part, was among the first interpreters to suggest that Machiavelli did not always mean exactly what he wrote, especially regarding principalities; and yet when treating Machiavelli's views on republics, Rousseau completely obliterates Machiavelli's explicit and implicit recommendations with respect to well-ordered popular government. Failure to heed the peculiar qualities and difficulties that characterize Machiavelli's writings (as well as a certain habituation to aristocratic norms) may partly explain what leads such vaunted interpreters astray. Thus do the two halves of the present study speak to each other: the chapters of Part I demonstrate how to read Machiavelli in a way that evades the insufficiencies of the three interpretations that I subsequently critique in Part II.

It would be difficult to overstate the influence that the Straussian and Cambridge schools of Machiavelli interpretation (addressed in Part II) have wielded internationally over the past five decades.[10] Strauss, on the one hand, and Pocock and Skinner, on the other, have established truly vast intellectual empires[11]—and yet, their respective students and disciples have seldom interacted with each other in meaningful ways. The present study may in fact stand as the first monograph that substantively engages both schools of thought, the first that takes equal and sustained aim at each of these two powerful hermeneutic traditions. Although the Straussian and Cambridge schools are most often understood to represent diametrically opposed ideological and methodological orientations, I demonstrate here that they share a common discomfort with Machiavelli's rough and tumble populism, with the democratic implications of his thought, and, perhaps not least of all, with his frequently expressed conviction that elites must be periodically held accountable through spectacular acts of violence.

The following remarks provide my provisional sketch of what Machiavelli presents as the effectual truth of virtuous politics, and the central role played by the vulgar within it, across his three major political works, The Prince, the Discourses, and the Histories.

Virtue, the Vulgar, and the Effectual Truth of Politics

Machiavelli's most famous work, On Principalities (1513), or, as it was subsequently titled, The Prince, announced a dramatic break with political doctrines anchored in traditionally moral and religious systems of thought. Unlike his classical or medieval predecessors, who took their political bearings from transcendentally valid or divinely sanctioned conceptions of justice, Machiavelli oriented himself, again, to the "effectual truth" of politics; that is, a politics oriented to how the world actually "is" rather than how it "ought" to be. Indeed, Machiavelli's brutally realistic advice seems intended to brazenly contravene all previous, socially respectable forms of political reflection. For instance, he boldly declares that it is safer for a prince to be feared rather than loved (if he must choose between these two forms of regard) because subjects love at their own pleasure while they fear at the pleasure of a prince. Moreover, Machiavelli steadfastly insists that violence and cruelty are necessary means of effective political action (even if their deployment must be circumscribed meticulously to avoid unintended, deleterious consequences for a prince's rule). Apologetically inclined commentators, such as Quentin Skinner (whose interpretation I will address in chapter 6), attempt to soften Machiavelli's radically severe political advice by consistently emphasizing, at the risk of morally sanitizing his lessons, the qualifications of the Florentine's doctrines contained in the preceding parentheses.[12]

Highly indicative of his unrepentantly disreputable and unorthodoxly realist approach to politics, Machiavelli blatantly rejects the ideal of philosopher kings whose perfect judgment might be even remotely approximated by the educated, wealthy, and prominent noblemen of worldly cities.[13] Exemplifying his profoundly anti-elitist political orientation, Machiavelli insists that there exist no few best men whose wisdom, prudence, or love of the common good can be counted upon to settle, with impartial justice, political controversies and crises. Defying the aristocratic preferences of previous philosophers and historians, as he states in the *Discourses* (D I.58), Machiavelli recommends in *The Prince* that individual princes militarily arm the vulgar common people, in whom the noble quality of *onestà* (honesty, decency, or justice) actually resides, and crush at every opportunity self-styled nobles or *grandi*, whose ambitious and avaricious motivations and machinations offer little more than oppression for the people and insecurity for a prince (P 9).

Machiavelli's preference for political arrangements that empower the people and contain elites was evident in his political career long

before he expressed it in his major writings. During his extensive service to the Florentine Republic (1494–1512), for which Machiavelli
performed vital administrative, diplomatic, and military duties, he
revealed himself to be a staunch defender of the city's popular assembly, the Great Council, and an outspoken advocate of a citizen
militia. The republic's aristocrats despised the Council and insisted
on altering the militia so as to render it, in quality and size, less alarming and intimidating to themselves. When the republic was overthrown through an aristocratic coup, foreign intervention, and Papal
intrigue that returned the Medici family to power, Machiavelli responded by writing to the restored princes, delicately advising them
to betray their untrustworthy allies among the nobility and to align
themselves instead with the recently disempowered Florentine people.[14] For his troubles, Machiavelli was implicated in an anti-Medici
conspiracy, tortured, imprisoned, and subsequently confined to internal exile. Several years later, Machiavelli repeated his advice that
the Medici ultimately re-empower the Florentine people at the expense of the family's aristocratic friends in an understudied but important memorandum on constitutional reforms.[15] As we will observe in chapter 5, Leo Strauss—often ingeniously but always
illegitimately—attempts to reverse Machiavelli's class partisanship
from the side of people to that of the nobles.

Machiavelli's Discourses (c. 1513–19) and Florentine Histories (c. 1520–
25) clearly exhibit the author's admiration for popular government,
even if, ever intriguingly, these works generally affirm rather than repudiate the moral and practical lessons of The Prince.[16] The "nearly
perfect" (if still ultimately flawed) ancient Roman Republic is Machiavelli's primary subject in the Discourses, while the embarrassingly
disordered, medieval Florentine republic takes center stage in the
Histories. In Rome, a prudent and virtuous founder, Romulus, organized the poor into armed legions and collected the wealthy in a senate (P 6; D I.9). In so doing, Romulus insured that future class conflicts between plebeians and patricians, which Machiavelli deems
natural and inevitable (P 9, D I.4–5), would produce two salutary
institutions: an office, the plebeian tribunate, dedicated to the welfare
of the common people, and large citizen assemblies in which the
people themselves freely discussed and directly decided legislation

and political trials (D I.2–8, D I.16, D I.58). I will delineate in chapter 4 Rousseau's elaborate attempt to undermine Machiavelli's democratic renderings of Rome's institutions.[17] For Machiavelli, such orders, created and sustained by intense but productive class conflict at home, as well as unprecedented territorial expansion abroad, herald Rome's singular greatness and its at least provisional value as a model to be emulated by all subsequent republics.[18]

To be more specific, in the *Discourses*, Machiavelli praised Roman institutions, undergirded by a full-scale citizen military, that both resulted from and then effectively re-channeled class-conflict: notably, the consulship and the tribunate—magistracies with year-long tenures of office reserved for, respectively, elite and common citizens; additionally, a senate and popular assemblies that kept noble and plebeian citizens unified among themselves and politically fixated on their natural class adversaries; and, finally, political trials where the entire citizenry renders judgment over individuals accused of political crimes—the closest real-world approximation, in Machiavelli's view, to fully objective political judgment.

By contrast with Rome, Machiavelli demonstrates in the *Histories* how badly ordered were both popular and aristocratic institutions in Florence. The Florentine people were constituted by the semipublic/ semiprivate institutional arrangements of the guild community, arrangements that reveal themselves to be politically deficient in two ways: the city's merchants and artisans, the *popolani*, were dispersed among twenty-one competing major, middle, and minor guilds; and the guild community excluded the vast majority of the city's freeborn, able-bodied male population, mostly employed as wool carders known as *ciompi, sottoposti,* or plebs. These disenfranchised and exploited workers proved amenable for cooptation by the city's ancient nobility (the *magnati* or *grandi*) against the guilds, or by a prospective tyrant like Walter Brienne, the so-called Duke of Athens, against the city as a whole. Moreover, in Machiavelli's Florence, rather than a proper senate, the dominant aristocratic institution was the semipublic/semiprivate Guelf Party, comprised of only half the city's nobility, which pursued domination over both rival Ghibelline nobles and common guildsmen. In a very un-Roman fashion, these adversarial, aristocratic Guelf and Ghibelline parties pledged loyalty to foreign entities, respectively, the Papacy and the German emperor, who periodically re-instigated social strife within the city.

In the *Histories*, Machiavelli illustrates how one Florentine individual after another emerged with the prospect of assuming the role of virtuous founder, for example, Giano della Bella (discussed in chapter 3) or Walter Brienne; yet each ultimately demurred from fully arming the entire people civically and militarily in good Romulan fashion such that social conflicts (not only between classes but especially among families and factions) persisted in episodically destructive rather than constructive ways. A "wise legislator," Machiavelli insists, could have imposed an appropriate constitutional order upon the Florentine Republic (FH III.1), which might have properly institutionalized social conflict along "natural" class lines (FH II.12). Instead, the city's either naively "good" leaders, like Giano della Bella, or imprudently "bad" leaders, like Walter Brienne, permit or encourage social discord to persist in ever more chaotic and variegated ways: specifically, intense conflicts among rival family cliques; between Guelf and Ghibelline nobles (and then "Black and White" Guelfs); between the so-called popular nobles of the richest guilds and middle class citizens of the middling/lower guilds; and, finally, through conflicts between various elite groupings and the city's plebeians, who were neither enrolled in nor represented by occupational guilds of their own. Machiavelli exhaustively chronicles how the republic's bleakly defective ordering and chronically tepid leadership resulted in its gradual enfeeblement: a steady decline measured ultimately by the civic corruption typified by the rise of the Albizzi oligarchy (1382) and the Medici principate (1434), as well as by geopolitical decline ultimately ratified by the invasion of Tuscany by the French in 1494 and the Spanish in 1512.

Machiavelli's descriptions of virtually every major Florentine figure in the *Histories* invite a comparison with his account of a Roman or an ancient leader in an earlier work.[19] Most pointedly, Machiavelli presents Giano della Bella as a civic leader confronted with the opportunity to become a Romulus, Moses or a Brutus: a defender of his own set of laws that concomitantly protect and benefit his people (D I.9; III.3, III.30; FH II.13). According to Machiavelli, those virtuous ancient leaders understood that new laws and the people's liberty must be secured by the blood of "the sons of Brutus," aristocratic abusers of the people and intransigent opponents of founders or reformers (P 6; D III.3, III.30). On the contrary, Machiavelli suggests that an undifferentiated notion of "goodness" prompts Giano to exit the city rather than, as did Moses or Brutus, resort to the force necessary to effectively enact his laws and ensure the enduring welfare of the common citizens of Florence—even though the armed people appear twice at his door begging for him to do so and pledging to him their military support.[20] In chapter 3, I demonstrate how Machiavelli maintained, throughout all his major political writings, a positive assessment of the common people's *virtù* and *onestà*; I contest scholarly orthodoxy which asserts that in the *Histories* our author presented the Florentine people and plebs to be civically and martially inferior in comparison with their ancient counterparts.

The *Discourses* and the *Histories* do, of course, present readers with striking contrasts, two of which are relevant here: firstly, Machiavelli repeatedly emphasizes the fact that the ancient Romans would consistently kill their own family members for the sake of civic well-being (e.g., Brutus, Virginius, Manlius Torquatus, among others), while the medieval Florentines constantly disrupt civic order by maiming or killing other citizens on behalf of aggrieved family, clan, or party members. And, secondly, rather than conquering other Italians militarily and vanquishing German, French, and Spanish enemies in battle, as the Roman Republic continually did, Florence, in Machiavelli's account, is conquered by these very same former subjects of that virtuous ancient republic. The political well-being of the Florentine Republic is consistently undermined (often through the pernicious or clueless meddling of the Roman Pontiff) by the German emperor and by French and Spanish monarchs.

Especially emblematic of Machiavelli's views on the salutary effect of institutionalized social conflict is his vivid account of Florence's Ciompi Revolt in Book III of the *Histories*. Since the city's oppressed woolworkers had no recourse to plebeian tribunes who might air their grievances and were unable to confront directly Florence's wealthiest and most prominent citizens assembled in a proper senate, the *ciompi* were compelled to pursue the city's elites house to house in a series of destructive but not especially bloody riots. These disturbances produced no longstanding progressive gains for Florence's poorer citizens, but rather facilitated conservative consolidation of power among the city's richest families (FH III.24).[21] From such entrenched oligarchic arrangements, Machiavelli shows how Cosimo de' Medici and his family successors—falsely presenting themselves as defenders of the people—rose to the ranks of commercial princes.[22] Rather than arm citizens, the Medici rendered the latter mere economic clients, definitively corrupting the city's civic life and ensuring its disastrous military dependence on foreign powers and mercenary warlords (FH IV).[23]

Why were Rome's founders and civic princes so virtuous and Florence's so hesitant and inept, especially with respect to arming the people civically and militarily? Throughout his writings, Machiavelli sometimes directly and sometimes more subtly blames Christianity for the weakness of modern republics and their leaders: unlike the teachings of previous, more robustly *political* belief systems, Christian tenets encourage passivity, subservience, and deferral of punishment to the next world—and, perhaps worst of all, such precepts promote an inflexibly undifferentiated view of "the good" among modern would-be founders and reformers (P 15; D III.1). These precepts seem to inhibit modern peoples and princes from behaving in the "bad" ways that actually prove salutary for political life. Ancient armed populaces often took matters into their own hands to discipline and punish those who commit sins against the public; moreover, ancient princes like Moses and Brutus never hesitated to eliminate rival threats to their new modes and orders that guaranteed the liberty and longevity of their peoples and polities.

Indeed, Machiavelli laments, Christian populaces suffer too long rather than instantaneously avenge ill treatment by abusive elites; as his narration of the Ciompi Revolt makes plain, when finally provoked to the point of a desperately spirited response, the *ciompi* strike out against their oppressors in undisciplined and ineffective ways. Florentine princes like the Medici, Friar Girolamo Savonarola and Machiavelli's own patron, Piero Soderini—all of whom maintained concrete ties of one kind or another with the Roman Catholic Church—seem hamstrung internally by Christian morality or externally by the Church's secular power from acting decisively to establish and maintain a healthy civic republic on the Arno (P 6; D I.52, III.3, III.9, III.30). In particular, Machiavelli avers, Christian princes seem especially incapable, on the one hand, of arming the people with little more than platitudes attesting to their goodness, and, on the other, of eliminating the metaphorical "sons of Brutus" who forever threaten "a free and civil way of life": that is, oppressive-minded elites who detest the people's liberty, bitterly resent their participation in politics, and oppose any reformer who attempts to limit their own aristocratic power and privilege.[24]

However, Machiavelli's reconstruction of Cesare Borgia's career, as I will discuss in chapter 1, raises the possibility that certain aspects of Christianity may prove congruent with ancient pagan practices and might serve as the basis of future virtuous princely and popular politics. As we will observe, while Borgia's anxiety over eternal dam-nation, and hence his inclination to believe in the possibility of for-giveness, may have ultimately spelled his political doom, other quasi-Christian aspects of his "spirit," Machiavelli intimates, portend significant political success. For instance: the commitment to the people's welfare signaled by the killing of one's own sons by both Brutus and the Christian God; the necessity of sins being paid for, to a spectacular extent, in this world and not the next (not merely once, but repeatedly); the necessity of scapegoating individuals such that princes take credit for good outcomes and that political rivals incur blame for the often obnoxious means deployed to achieve them; and the promise and experience of a real, if always qualified, domestic peace that serves to forge an intimate relationship between princes and peoples.

Speaking more transhistorically, scholars often blindly misappre-hend Machiavelli's concrete impact on practical politics and consti-tutional forms in the modern world. After all, the "republicans" of the broad Enlightenment era drew upon the Florentine's prescriptions in a highly selective fashion: they only partially adopted his call for neo-Roman full militarization of the people, and they almost completely rejected the democratic institutions and practices that Machiavelli hoped would be demanded by such newly armed citizenries. They explicitly rejected, as exemplified by the case of Rousseau (chapter 4), Machiavelli's call for modern plebeian tribunates, and for assemblies in which common citizens themselves freely discuss and equitably enact public policy. Instead, the framers of modern constitutions opted exclusively for offices filled through general elections, in which the people might choose the most wise and prudent (in reality, the richest and most prominent) individuals, and for elected assemblies of notables that would purportedly represent the interests of common people in a faithful and effective manner.[25]

Machiavelli achieved perhaps his greatest practical influence, and hence earned his greatest infamy, in literatures associated with "reason of state," a phrase he never used.[26] Architects of the European absolute monarchies appropriated Machiavelli's apparently cynical, amoral doctrines, but decisively severed these from his own normative, populist cum democratic concerns. They successfully elevated individuals to the status of national monarchs—Tudors, Stuarts, Valois, Hapsburgs and Hohenzollerns—and certainly helped subordinate traditional aristocracies to these dynasts' authority. But by relying on professional militaries and by endorsing representation of the public's interest, modern state-builders failed to empower the people to the full extent that Machiavelli recommended. The economic dependence of these modern princes—and, notably, of the bureaucratic states that succeeded them—on newly emerging capitalist aristocracies would leave the citizens of modern republics without robust recourse to the military or civic arms that the Florentine thought eternally necessary for the defense of their liberty against rapacious elites.[27] In chapter 2, I argue that Machiavelli prescribed socioeconomic conditions of substantive equality for the realization of liberty within well-ordered popular governments; and, in fact, that he directly attributed the collapse of the world's greatest democratic republic, ancient Rome, to its failure to stem the otherwise inevitable rise of economic cum political inequality.

PART I

1

The Passion of Duke Valentino

CESARE BORGIA, BIBLICAL
ALLEGORY, AND *THE PRINCE*

AFTER ROUGHLY FIVE HUNDRED YEARS, no consensus has yet emerged over Niccolò Machiavelli's religious views. Despite his discernable anticlerical political stances, many scholars continue to insist that Machiavelli's orientation toward religion remains largely within the ambit of orthodox Christianity.[1] Others take the opposite view: not only was Machiavelli a virulent anti-Christian, but his writings are motivated by nothing less than a desire to eliminate religiosity from human existence and to establish an atheistic world order.[2] This chapter accomplishes little to settle this issue. It merely explores the way that Machiavelli employs Christian allegory at critical junctures of *The Prince*,[3] specifically, when he discusses the political career of the crucial figure Cesare Borgia. I will show definitively that Machiavelli draws on deep knowledge of the Gospels and enlists Christian imagery and doctrine to impart his political lessons through the example of Borgia. Whether he does so entirely to refute Christianity or whether he thinks that his novel political science, his "new modes and orders," appropriates and advances certain Christian tenets (in religious or irreligious ways) remain very much open questions.

Machiavelli's use of Borgia has always posed a puzzle for interpreters of *The Prince*. Those who denounced the scandalous quality of Machiavelli's *piccolo libro* argued that the laudatory presentation of

Borgia—ambitious, cunning and brutal—proved that Machiavelli cared little for piety, morality, good government, or basic decency. In attempting to shield Machiavelli from such charges, no less a luminary than Jean-Jacques Rousseau insisted that Machiavelli's use of Borgia was instructively ironic: Machiavelli did not mean for Borgia to serve as an exemplar of anything other than the kind of vicious tyranny that inevitably emerges in circumstances where republican government is absent.[4] Interpreters more willing to take Machiavelli at his word detect in the example of Borgia Machiavelli's straightforward confrontation with the dire political realities of his day: Jacob Burckhardt, for instance, understood Machiavelli's account of Borgia's career to illustrate how a ruthless, mendacious warlord could use the authority of the papacy to accumulate power and even create circumstances where the papacy itself might be converted into a proper hereditary monarchy; that is, into a more traditionally effective principality capable of expelling foreign invaders and unifying Italy.[5]

My interpretation highlights the Biblical resonances that incontrovertibly characterize Machiavelli's account of the rise and fall of Borgia, the paradigmatic "new prince" of *The Prince*; a Christological "prince of peace" whose subjects, and Machiavelli himself, call by the exalted title "Duke Valentino." I agree with Rousseau that everything Machiavelli wishes to communicate concerning Borgia's career is less than obvious, but I dispute his contention that Machiavelli means for Borgia's "virtue" and "spirit" to serve anything less than exemplary purposes, both negative and positive.[6] Like Burckhardt, I believe that Machiavelli has in mind prescriptive intentions and practical goals as he chronicles the duke's career, which Machiavelli presents in unambiguously religious terms, but which he puts toward deeply ambiguous religious ends.

Machiavelli's "Duke" and the People's Prince of Peace

In chapter 7 of *The Prince*, Machiavelli upholds Cesare Borgia as the best example of someone who came to power through fortune—that is, through some other prince's power—but who almost solidified his own authority through virtue—that is, with his own arms and efforts. Machiavelli presents Cesare as an explicitly inferior example to the unequivocally successful if problematically mythic princes whom the Florentine discusses in the previous chapter: Moses, Romulus, Theseus, Cyrus (P 6); founders of peoples or religions who came to power exclusively through their own virtue and arms.

This deficiency notwithstanding, Machiavelli goes to great lengths to associate himself both with Cesare Borgia, personally, and, via Borgia, with the common people as a class. In the first place, he uses phrases to describe Cesare that he applies to himself in the book's "Dedicatory Letter": both he and Borgia, Machiavelli writes, egregiously and unfairly suffer "fortune's malignity" (P DL, P 7). Curiously, the only instances where Machiavelli inserts himself as an interlocutor within the pages of *The Prince* occur in the two chapters (P 3 and P 7), where Cesare figures prominently. In these two chapters Machiavelli mentions that Cesare was called "Duke Valentino" by "the people," or "by the vulgar"; and then Machiavelli himself, in a popular or vulgar manner, exclusively refers to Cesare as "the duke" for the duration of his account of Borgia's short but striking career (P 3, P 7). Machiavelli alludes to the circumstances through which Pope Alexander VI formally acquires for his son, Cesare, a noble title: while granting the French King's request for an annulment of his marriage, the Pope also elevates the king's minister, the archbishop of Rouen, to the rank of cardinal; in return, the Pope secures from the king a title for Cesare, "Duke of Valentinois." However, Machiavelli suggests that Cesare, through his own accomplishments, earns the title "duke" in the eyes of the people, and, evidently, in the eyes of Machiavelli as well. The people's judgment, apparently, not that of popes and kings, is what ultimately matters to Machiavelli. Again, the Florentine insists on calling Cesare "Duke Valentino" precisely because that is what the people do.[7]

As Machiavelli famously remarks elsewhere in *The Prince*, the people are fascinated by appearances and outcomes; but since "in the world abide none but the vulgar," appearances and outcomes may be, in the end, all that count (P 18). While this remark is often taken as Machiavelli's criticism of popular judgment—that is, as an expression of his contempt for the people's shallowness—Machiavelli's self-association with the duke and with the people (with both the virtuous and the vulgar) actually affirms the validity of this perspective. Indeed, while serving as advisor and minister to Piero Soderini, chief executive of the ill-fated Florentine Republic of 1494, Machiavelli wrote to Soderini's nephew, in words that presage *The Prince* by seven years: "I am looking not through your glass [i.e., that of a young patrician], in which nothing is seen but prudence, but through the glass of the many, who have to judge the end of things as they are done, and not the means by which they are done."[8] Machiavelli hereby asserts his concern with ends, with outcomes, over means because these are the people's chief concerns. Neither Machiavelli nor the people, it would seem, can afford the luxury of fussing over means, as do the few. The direct relationship between the people and the duke—the bond between them forged by the people's appreciation for outcomes delivered by the duke—increases in importance throughout Machiavelli's account of Borgia's career in *The Prince*. In fact, Machiavelli celebrates it, or, as we will see, he consecrates this relationship, this bond.

Again, Machiavelli first introduces Cesare as the natural son of Pope Alexander VI in chapter 3. Cesare enjoys prominent—indeed religiously exalted—parentage and patronage. However, he was born out of wedlock, which, in a considerable sense diminishes, perhaps even vulgarizes, the quality of his origins. Like those of many founders and prophets, Cesare's beginnings are ambiguously exalted and humble, theologically validated yet transgressive in a conventionally moral sense. What is immediately important for Machiavelli is that Cesare inherits someone else's conquests and kingdoms. The very next chapter (P 4) seems to emphasize this point as it concerns the fate of territories conquered by Alexander after his death, even if the Alexander invoked here is not the Borgia Pope mentioned in the preceding chapter, but rather Alexander of Macedon. Machiavelli instructs readers that Alexander the Great's conquests would have been easy to maintain if his successors had been united—that is, for instance, if he had left behind a son who was a worthy successor.

A venerable tradition, most notably represented by Dante, recognizes the Roman Caesars to be the heirs of Alexander: the emperors built upon his example in order to conquer the world.⁹ Indeed, Machiavelli remarks how Julius Caesar imitated Alexander, just as Alexander and Scipio imitated, respectively, Achilles and Cyrus (P 14). A central question in these early chapters of *The Prince* is whether *this* Caesar, Cesare Borgia, is capable of maintaining and building upon the foundations that he inherits from *his* Alexander. In fact, since the ancient and modern Caesars and Alexanders are spelled the same way in the Italian text, Machiavelli often compels his readers to pause and reflect upon which "Cesare" or "Alessandro" he may be discussing at any particular moment. More specifically, Machiavelli graphically, visually prompts readers to consider whether, or to what extent, this Holy Father and his natural son appropriately imitated their more renowned ancient namesakes. Machiavelli invites readers to consider the similarities and differences between these ancient and modern examples with identical names: do Alexander and Cesare accomplish as much as their ancient counterparts? By calling Cesare by another name, Duke Valentino, does Machiavelli suggest that he could have established something new and different in comparison with the accomplishments of the ancient conquerors, or does this renaming only accentuate how far short the pope and the duke ultimately fall?

The Parable of Cesare Borgia

Machiavelli reports that Pope Alexander initially cannot find arms to help support Cesare's military endeavors, specifically his attempt to reconquer the Romagna for the papacy, because all his potential allies worry about increasing the Church's territorial reach (P 7). In response to this impasse, Alexander shakes up Italy to distract and disorient his adversaries. The Pope encourages the Venetians to bring France into Italy from whom, in turn, Alexander acquires arms to help Cesare wage battle against the Venetians (P 7). In short, Alexander effectively tricks the French into helping him take the Romagna, and then he places Cesare in charge there. But despite the fact that the duke takes the province with troops provided to him by others (that is, by the Church, by the Venetians, and by the French) Machiavelli demonstrates Borgia's capacity to behave "virtuously" when he describes how the duke himself handles these dubiously loyal troops and their commanders.

Cesare recognizes immediately that these inherited troops are unreliable: they are either too "cool" and, hence, reluctant to fight, or too much of a threat; that is, too readily inclined to turn against their new captain (P 7). The duke flatters, bribes, or corrupts most of the lords who provide him arms and who pose threats to him, thus winning them over. In the paragraph describing these actions, a transformation takes place, a transfiguration of sorts: it begins with the proper nouns of "Alexander" and "the pope" undertaking the primary actions, but after the deployment of some indefinite pronouns, it concludes with "the duke" or "Valentino" as prime actor in the proceedings.[10] This is where Machiavelli's narrative starts to take on strange overtones. One of the lords with whom Cesare has recently been at odds, and from whom the duke needs arms, is Pagolo Orsini. Orsini apparently has two names: although Machiavelli refers to him elsewhere by his actual name, Pagolo,[11] here he calls him "Signor Paolo," Mr. Paul. The duke wins over Paolo with gifts, including horses. Machiavelli neglects to inform readers whether or not this Paul with two names falls off one of these horses. Rather, the most important point seems to be that Cesare converts Paul, his erstwhile adversary.[12]

The duke then enlists the aid of Mr. Paul to convert the rest of Cesare's enemies. Through Paolo's mediations, Cesare invites them to a celebration of reconciliation, as Machiavelli describes it, in the coastal city of Senigallia (P 7). The participants are not quite aware of it, but this will be their last supper. Unlike other notable last suppers, however, this gathering will not conclude with its host suffering betrayal, arrest, and then execution.[13] Rather, the duke consummates this gathering of reconciliation by having his guests strangled. As a Florentine emissary, Machiavelli was present in Senigallia to observe, firsthand, the duke's actions on this New Year's Eve of 1502. Indeed, here in chapter 7 of *The Prince*, Machiavelli writes generally as if he were a chronicler of the duke's life, having both observed and spoken with Valentino. Machiavelli repeatedly insists that he wishes to record the duke's sayings and actions so that those who had not experienced them firsthand might follow them in the future.[14]

After the assassinations at Senigallia, Cesare no longer depends on the arms of others—at least in his efforts to acquire power. But the task of maintaining power is a different matter altogether: dependable subordinates will prove necessary for the consolidation of the duke's new authority within the Romagna. Cesare finds the province badly disordered; the local barons would rather "exploit than correct their subjects," as Machiavelli writes of the crimes, feuds, and insolence that plague the people there (P 7). To help him bring peace and obedience to the Romagna, Cesare resorts to a "kingly arm"; he promotes the "cruel and able" Remirro d'Orco to do the job for him (P 7). Remirro succeeds at this task—eliminating the lords and disciplining the people—and consequently gains a great reputation for himself.

Perhaps not surprisingly, Machiavelli reports that Cesare begins to fear that Remirro's excessive authority and "the rigors" that it entails will become hateful to the people (P 7). However, he leaves it unclear whether Cesare fears that such hatred will be directed toward Remirro or Cesare himself. Or perhaps what most disturbs Cesare is the reputation that Remirro has acquired for himself as much as, or more than, the hatred he arouses within the people. Will the people blame the prime actor or the mere instrument? The prince himself or his kingly arm? And who exactly is the prime mover in these circumstances? Remirro, who did the dirty work of making the Romagna peaceful? Cesare, who ordered Remirro to do so? Alexander, who effectively gave Cesare the Romagna? Or Machiavelli, for that matter? After all, Machiavelli has put them all there, at least in the context of this little parable.

Initially, it seems as though the establishment of legal and representative institutions will alleviate the people's anger over being rendered "peaceful and united" via cruelty and violence, even if the corrupt and oppressive lords bore the brunt of Remirro's harsh modes: Cesare establishes a court with a respected presiding officer and representatives from all parts of the region (P 7). In conventional Weberian terms, the policies of a new prince must be enacted, at first, by agents with whom he has a directly personal relationship, and then subsequently by more formal and impersonal institutions. According to Weber, this can eventually lead to the establishment of a legally rational form of government, such as the modern *Rechtsstaat,* one that is free, at least theoretically, of any personal relations of subordination.[15] Certainly, the duke seems to be transitioning from rule through a henchman—Remirro had been Cesare's major domo—to procedurally based governance in the Romagna. However, formally rational institutions are not sufficient for either Machiavelli or Cesare at this point in the latter's mission to establish a state in North-Central Italy. Routinized administration is not all that the duke provides the people; he also brings them food for their souls. Machiavelli suggests that, on the one hand, Cesare wishes to purge the people's "spirit" of their hatred more fully, and, on the other, that he wants to show them from whom the cruelty that ordered the province really derived: not from Cesare but from his minister (P 7).

As Machiavelli tells it so unforgettably, one morning in the town square of Cesena, the people find Remirro in two pieces, *in dua pezzi,* with a bloody knife and a piece of wood beside him (P 7). As anyone even slightly acquainted with *The Prince* knows, Machiavelli, who was there, reports: "This ferocious spectacle at once satisfied and stupefied the people" (P 7). There are myriad ways of interpreting this satisfying and stupefying *spettacolo.*

One way is to think of it as an illustration of specific Machiavellian precepts. Earlier in *The Prince,* Machiavelli claims that anyone who is the cause of another's ascent to power will himself come to ruin. He concludes chapter 3 by emphasizing the danger faced by anyone who has helped someone else come to authority because a prudent, newly powerful prince will naturally fear the industry or force of their own lieutenants and will vigorously counteract the potential threat that they pose. In short, one becomes a threat to the very person one helps to gain power, and if that person is at all astute they will neutralize all erstwhile aids as potential threats. In the case at hand, Remirro solidified Cesare's power for him and receives bodily bisection as his reward. However, Remirro may also have gone too far and thus may have deserved his fate: Machiavelli notoriously instructs elsewhere that it is better for rulers to be feared than loved, but that princes must avoid hatred in order to be truly secure (P 17, 19). Fear maintains subjects within boundaries fixed by their appetite for self-preservation; hatred impels them to transgress such boundaries once their desire to kill exceeds their appetite to live. Hatred is precisely what Remirro's cruelty generated among the people, a "spirit" that the duke decides he can scarcely afford.

But Cesare and Remirro are both described as cruel by Machiavelli. Why is the duke's cruelty preferable? Why does his cruelty result in fear but not hatred? In a celebrated discussion, Machiavelli contrasts Cesare's cruelty to the supposed kindness of the Florentine republic in dealing with subject cities, like Pistoia (P 17). Florentine "charity" permitted the continuation of the disorders—discord, rebellion, civil war—that cost Pistoia more lives than the single, solitary life (Remirro's) that Cesare expended at a stroke for the sake of all of the Romagna's people. In this sense, at least, Cesare's cruelty is more Christian than is Florence's charity.[16] It is a Christian tenet, after all, that one individual be sacrificed for the sake of everyone else; one person, Jesus Christ, must pay for everyone else's "sins," *peccati* (one of Machiavelli's favorite words).[17] Indeed, one might consider whether the block of wood that Cesare left near Remirro's two bodies is a visual allusion to the cross and to the ultimate meaning of the Crucifixion.[18]

Further reflection yields additional interpretive possibilities. Later, in chapter 21, Machiavelli advises princes on the subject of holidays: At suitable times of the year a prince should entertain the people with festivals and spectacles—*spettacoli*, the plural form of the same word he uses to describe the Remirro incident (P 21). Machiavelli need not mention something that almost anybody reading *The Prince* at the time would have known: Remirro was cut in two pieces on December 26, 1502. Given this fact, Remirro's death is a Christmas present, or more specifically, a St. Stephen's Day or Boxing Day present, for the people of the Romagna. Christmas is a festival celebrating God's covenant with mankind, His promise to redeem humanity.[19] The day after, the feast of St. Stephen, is the holiday when European nobles traditionally bestowed provisions in leather boxes to the poor so that they might enjoy sustenance through the balance of the winter. Machiavelli's duke, it seems, has provided sustenance for the common people's "spirit" with a holiday spectacular. Perhaps this is part of Machiavelli's lesson that a prince must always appear to be generous or pious (P 16, 21). Or maybe there is an even more substantive message behind appearances or even behind the appeal to appearances in this circumstance.

After all, as all good Christians try to teach their children, the spirit of Christmas entails much more than presents and pageants. The Holy Father sends his son to save the people, to bring them peace and unity on earth. Cesare is also a prince of peace sent by his holy father to the people of the Romagna. In this sense, Remirro's execution at Christmas is a covenant, a promise of faith. Indeed, perhaps the duke is thinking of Christmas, as it was traditionally understood, as a season rather than a day, a season comprising several important feast days. After Christmas Day and St. Stephen's Day, the next major feast in the Christian calendar is a reminder of another covenant between God and His people. Until fairly recently, the Feast of the Circumcision, celebrated on January 1, was the day when Roman Catholics acknowledged Jesus's ties to the Jewish people: The fact that Jesus came not only to bring new laws but to fulfill old ones as well. Jesus, like all Jews since Abraham, bore the physical mark of God's covenant with Israel, a covenant signified by a cutting, a severing of one's member.[20] Remirro, we should recall, was Cesare's "kingly arm," his princely extension—in several senses, his extremity (P 7). He is a prominent symbol of the duke's authority, a political phallus, if you will. I suggest it to be noteworthy that Remirro would be severed and publicly rendered in two bloody pieces during this significant holiday season in the Christian liturgical calendar.

What might be the substance of the covenant between Duke Valentino and the people of the Romagna? Cesare sets up courts establishing law and accountability and then jettisons the part of himself that resorted to extraordinary, extralegal violence. He dismembers himself from the very body that signifies excessively cruel, hate inducing violence. He dramatically cuts himself off from the very embodiment of arbitrary violence. In Machiavelli's account, the duke leaves the bloody knife behind at the scene of the crime. In some sense, this conveys the message: "I didn't do this, Remirro is responsible." The knife symbolizes Remirro's excessively cruel policies, and so it remains with him. Yet, the duke may be communicating a deeper, more profound form of separating, of distinguishing *that* from *this*. The duke also seems to say: "Now that the Romagna is well-ordered, I have no use for either Remirro *or* a knife." Going forward, a prince would certainly have recourse to a sword, while commanding troops or at the behest of the courts, but not a knife, which is functionally and symbolically a very different instrument. Indeed, Machiavelli later remarks how a prince who misuses cruelty and rouses his subjects' hatred must always "keep a knife in his hand" (P 8). On the contrary, a prince who uses cruelty well, who provides good government and avoids popular hatred, can afford to rely on laws and representative institutions. He need not avail himself of criminal means; he can leave behind the criminal weapon and perhaps even criminality itself.

Now we are in a position to understand more fully why the vulgar call Cesare by the exalted title "Duke Valentino." At the Feast of the Circumcision, Roman Catholics traditionally celebrated the consecration, by blood, of Jesus's name and its affiliation with the alternative name of "savior." The common people of the Romagna seem to understand the name "Valentino" in precisely this sense. The people may be aware of the behavior that Machiavelli catalogs in *The Prince*: that Cesare wages war and lies, strangles, and betrays his way to acquiring and consolidating power in the Romagna. Moreover, they may be cognizant of the rumors surrounding Cesare that were so ubiquitous at the time that Machiavelli does not even bother to mention them: that Cesare kept his sister as a concubine, that he slew his own brother, and that he raped and murdered the boy prince of Faenza—this, after guaranteeing the child's safety in return for the town's surrender.[21]

However, as far as the people are concerned, the following facts pertaining to "the end of things" are much more consequential: Duke Valentino beat down the nobility who misruled the people for so long; he ended the arbitrary violence that continually plagued them; and he established judicial and representative institutions on their behalf. In short, Valentino provided "good government" to them and allowed them to "savor well-being" (P 7). The people, recall, are concerned with outcomes and appearances more than the means that bring them about. Well-being and good government are tangible outcomes that satisfy the people. The bloody execution of Remirro stupefies them into accepting the appearance that the duke is less than fully complicit in the cruel policies that Remirro employed to deliver good government and well-being. The people know the good ends provided by the duke; they choose not to know that the evil means employed to bring them about, at least to some extent, belong to him as well.

Through his description of Cesare's actions, an account that would not fail to impress Max Weber, Machiavelli draws the blueprint that state-builders like the Tudors, Bourbons, Hohenzollerns, and their illustrious ministers would follow in creating the national dynastic states of Europe. Weber demonstrates that the modern state rests upon an historically unprecedented level and extent of popular legitimacy; a kind of popular legitimacy described and foretold by Machiavelli in his account of Cesare Borgia.[22] Despite oft-quoted passages where Machiavelli pronounces on the ingratitude of men or the fickleness of humanity (P 17), when the Florentine describes the behavior of "the people," specifically as a class, he emphasizes this fact: as the duke's political good fortune starts to fade with his father's death, his own ill health, and the election of an unfriendly pope, the people of the Romagna do not erupt into anarchy, rebel against his rule, or invite foreign forces to invade. On the contrary, they wait faithfully for the return, the second coming, of the prince who had brought them peace (P 7). The people's faithful obedience is the reward for a prince who suppresses the nobility, curtails arbitrary violence, establishes law—the very stuff of modern state legitimacy. While modern state-builders did not put down roots into popular soil as deeply as Machiavelli recommended,[23] they nevertheless forged more intimate ties with the people than did many of their historical antecedents.

Machiavelli is the first major thinker in the history of political thought to favor the people unequivocally over the aristocracy when discussing the stability of principalities and republics. As he asserts in chapter 9, princes may establish their power on the social foundation of either the people or the nobles, the *popolo* or the *grandi*. These classes are motivated by two opposing "humors" that exist in every polity: the people's desire not to be dominated and the nobility's desire to oppress the people (P 9). According to Machiavelli, these humors interact to cause principality, liberty, or license. When the parties successfully interact, liberty or a republic is the result; when their conflict approximates civil war, the result is license or anarchy. But, for Machiavelli's purposes in *The Prince*, when one part of the polity is not enjoying adequate satisfaction of their humor—when the *grandi* are not oppressing the people with some level of gratification, or the people are not living free of such oppression to a sufficient extent—one, the other, or both, will raise up a prince who enables them to do so (P 9).

Machiavelli provides several reasons why a prince should forge an alliance with the people instead of the great. He warns that the prince who has been elevated by the nobles is always in danger because the nobles view the prince as just one of their own whom they can unmake at any time and replace with another from their own ranks (P 9). On the contrary, the people afford the prince much more leeway since they do not assume, as do members of the *grandi*, that they can rule as well as he can. Moreover, Machiavelli avers that it is an easier task to side with the people: the nobles cannot be satisfied as readily as the people because their desire to oppress is infinite, while the people's desire not to be oppressed is fixed (P 9). The people will be pleasantly surprised when they are not oppressed, while the nobles will always be unimpressed by a prince's efforts; they inevitably assume that more could be done to facilitate their oppression of the people. Machiavelli also suggests that it is much less dangerous to side with the people: when offended, the worst the people will do is to abandon a prince; but a disaffected nobility is rather likely to kill him (P 9). The example of Duke Valentino demonstrates that the people will remain faithful if a prince has successfully defended them from the great and quelled the disorder that corrupt rule by the few invariably entails.

To quote Machiavelli at this point: "let us return to where we left off," or resume where "we parted ways" (*Ma torniamo donde noi partimmo*) (P 7). He utters this phrase immediately following the description of the Remirro *spettacolo*. After recounting a story about cutting, severing, and separating, Machiavelli points to a rupture, a disjuncture, in his narrative: where, indeed, did we "leave off," or "part ways"?

Fortune's Malignity or Deficient Virtue?

Duke Valentino seems to have acquitted himself pretty well at this point in Machiavelli's account. He has strangled enemies, cut to pieces erstwhile friends, and won over the people. In short, he has eliminated all those on whom he might have depended—except for the people. Dependence on the people is, after all, the only infringement on absolute autonomy that Machiavelli countenances in *The Prince*. But there is still Cesare's initial dependence on his father to consider. Pope Alexander VI, who had disappeared from the proceedings, returns to the narrative. Machiavelli reports that Cesare was secure in the Romagna and could have proceeded with further acquisition in Italy *if* Alexander had lived (P 7). The duke's father, the Pope, is dying and his successor will likely take away what Alexander had given him. A new prince will take away Cesare's patrimony, and Machiavelli expresses the following with brutal frankness: men more easily forget the death of their father than the loss of their patrimony (P 17). The duke may not mind the passing of his father so much as what it portends for his own inheritance. In a race against the clock, in a race against mortality, initially his father's mortality, Machiavelli recounts how Cesare sets about eliminating the blood lines of all those he has heretofore despoiled. In other words, he kills everyone in Rome whom *he* has deprived of *their* patrimonies. The duke must liquidate the heirs of anyone he has already robbed or killed; in so doing, he must remove a new pope's opportunity for moving against him and retaking the Romagna. In Machiavellian terms, Cesare does not want to give a "new founder" the occasion to exploit someone else's loss into the new pope's gain. He must not give a new Moses, Romulus or Theseus disgruntled or dispossessed persons to redeem at the duke's expense (P 6).

As Dante, for one, had documented years before, possessions like the Romagna were plums that pontiffs consistently dispensed as patronage to clients and relatives.[24] Machiavelli's own *Florentine Histories* reads like a litany of invasions by French, German, Neopolitan and Spanish forces who have been summoned by new popes hoping to dislodge the clients of their predecessors from Central Italian territories.[25] Thus, the threat posed to the duke's new principality by the papacy, his initial source of power, is very real indeed. As Machiavelli intimates throughout *The Prince*, a prince of any ability faces a daunting task in attempting to fortify a territorial base in North-Central Italy. Given the structure of the papacy and its status in Italy, such a regime would have to be established under papal auspices but could not be maintained under the same. Machiavelli observes that the papacy is too strong to allow a rival power that might unify Italy to emerge in the region, and yet it is too weak to do so itself (P 11). The papacy has no army of its own, papal elections are influenced by foreign powers, and the reign of a single pope tends to be quite short— Machiavelli estimates about a decade (P 11). More conventional monarchies, on the contrary, control their own arms, determine succession in a hereditary fashion, and do not depend on the life span of any particular prince for success, since political projects can be maintained across the life spans of fathers, sons, grandsons, and so on.

But Machiavelli insists that the duke, despite the odds stacked against him, could have accomplished several tasks before his father's death that would have secured his own power—four last things, as it were (P 7).[26] In addition to eliminating enemies whom he previously despoiled, Cesare must win over the nobles in Rome to keep the new pope in check. He must control as much of the College of Cardinals as he can so as to influence the election of the next pontiff. And he must acquire as much territory as possible so as to survive a first assault should the new pontiff attack him. The duke accomplishes most of these by the time of Alexander's death: Machiavelli describes with relish how the duke kills almost everyone he can get his hands on; how he wins over the Roman gentlemen; and the fact that he gains control of a sufficient number of cardinals to block anyone from the seat of St. Peter, if not enough to elect his own choice. Moreover, Cesare attempts to expand his conquests to include nearly all of Italy not already controlled by France, Spain, Milan, the Florentines or the Venetians. If he could have accomplished this successfully, Machiavelli suggests, the duke would have stood by himself as "arbiter of Italy," depending no longer on fortune but only on his own considerable virtue.

Yet Machiavelli writes that Alexander died five years after "he" had begun to draw his sword. It is not exactly clear to whose sword—Cesare's or Alexander's—Machiavelli refers. As Machiavelli begins to recount the duke's demise, the distinction between father and son is once again ambiguous: Cesare's mission is jeopardized only a few years after he had set about his father's business. Alexander left the duke with just the Romagna secured, while all the others, as Machiavelli describes them, hover "in the air" (P 7). These other potential conquests remain unreal, ideal cities—kingdoms not of this world.[27] In other words, the duke's imperium, arguably the most important polity described in *The Prince*, is very much the kind of imaginary republic and principality that Machiavelli dismisses when he boasts about his own purported concern with, above all other things, "effectual truth" (P 15).

Late in the account of Cesare's fall from grace, Machiavelli adds to the duke's woes by reporting the following: not only is the father dying but the son, Cesare himself, is seriously ill in the midst of this political crisis (P 7). The duke finds himself suffering from a life-threatening illness and is caught, incapacitated, between the hostile armies of France and Spain. Machiavelli insists that if Cesare had not been so sick, he would have pulled off the task—easily. One of the resources that the duke clearly possesses is the popular basis of his power: again, despite his vulnerabilities, Machiavelli states that the Romagna does not rebel against Cesare. The people are certainly not one of the duke's problems; they keep their covenant with their prince of peace. And here Machiavelli re-inserts himself into the story as one who witnessed the young prince's actions firsthand and who subsequently put Cesare's words and actions to parchment. Machiavelli, who was present in France at Cesare's political birth, relates how he conversed with the duke in Rome on the day the new pope was "created," effectively the day of the duke's political death (P 7). Cesare tells Machiavelli that he had carefully considered what would happen when his father eventually died, but not the fact that he himself would be so direly ill in such circumstances as well. Apparently, a son interested in a patrimony may consider a father's death but not his own mortality. Part of the duke's illness seems to have something to do with a certain understanding of mortality, or, as it were, a belief in his own immortality. But why should the young duke be concerned with his own death? What perverse and unnatural way of thinking focuses on the death of a son rather than the death of a father? Fathers are supposed to die; sons grow to become fathers, at which time, according to the natural course of things, they may die.

Cesare admits to his chronicler that he never considered such a thing. And Machiavelli does not reproach him for this. He tells readers that he cannot blame the duke (P 7). The duke, recall, like Machiavelli, suffered from terrible bad luck, from "fortune's excessive malignity." But this exoneration is not Machiavelli's final word: It turns out that Cesare made a mistake. His fate was in his own hands, after all; it rested with his own free choice or free will. What is this mistake? Caesar allows Julius to become Alexander. That is, the duke allowed Giuliano della Rovere—a man he had offended—to become Pope Julius II. Machiavelli suggests that Cesare could have vetoed the candidacy of any cardinal, and he could have safely permitted the election of a French or Spanish cardinal who might not have turned against him immediately. Instead, taken in by Giuliano's assurances, the duke sanctions the election of a prince he has wronged who consequently deprives Cesare of his state. This mistake violates another important Machiavellian maxim: Great men never forget an old injury (P 7). In this light, Cesare's ultimate mistake is that he believes in forgiveness.[28]

How is this possible? Earlier in the parable, Cesare Borgia certainly seems to hold no stock whatsoever in forgiveness—in fact, belief in it serves as a weapon that he ably wields against others. The duke preys on his enemies' belief in reconciliation, luring them under this very pretext to a holiday gathering where he proceeds to murder them. In this instance, it is not so much that the duke forgives, but rather that he "deceives" himself into thinking that others forgive him. And why should he not think this? Anybody reading this account at the time would know that Cesare himself had not offended Giuliano, as Machiavelli states misleadingly. The duke had not caused any harm to Julius. Alexander, the duke's father, had offended Giuliano by exiling him from Rome for ten years. Cesare has spent this whole passion play attempting to free himself from dependence on the Holy Father. He wants his patrimony from his father, but without dependence on him. But the offense committed against Julius, every bit as much as the territory of the Romagna *is* Cesare's patrimony. Machiavelli's lesson seems to be that the duke is more dependent on his father than he can possibly estimate; he does not consider that he might be held accountable for offenses committed against a great man by his forbearer. The advice seems to be: do not allow someone to come to power that you or your family has offended. (One wonders if the Medici Prince to whom Machiavelli dedicates this book apprehends and heeds this lesson. Just because a different Medici, Giuliano, sacked, tortured, and confined Machiavelli to internal exile for his republican allegiances, should Lorenzo, his successor, trust this book-bearing office-seeker?)

Or, perhaps there is another dimension to Cesare's sickness. Perhaps Borgia's life-threatening illness prompts him to entirely reevaluate the significance of forgiveness. Cesare is a good Catholic boy—or, at the very least, he is a son of the Church. In confronting, for the first time, his own mortality, Cesare may be compelled to consider a different set of "last things" than the expressly political ones that Machiavelli lists above. Not to be too judgmental, but Cesare is a sinner—a rather extravagant one—who may, on the point of death, be examining his conscience and contemplating the dire consequences of his many iniquities. As a Christian he may conclude that the salvation of his eternal soul requires forgiveness for the nearly innumerable mortal sins that he has committed in his young life. And what better father confessor could Cesare hope for than a warmly assuring and accommodating cardinal, and potential pope, like Giuliano? Indeed, great sins may require remittance by a commensurately great spiritual authority.

At this moment of weakness in body and soul—actually, Machiavelli might insist, weakness "of the brain" (D III.6)—Cesare is susceptible, in a way that would have been impossible at any previous moment of his life, to deception by a father figure falsely promising him forgiveness. While mourning, at least to some extent, the loss of his own not-so-holy natural father, and while perhaps pondering with fear and trembling the looming severe judgment of his Heavenly Father, Cesare accedes to Giuliano's request to be created the Holy Father in Rome in exchange for a promise of absolution and the con-

tinued security of the duke's state. Cesare's spiritual need for forgiveness of his sins against God, as much as his mistaken faith in Giuliano's willingness to forgive past wrongs of a more personal quality,
Machiavelli intimates, is the ultimate cause of the duke's ruin.

Each of the following factors emphasize the extent to which Borgia's political viability is tied to the authority of three persons (respectively, Alexander, Julius, and God): the coincidence of Cesare's
illness and his father's demise; the ease with which a would-be pope
exploits Valentino's vulnerability; and the inducement toward credulity generated by the duke's confrontation with mortality. Even
though Cesare did everything he could, he underestimated just how
much he was always his father's son—or, rather, some father's son—
and hence not ultimately his own man.

Clearly extrapolating from Machiavelli's account of Borgia in *The
Prince*, Burckhardt, as mentioned above, insists that a physically
healthy Cesare would have been able to intimidate the College of
Cardinals into electing his choice as pope—or that he might even
have engineered something more drastic like annihilating the papacy
as such.[29] Machiavelli, however, suggests that Cesare suffers from a
spiritual cum psychological sickness in this moment of crisis that in-
hibits him from operating with his characteristic cunning and ferocity. A certain Christian frame of mind, Machiavelli intimates, presently inclines the duke to act, in Rome, in a manner diametrically
opposed to how he previously behaved in Senigallia or Cesena. Instead of exploiting the notion of reconciliation to his own advantage
against Giuliano and ruthlessly entrapping and killing en masse his
adversaries in the College of Cardinals—as he did when dispensing
with previous enemies—Cesare now seems disposed toward seeking
forgiveness for his sins and disinclined to commit outrageous acts of
impiety.

Even if, in the manner that Burckhardt recommends, the duke had
prevented the election of a successor to his father in Rome, it is fair
to assume that the non-Italian powers who had long benefited from
the papacy's presence there would certainly have concerted in a vigorous effort to reinstate it. Indeed, the duke could have declared the
Holy See a hereditary office and appointed himself pope. But this
radical change in the nature of the institution—this secularization or

normalization of it—likewise would have provoked a violent reaction on the part of the rest of the kingdoms of Christendom. Alternately, the duke might simply have claimed as his patrimony all of the Church's secular holdings in Italy and dared the foreign powers to relocate the Court of Rome elsewhere, if it was so important to them. If not Switzerland as a site—which Machiavelli jokingly suggests to emphasize the papacy's unlimited capacity to corrupt even the most virtuous regions of the earth (D I.12)—Cesare might have insisted upon, say, Avignon as a re-established location for the Holy See. But besides wishing to keep at a relatively safe distance from themselves the irresistible corruption that, according to Machiavelli, the papacy brings to any province it inhabits, France, Spain, and the German emperor would have worked exceedingly hard to re-establish the Holy See in Rome. They benefited greatly from its location and functioning: the workings and very structure of the papacy insured frequent occasions for them to meddle in Italian affairs and invade the peninsula.

Conclusion: The Gospel according to Niccolò

In the foregoing discussion I have revisited Machiavelli's account of the rise and fall of Duke Valentino. Cesare Borgia, like other famous founders, was of questionable birth and a foreigner to the people he attempts to reconstitute as subjects. This illegitimate child of Spanish descent rises to the rank of almost-arbiter of all of Italy. Having taught *The Prince* for some years, I am always amused by students' assumptions concerning Cesare's ultimate fate. Machiavelli writes that the duke was deathly sick but never states that he actually dies. Yet, in discussions students inevitably and overwhelmingly refer to Cesare's *death*, as if he perished from his illness or was executed by Pope Julius. Machiavelli makes no reference to Cesare's fate beyond his political failure. If one goes looking for the duke's body in the book, one will find it missing. Contemporary readers would know that Cesare was stripped of his power by Julius and imprisoned, only to escape and die in battle as a middling military captain in Spain. However, textually, the body is nowhere to be found. In a book littered with corpses, the duke's body disappears.[30]

What are we to make of the Biblical, and especially Christian, allegories that make Machiavelli's account of Borgia's career read so much like a Gospel? Many notable scholars consider Machiavelli to be something less than an enthusiastic supporter of Christianity.[31] Is Machiavelli committing subversion-through-imitation with this allegorical rendering of Borgia? After all, the Antichrist is expected to arrive appearing very much like his holy alter ego, despite his very different ultimate intentions.[32] Interestingly, in the "First Decennale," Machiavelli pronounced that Borgia's fall was a fate befitting all such "rebels against Christ."[33] In this sense, Machiavelli's Duke Valentino appears nothing other than a rather devoutly antichristian exemplar. Indeed, to render Christian themes, motifs and tropes, as Machiavelli does, so violent, conspiratorial, and cynical certainly seems to entail a subversion, perhaps a wholesale inversion, of Christian morality. After all, at the Last Supper, Jesus does not have Judas strangled. Moreover, Jesus does not offer His Father some other guy, a stooge like Remirro, to serve as the sacrificial victim in the Passion Play that redeems all of humanity. This much is clear. But are Machiavelli's alterations of the Gospels inherently or comprehensively antichristian? Does he turn all of the Christian elements that he appropriates against Christianity itself?[34]

To be sure, Machiavelli explicitly claims that strict adherence to Christian doctrine has weakened the princes and republics of Italy, and that excessive tolerance for the Roman Church's secular power has kept the peninsula from being unified and hence incapable of resisting frequent incursions by France, Spain and the German emperor. Nevertheless, Machiavelli writes in the *Discourses* that the problem with Christianity is not so much "our religion" itself as much as reigning interpretations of it (D II.2). Recent reformers like St. Dominic and St. Francis, he suggests, misemphasize certain aspects of the Christian religion: they emphasize the poverty and self-abnegation of Christ's *life* and preach the deferring of punishment for the wicked into the next world. That is, Machiavelli implies, they do not emphasize the true meaning of Christ's *death*: the fact that sins must be paid for with blood in this world, not the next. And here, I believe, is a clue to the further significance of Remirro and circumcision. Of course, the piece of wood conjures the image of the cross on which Jesus's broken and bloody body is sacrificed for the salvation of mankind, much as Remirro is spectacularly sacrificed for the salvation of the Romagnol people. However, Jesus was not merely crucified, he was also circumcised; and Christians do (or did) celebrate this link with Judaism. With this allegorical rendering of Remirro's execution as crucifixion cum circumcision, Machiavelli seems to recast a link between the two traditions, the two Bibles. Moses, of course, is Machiavelli's archetype for an armed prophet, while Savonarola, a Christian *Frate*, serves as his reviled poster child for Christianity's lack of arms (P 6).

But the parable of Cesare Borgia suggests that Christianity offers unprecedented possibilities for founding princely authority upon popular legitimacy—opportunities that Theseus, Cyrus, Romulus, or even Moses did not fully explore. What if a prophet could redeem the people, as Christianity teaches, more widely and substantively than did the ancient founders, without that prophet having to sacrifice himself for their sins? Machiavelli recounts with delight the "infinite" numbers of envious rivals to his authority that Moses killed rather than allowing himself to be usurped by them (D III.30). Moreover, what if one could in principle champion the weak, as does Christianity, but not in practice leave them weaponless, as did the most important unnamed, unarmed prophet in *The Prince*? Importantly, Machiavelli emphasizes that Borgia begins to militarily arm and train the people during his reign in the Romagna (P 9). Furthermore, in the *Discourses*, Machiavelli suggests that regular public executions of prominent citizens, reminiscent of both the Remirro *spettacolo* and Jesus's Crucifixion, are the surest ways for republics to protect the many from abuse by the few (D III.1).

Clearly, Duke Valentino learned only half of these lessons. On the one hand, he kills Remirro rather than himself in a blood rite of popular redemption, and engages in efforts to empower the people militarily. However, on the other hand, he trusts too much in the possibility of reconciliation among enemies, especially "great men," when he allows Giuliano to become Pope. Nevertheless, Machiavelli and his duke do point the way for princes to interact more directly with their peoples than did all the armed prophets named in *The Prince*. In fact, they do so in a manner not unreminiscent of the world's most famous unarmed prophet.

There are suggestions throughout *The Prince* and *Discourses* that Machiavelli wishes to emphasize the sword as a symbol of Moses rather than of, say, St. Paul. Paul, after all, is often considered the true founder of Christianity. Like Machiavelli's Signor Paolo, who facilitates both Cesare's consolidation of power as well as Machiavelli's written account of it, St. Paul makes possible our knowledge of Jesus's words and deeds. The sword signifies the triumph of Moses over unbelievers within his own ranks and over foreign enemies; in Christian iconography it signifies Paul's martyrdom. Who is the better "armed prophet," to use Machiavelli's term? The answer seems obvious.[35]

We should, however, consider whether Machiavelli thought it possible for a successful founder to be armed with a book, as well as, or in lieu of, a sword. Moses, Jesus, Paul, and Machiavelli were most fiercely armed with books—books that either they themselves composed or whose authorship was in some extended sense attributed to them. Books, in the right circumstances, allow one to succeed even when conventional weapons fail. The image of a prophet armed with a book prompts us to rethink the definition of political success. After all, books attributed to the executed Jesus, the assassinated Moses, the outmaneuvered Borgia and the sacked and tortured Machiavelli allow such prophets to succeed despite short-term failures—even to succeed after their deaths and thus to win their greatest victories posthumously, in a kind of after-life.

Despite the duke's failure, through Machiavelli's recounting of his deeds and words, the Florentine still offers Cesare as the best example for new princes who must rely on fortune—and that is, in reality, all new princes. Machiavelli emphatically reminds us that, despite his shortcomings, the duke is still deeply deserving of notice and imitation. Success reconceived along these lines invites readers to rethink whether this book, *The Prince*, known above all others for a fixation on practical, real-world success, is in actuality an exercise in political idealism, an elevation rather than denunciation of hypothetical, ideal regimes. Machiavelli may feign indifference to republics and kingdoms that no one has ever seen (P 15), but how else would one characterize Cesare Borgia's kingdom that, as Machiavelli concedes, proved ultimately to be made of "air" (P 7)? Indeed, how factual or real is the united Italy invoked in the final chapter of *The Prince* (P 26)?

2

"Keep the Public Rich and the Citizens Poor"

ECONOMIC INEQUALITY AND POLITICAL CORRUPTION IN THE *DISCOURSES*

ECONOMIC INEQUALITY is perhaps the greatest threat to the civic liberty that republics, ancient and modern, promise to their citizens. Liberty depends first and foremost on political equality: every citizen ought to influence law- and policy-making in a relatively equal way; at the very least, government ought to be responsive and accountable to all citizens on a fairly equal basis.[1] Yet the freedom so prevalent in republics invariably allows those citizens who accumulate greater material resources (and longer term, the cultural capital of personal and family reputation) to enjoy such advantages at the expense of less privileged citizens. Put simply, economic inequality inevitably undermines political equality, and, hence, liberty itself.[2] This fact ought to be especially alarming today as socioeconomic inequality rises precipitously in contemporary democracies like the United States and in others throughout the world.[3]

Civic liberty permits wealthy citizens to bring their economic resources directly to bear on politics: various forms of clientelism and bribery are ubiquitous within the politics of *all* republican or democratic polities. Marginally legal buying of influence or peddling of favors, as well as blatantly illegal political corruption, in all times and all places, enable a polity's few richest citizens to exert

excessive influence over the formulation of laws that are supposed
to benefit the majority.[4] Moreover, wealth enables certain citizens
to cultivate a greater reputation, a more distinctive appearance, and
better public speaking skills. Consequently, both audiences within
ancient assemblies and voters within modern electoral contests have
tended to bestow disproportionate favor on wealthy individuals.[5]

I begin this chapter by sketching attempts made by various ancient republics—specifically, Athens, Sparta, and Rome—to confront, constitutionally, the threat posed to liberty by economic inequality. Readers will perhaps not be shocked to learn that none of
these constitutions were terribly successful at defending civic liberty
from the corrosive and corrupting influence of economic inequality.[6]
Subsequently, I turn to Machiavelli's analysis of the Roman Republic
in the *Discourses* for clues that might instruct us how ancient republics perhaps ought to have better contained the corrupting influence
of economic inequality.[7] In particular, I hope that Machiavelli's engagement with the crisis associated with Rome's Agrarian Laws will
prompt readers to think more creatively about how to protect, in his
words, "the free and civil way of life" from the "great avarice and ambition of the few" (D I.40).

Scholars have tended to underestimate the central role played by
economic inequality in Machiavelli's diagnosis of political corruption. Intellectual historians who emphasize Machiavelli's purported
fidelity to the traditions of Roman or Florentine "republicanism," and
political theorists whose ideological conservatism inclines them to
neglect, dismiss, or distort the democratic character of Machiavelli's
political thought, both attribute Machiavelli's critique of corruption
in the Roman Republic to sources other than rising inequality.[8] Instead, they accentuate the following as the main causes of the civic
corruption that, according to Machiavelli, eventually destroyed the
republic: a decline in the Roman people's moral virtue, manifested
by degenerating civic mores and customs or increasing support
among the Roman people for leaders, such as Gaius Marius and
Julius Caesar, who promise redistributive reforms in exchange for
tyrannical authority.

To whatever extent such scholars acknowledge the fact that
Machiavelli considered economic inequality to be a political prob-

lem, they are inclined to the opinion that he viewed this affliction to be, in good republican or conservative terms, one whose potential cure was worse than the actual disease.[9] In what follows, I will argue that Machiavelli demonstrates, throughout the *Discourses*, that developments such as the decaying of the Roman people's mores, customs, and morality, or their increasing "adoration" or "favoring" of demagogues who promised economic redistribution (D I.5, D I.37), are fully attributable to deeper structural causes—socioeconomic causes generated by Rome's nobility and senate, whose efforts to amass ever greater wealth through imperial expansion resulted in the collapse of the republic.[10]

Economic Inequality in Ancient Republics

How did ancient republics attempt to mitigate the threat posed to liberty by economic inequality? Democratic Athens established the following informal truce between rich and poor citizens: the demos would not "soak the rich" through democratic institutional arrangements that favored the poor, so long as the wealthy did not use their vast economic resources and public prominence to compromise political equality, or *isonomia*.[11] As Demosthenes famously exclaimed: "The elite have great wealth, which no one keeps them from enjoying; therefore, they must not keep us from enjoying the security which is our common possession—the laws."[12]

The laws of the Athenian constitution politically empowered poor citizens in three primary ways: through a legislative assembly open to all citizens; executive offices distributed by lottery; and political courts comprised of large subsets of randomly selected citizens. In the Athenian assembly, the *ekklêsia*, every citizen was entitled to initiate and discuss legislation, laws over which ultimate decisions were decided by majority vote. Furthermore, any citizen who was willing and able to stand for executive or judicial office could submit their name for inclusion in the political lotteries that appointed magistrates and jurors. When public funding subsidized these forms of political participation, Athenians distributed direct political power among a greater proportion of its citizenry than any government in history. Of course, property qualifications, slavery, and the political exclusion of free women and foreigners are unavoidable issues to consider in this context.[13] Nevertheless, Athens, at its most democratic, empowered a greater number of the poor to participate in actual rule than any other political regime, before or since.

The Athenian demos jealously guarded the border between socioeconomic and political power—that is, between economic inequality and political equality—through the large citizen juries and the practice of ostracism. Former magistrates and, indeed, any citizen at all could be indicted by any other citizen and be tried before the large citizen juries for behavior deemed threatening to the democracy. Moreover, if wealthy or prominent citizens were suspected of exerting excessive influence in assembly, in the regime's few elected offices, or in any manner whatsoever, the demos might ostracize them, effectively exiling such individuals for as long as a decade.

Aristocratic Sparta, by contrast, attempted to secure its own ideal of civic liberty by substituting economic equality for political equality.[14] Sparta's reputed founder, Lycurgus, established strict economic equality at the outset, for which he compensated prominent families and individuals with fairly insulated political authority; although denying them their traditional economic advantages, Lycurgus entrusted the city's aristocracy with preeminent political power. Sparta's two oldest, most esteemed families shared joint rule in the republic's dual monarchy and other prominent families were granted dominance over the republic's most important political body, the senate. Moreover, the republic's highest magistrates, the ephors, were appointed, not through lottery, but through election in Sparta's popular assembly—which itself was much weaker than popular assemblies in either Athens or Rome.[15]

Lycurgus purportedly established economic equality by distributing land equally among all citizens, by banning foreign trade, and by imposing strict sumptuary laws. Under such circumstances, Spartan citizens could plausibly claim that they were ruled, not by a wealthy few, but by the most experienced and wise among the citizenry. This conclusion ought not appear as foreign to us as it might first seem; after all, a powerful strand of modern republican political thought identifies true liberty, not with equal distribution of access to self-rule among citizens, but rather with rule by the best citizens. Modern republics and "republicanism," however, make little or no effort what-soever to ensure that these few best are not, in fact, simply the rich or their clients.[16]

Thus, while Athens was an economically inegalitarian political democracy, and Sparta an economically egalitarian political oligarchy, we can, in some way, conclude that ancient Rome was a combination of both. The Roman republic was both politically oligarchic and democratic; while Roman society was economically inegalitarian in profound ways, Roman citizens enjoyed extensive, indeed, almost unprecedented, opportunities for upward socioeconomic mobility.[17] Polybius famously depicted the Roman constitution as a composite of parts affiliated with other, more simple regimes: the Roman mixed regime contained a tamed monarchical power in its chief magistrates, the consuls; a contained aristocratic power in the Roman senate; and a fairly constrained popular power in the tribunes of the plebs and the citizen assemblies.[18]

When the political role of wealth is taken into account, it is clear that Rome's richest, most prominent families dominated, at first formally and then informally, the consulship and the senate. Assemblies where votes were weighted in favor of wealthier citizens annually elected Rome's two consuls. The consuls, originally drawn exclusively from the patrician class, were charged with the highest administrative and military duties. The senate, ostensibly just a deliberative and advisory body, nevertheless enjoyed substantial influence over the republic's fiscal and foreign policies. Senatorial mentoring of consuls, plus the prospect of former consuls joining the senate, ensured that this body, composed of the republic's wealthiest citizens, exercised exorbitant sway over the republic's supreme magistrates. Rome's armed poor, the plebeians, responded to the political monopoly enjoyed by Rome's nobility in two ways: first, by instigating the establishment of the tribunate, a magistracy for which the very wealthiest citizens were ineligible; and second, by increasing the importance of citizen assemblies more closely approximating majority rule over those in which voting was weighted in favor of the wealthy.

The ten tribunes of the plebs, annually elected exclusively from plebeian ranks, were charged with popular advocacy. As bearers of veto power over most of the workings of Roman government, and as the chief agents of public indictments for political crimes, the tribunes possessed the means to block policy proposals and punish magistrates and prominent citizens for violating the liberty of the citizenry or for corrupting the republic's civic life. Furthermore, over the course of the republic's history, legislative and judicial power shifted from the oligarchically structured centuriate assembly to assemblies where the tribunes presided, and where patricians were excluded or where they could be outvoted by a majority of poorer citizens.[19]

Thus, we might understand the Roman Republic to sit on a sociopolitical continuum somewhere between Athens and Sparta: some political institutions directly empowered the wealthy, while others directly empowered the poor. Moreover, upward socioeconomic mobility, exemplified by the careers of notable "new men," allowed Romans to insist that their republic was not dominated by a hermetically sealed wealthy caste of senatorial families.

As I mentioned at the outset, none of these republics' efforts to block, mitigate, or forestall the corrosive influence of economic inequality upon civic liberty worked very well—or at least, they did not work effectively for very long. Even though Athenians permitted the wealthy full enjoyment of their economic advantages, democratic Athens nevertheless proved particularly susceptible to oligarchic coups. The people's harsh political treatment of the wealthy, whether real or merely perceived, motivated Athenian oligarchs to overthrow the democracy—although, usually on the pretext that the demos was guilty of egregious political or military mismanagement. When analyzing these coups and what they say about the stability of Athenian democracy, it is very difficult to disaggregate two factors: the unprecedented pressure placed upon Athens by the Peloponnesian War and the Athenian elites' longstanding resentment toward the democracy that severely curtailed their political power.[20]

Nevertheless, history has been quite kind to the enemies and critics of Athenian democracy. The vast majority of philosophical and historical accounts consistently deride the Athenian demos for unjustly ordering the execution of roughly half a dozen citizens: specifically and notoriously, Socrates and the five Athenian commanders at the battle of Arginusae. The Western Great Books tradition focuses far less extensively on the thousands of Athenian democrats murdered by the oligarchs, more or less in collusion with foreign enemies, during the city's two principal oligarchic coups in 411 and 404 BCE.[21]

As for the Spartans, despite the severity of Lycurgus's proscriptions on wealth acquisition, economic inequality greatly expanded in the Lacedaemonian republic; the royal and noble families, who were meant to enjoy only political authority, soon amassed fabulous wealth, with which they progressively marginalized and oppressed common Spartan citizens. In response, the reform-minded kings— Agis, ineffectually, and Cleomenes, with some success—attempted to reinstitute Lycurgus's laws. However, these kingly efforts aimed at restoring economic equality resulted in violent, bloody intra-elite conflict within the republic, conflict that arguably contributed to Sparta's military and political decline. Indeed, as recent scholarship has suggested, Spartan laws aimed at achieving economic equality may have originated with Cleomenes himself and may have been only mythically attributed, after the fact, to Lycurgus, in order to legitimate such policies.[22] Be that as it may, the controversies and instability that emerged as a result of these laws accentuate how difficult it is to peacefully legislate economic equality within republics.

In the Roman Republic, economic inequality, already quite pronounced, was wildly exacerbated by the expansion of Rome's empire with dire consequences for its citizens' liberty at home. As Rome's army spent ever greater periods of time farther away from the city and, eventually, from the Italian peninsula, its citizen soldiers became increasingly impoverished and its commanders increasingly powerful. I will discuss Machiavelli's view of this critical trend in greater detail below.[23]

For various reasons, the constitutional arrangements of Athens, Sparta, and Rome unsuccessfully prevented those republics' wealthiest citizens from corrupting civic liberty and from undermining the free status of their polities. I turn now to Machiavelli's analysis of civic liberty, economic inequality and political corruption in the Roman context. Machiavelli's account offers intriguing counterfactuals that might help us think more fruitfully about the problem of wealth and freedom in republics more generally. In particular, I focus on Machiavelli's treatment of the Brothers Gracchus, Roman tribunes whose efforts to enact economic reforms represented the last stand of Roman civic liberty in the face of oligarchic predation and corruption. First, however, I offer some general considerations on Machiavelli's views on the proper role of socioeconomic equality in healthy republics.

Machiavelli's Egalitarian Politics

Did Machiavelli hate the rich? I have argued elsewhere that Machiavelli deeply distrusted wealthy citizens, that he gravely worried about the negative impact their economic advantages visited upon republics, and that he consequently recommended treating them with harsh recourse to address political inequality.[24] The historical record establishes firmly that during his career as a public servant for the 1494–1512 Florentine republic, Machiavelli was a steadfast, partisan enemy of the wealthy Florentine *ottimati* who opposed the popular government. Recent historiography adds to evidence provided in earlier biographical accounts supporting the view that Machiavelli was an enemy of the aristocrats, conceived not only as a political but also as a socioeconomic class.[25] In particular, Jérémie Barthas's work documenting Machiavelli's deeply antagonistic relationship with the Florentine aristocrats accentuates the political problems that the *ottimati* posed for the popular government and identifies a particularly acute financial crisis they created and exacerbated.[26]

Barthas shows convincingly that Machiavelli's famous militia plan in Florence was intended not only to achieve a valuable military goal but also a salutary socioeconomic one: Machiavelli proposed the plan to stem the massive amounts of money that wealthy citizens were accruing from the city's funding of mercenary arms, thus intensifying inequality within the city. Machiavelli's militia proposal would have put an end to the favorable loans that wealthy families were extracting from the republic at exorbitant rates of interest. This, as much as any fears that the aristocrats harbored of a militia serving under the command of Gonfalonier Piero Soderini, generated the *ottimati*'s opposition to the militia plan and intensified their contempt for its chief advocate and author, Machiavelli. In any case, such contextual considerations make it difficult to imagine that such intensely personal and policy-related antagonism between Machiavelli and the wealthy Florentine aristocrats would not make its way, to an important extent, into Machiavelli's writings.[27]

In this light, we must consider the praise that Machiavelli's political works express for egalitarian conditions in healthy republics, generally, and in contemporary Swiss and German republics, more specifically (D I.55–56).[28] After all, such equality is only instituted and maintained by policies that, in Machiavelli's words, "keep citizens poor and the public rich" (D I.37); modes and orders that, he avers, "turn the rich away empty handed" (D I.26). As Machiavelli reiterates later in the *Discourses*, "it is most useful to order a free way of life such that the citizens are kept poor" (D III.25). In the ancient context, Machiavelli repeatedly invokes the civic necessity of maintaining relative economic equality, often coupling it with the importance of sustaining an armed citizenry: "the public must be kept rich and private citizens poor, and military exercises maintained with the utmost seriousness" (D II.19); moreover, to insure that truly worthy individuals are esteemed in peacetime, Machiavelli recommends both "keeping all the citizens sufficiently poor such that they cannot corrupt themselves or others with riches . . . and maintaining military orders such that war-making is always possible and reliance on respected citizens is always necessary" (D III.16). Egalitarian and martial republics lead an uncorrupted way of life, and they repute militarily virtuous rather than economically powerful citizens.

Machiavelli devotes chapter 10 of *The Prince* to the social conditions requisite for principalities to maintain martial virtue and sustain enemy sieges, but he uses the Swiss/German republics as his chief example. In this context, Machiavelli mentions several public provisions intended to insure the material sustenance and prosperity of citizens (including, the socioeconomic well-being of "the plebs") during conditions of war (P 9). Likewise, in the *Discourses*, Machiavelli emphasizes how the Swiss and German republics "kill all" the rich "gentlemen" with whom they come in contact (D I.55). They do so to insure that such gentlemen—who venture forth from the security of their fortresses to plunder the countryside and expropriate the peasantry with impunity—never secure footholds in their lands. As a result, Machiavelli concludes, these Swiss/German republics live "very armed," "very free" and in "broadly equal" social conditions (D I.55, D II.19).[29] We are now perhaps better positioned to examine Machiavelli's critique of increasing economic inequality cum political corruption in the Roman Republic and the Gracchi's efforts to reverse this trend through passage of Agrarian reforms.

A Roman Crisis in the Florentine Context

In the *Discourses*, Machiavelli famously defies consensus among commentators on the Roman Republic: unlike his predecessors, the Florentine attributes the flourishing of Rome's freedom and greatness to "the tumults" resulting from the domestic conflicts that frequently ensued between the wealthy nobles and the common people.[30] But Machiavelli also concedes that class conflict ultimately contributed to the ruin of Rome's free way of life after the plebeian tribunes Tiberius and Gaius Gracchus attempted to institute redistributive economic reforms (D I.4). The Agrarian Laws, sponsored by the Gracchi, limited the amount of public lands any citizen could hold, and it redistributed to the plebeians public lands already held in custody by wealthy Romans.[31] In Book I, chapter 37, Machiavelli marks the reform efforts of these ill-fated brothers as a decisive moment in the history of the republic.

On separate occasions, the Roman nobility infamously eliminated each of the brothers in a dramatically public fashion. In 133 BCE, senators and their clients murdered Tiberius in the open air of the republic's civic space, after he successfully resisted their efforts to block passage of the laws and his reelection as tribune. A decade later, they desecrated the body of his brother, Gaius, who had committed suicide after his term as tribune failed to prevent a conservative rollback of his brother's agrarian and judicial reforms. Apparently taking these lessons to heart, all future "reformers" would enter the Roman Forum accompanied by armed legions.

It is worth noting that Machiavelli's description of Rome's decline after these events invokes the "time of" the Gracchi, or the "scandals" and "contentions" that arose in response to their policies (D I.37, D III.24). Machiavelli attributes this decline neither to the brothers themselves nor to the content of their land reform proposals. Actually, he concludes his account (1) by criticizing the "prudence" that the brothers exhibited in attempting to enact substantive land reform rather than their actual "intentions" in wishing to pass such reforms; and (2) by validating the necessity of laws precisely like those that the plebeians demanded and that the Gracchi proposed and promulgated (D I.37). But why does Machiavelli take readers through an obviously confusing and circuitous route to such conclusions?[32] I suggest that for Machiavelli's wealthy patrician audience, typified by the *Discourses'* dedicatees, economic redistribution is a delicate issue.[33] Hence, it is crucial that we examine Machiavelli's ambiguous presentation of the brothers' reform agenda with great care.

Machiavelli's discussion of the Gracchi's careers initially appears to condemn both the brothers and the Roman plebs (D I.37). Apparently agreeing with the position of aristocratic critics of the plebeians whom Machiavelli himself attempted to refute during a debate that he staged earlier in the *Discourses* (D I.5), here he reiterates the assertions of his erstwhile opponents: "the Roman plebs considered the *necessary* security that they gained against the nobles through the creation of the tribunes to be insufficient; once they achieved that, they immediately began to agitate out of *ambition*, desiring to share the nobles' honors and resources as the things that men esteem most of all" (D I.37, emphases added). One might plausibly read this statement to mean that the plebeians were justified in desiring the tribunate because necessity dictated the creation of a magistracy that would protect them from domination exercised by the nobles, but that Machiavelli condemns the plebeians for then aspiring after consular offices and a share in the nobility's wealth because they were motivated only by ambition and greed.[34]

These are curious statements considering that elsewhere in the *Discourses* Machiavelli explicitly endorses the opening of the consulship to the plebeians, because it permitted the Roman Republic to avail itself of virtue wherever it resided, among both "the nobles and the ignobles" (D I.30) and enabled the republic to benefit from an influx of political "youth" represented by the plebeians (D I.60). Moreover, earlier in the work, Machiavelli emphatically declares that the common people only desire to reduce or share in the wealth of rich citizens when they observe that latter using such wealth "inappropriately," that is, to further their efforts at political oppression (D I.5). Finally, even in the bulk of chapter 37, and elsewhere (e.g., D III.24), Machiavelli presents details of the circumstances, discussed at length below, in which offices and wealth also proved to be necessary means by which the plebs might protect both their liberty and that of the republic, circumstances of gross economic inequality between the *grandi* and the *popolo*. And yet, in the context of his discussion of the Agrarian Laws in Rome, Machiavelli invites readers, at least initially, to understand him to be criticizing the Roman people for excessive political ambition and inappropriate economic greed.

In a Florentine political culture still deeply scarred by the violent, destructive Ciompi Revolt (1378) and its aftermath, Machiavelli treats political efforts to address economic inequality and its political ramifications quite gingerly. To be sure, the Ciompi were defeated and the widely participatory republic that emerged after the Revolt was ultimately undermined by aristocratic usurpation.[35] Nevertheless, the purported excesses of the *ciompi*'s behavior and demands would play an important role in Florentine humanism's efforts to legitimate both the Albizzi oligarchy and the Medici principality that subsequently ruled the city.[36] Similarly, in ancient Rome the supposed extremism of the Gracchi's agenda and actions had played a central role in legitimating conservative agendas both radical, in the case of Sulla, and more moderate, as espoused by Cicero.[37]

Therefore, Machiavelli's immediate Florentine audience of humanist *ottimati* might easily associate plebeian demands for the consulship and for agrarian legislation in Rome with the political and economic demands of lower guildsmen and unguilded workers during the Ciompi insurrection a century and a half before Machiavelli wrote the *Discourses*. The woolworkers had demanded debt relief, the right to organize themselves as a guild, and guaranteed seats in the *Signoria*, the republic's chief executive committee. Machiavelli's reticence to explicitly endorse the radically reformist agenda of either the Gracchi or the Ciompi may account for the fact that, in the *Discourses*, Machiavelli writes in such a way that many interpreters consider the Agrarian Laws—and hence also the plebs and the Gracchi who, respectively, clamored for and advanced them—to be the

main cause of Rome's destruction.[38] Upon closer inspection, however, Machiavelli argues that the actual cause of the republic's corruption and collapse was not the Agrarian Laws but rather the deeply
and increasingly inequitable circumstances to which the laws were
merely an inevitable and even necessary response.[39] Again, Machiavelli remarks explicitly in this context, "well-ordered republics must
keep the public rich and citizens poor" (I.37). This statement signals
Machiavelli's preference for socioeconomic conditions more egalitarian than those that actually characterized his paradigmatically
"perfect" republic, Rome—and certainly more egalitarian than
those that characterize his own problematically inegalitarian republic, Florence (D I.3).[40]

Senatorial Sources of Economic
and Political Inequality

If Machiavelli is not in fact a full-scale critic of the Gracchi and the
Agrarian Laws, then what are we to make of his assertion that "there
must have been a defect in this law" (I.37)? The Florentine's invocation of this "defect" initially seems to constitute a critique of retroactive law. As Machiavelli declares: "it is exceedingly imprudent to attempt to correct an emerging disorder within a republic through a
law that looks very far back into the past" (D I.37). This obscure statement implies that retroactive law is especially obnoxious to those it
targets; in this case, one cannot expect to take property away from
those who have managed and benefited from it for an extended pe-
riod of time without provoking them into uncivil behavior. And yet
this cannot be the definitive answer to the puzzle of the "defect" supposedly inhering within the Gracchan legislation. After all, Machiavelli reports that the Roman nobles were just as enraged by the law's
prohibition of their gaining more wealth *in the future* as by the law's
redistribution of wealth that the senatorial order already controlled.
Not only, he writes, "did the greater part of the nobility, who held
more land than was permissible under this law, have to give it up,
but dividing among the plebs the fields appropriated from enemies
deprived the nobles opportunities to get richer." Machiavelli thereby
insists that the senate was angered at the prospect of losing new

revenue sources, since the agrarian reforms were intended to distribute among the plebeians, in actual practice rather than just in theory, newly conquered lands.

Machiavelli invokes another sense of timing, or poor-timing, when he remarks further: "Either [the Romans] failed to enact the law at a sufficiently early juncture such that it did not have to be constantly readdressed, or they delayed to such an extent that revisiting it became the cause of scandals" (D I.37). In other words, agrarian legislation—although demanded by the plebeians early in both Livy's and Machiavelli's accounts of the Roman Republic—was neither instituted at a sufficiently early moment nor, as a result, was it successfully preserved or reinforced at some later time. The fatal fault, therefore, resides not in the laws themselves, but rather, according to Machiavelli, in the fact that they were not instituted until it was too late for them to be fully efficacious upon enactment or to be passed without violent opposition. What, to Machiavelli's mind, accounts for the fact that the laws were promulgated only very late? Or, rather, who prevented the laws from being passed even though they were appropriately discussed and proposed very early in the republic's history?

There were good reasons for the plebeians to clamor for agrarian legislation from the earliest days of the republic. As Livy reports, while plebeian soldiers were in the field, senators and their clients foreclosed on their lands at home; consequently, the soldiers could no longer pay their debts since they lacked yields from farms that they left uncultivated while fighting for the republic. The senatorial class then worked these lands with the cheap labor of slaves such that increasingly impoverished and unemployed citizen-soldiers fell into debt bondage or, later, stopped having children who could repopulate the army.[41] Moreover, the foreign territories that the citizen-soldiers conquered in these victorious wars, and the riches that they yielded—which were supposed to become the property of all Roman citizens—fell into the "custodial care" of Roman nobles.

According to Machiavelli, the Roman nobility—"the greater part" of which was, in fact, composed of Rome's wealthiest citizens—apparently refused to recognize that the public good necessitated sharing these spoils with the people and, hence, limiting economic inequality within the republic (D I.37). Instead, the nobility associated the common good with their own economic privilege: as Machiavelli observes, "they assumed that they were defending the public by vigorously opposing" agrarian legislation that distributed land to the plebeians. Many interpreters suggest that Machiavelli understands the Roman nobility to be driven primarily by a desire for glory or honor rather than by the baser appetite for acquiring and preserving wealth.[42] Yet, Machiavelli observes, when discussing the Agrarian Laws, that the Roman nobles, after protracted delays, "always conceded offices to the plebs without resorting to extraordinary scandals" (D I.37). However, when it came to property, he declares quite explicitly that the nobility defended their economic privilege with the utmost "obstinance," first through protracted delays and eventually through violence.

Recall that this property that the nobles considered their own was actually won for Rome by the plebeians through the sweat and blood of combat, property that in theory the plebs owned but that in practice the nobles exploited to their own benefit. Moreover, this obstinance invoked by the Florentine is an explicit, if politely understated, reference to the butchery that the senators inflicted upon the Gracchi and their supporters in defense of economic inequality. Machiavelli suggests that this fact demonstrates "how much more than offices men value property"—and, as it often does, "men" here refers euphemistically to members of the nobility (see, e.g., D I.3). Clearly, Machiavelli understands the nobles to value material goods much more highly than they do their reputation and prestige, their honor and their dignity.

Thusly motivated to aggrandize themselves economically at the expense of the plebs, the nobles comprising Rome's senate, in Machiavelli's account, began to send the republic's armies "to the outskirts of Italy and beyond" to acquire lands that poor plebeians could not feasibly make profitable even if they were to own them (D I.37). This senatorial strategy, according to Machiavelli, worked in the following way: since the fields of Rome's new enemies "lay far beyond the eyes of the plebs, and in places where they could not easily cultivate them, they desired them less" (D I.37). These distant lands, in time, were to become an unlimited source of revenue for the few wealthiest

Romans who could afford to maintain them—a source of revenue that inevitably exacerbated the inequality that already existed at home between the nobles and the plebeians.

Furthermore, the nobles' self-enriching imperial policy also made military commanders inordinately powerful (D III.24). According to Machiavelli, senatorially driven acquisition of territory farther and farther afield from Rome and Italy necessitated the prolongation of military commands: the senate encouraged the creation of pro-consuls who required more than the customary, annual term of office to conquer and maintain the distant lands that were the ever-expanding source of the nobility's streams of revenue. Machiavelli concedes that the plebeians initiated the practice of prolonging terms of office: they re-elected tribunes who most effectively defended them against the oppressive behavior of the nobility, and who most deftly resisted the nobility's efforts to obstruct proplebeian reforms. But Machiavelli argues that, by pursuing the expansion of an ever more profitable empire, the senate converted repeated reappointment into the practice that eventually undermined the republic's "free way of life."

Put simply, this policy laid the groundwork for the phenomenon that would come to be known as Caesarism: fewer captains received military experience, hence necessitating the republic's reliance on an ever smaller cadre of commanders; moreover, the increasingly prole-tarianized citizen-soldiers became economically dependent on these very generals with whom they lived for years at a time away from the city. Such circumstances generated the conditions for the civil wars that would destroy the republic: warlords such as Marius and Sulla, Pompey and Caesar, Antony and Octavian would eventually confront each other at the head of armies composed of what were effectively personal clients rather than Roman citizens (D I.37, D III.24).

Therefore, are the plebeians of republics naturally or inevitably inclined to bestow adoration or favor upon would-be tyrants such as Marius and Caesar, as conservative critics ancient, modern, and contemporary charge? The overall thrust of the *Discourses* suggests that the answer is no. Machiavelli demonstrates over the course of the work that when the Roman people are not forced to choose between political liberty and economic well-being, they ultimately resist tyrannical figures who promise economic redistribution, such as Manlius Capitolinus, Spurius Cassius, and Spurius Maelius (D I.8, I.24, I.58, III.1, III.3, III.8, III.28). However, when the people are reduced to socioeconomic desperation and are shut out of substantive participation in their republic's politics—as Machiavelli insists, the Roman people increasingly were after the Punic Wars (D I.18, DI.37)—they may indeed follow a tyrant who offers them economic relief and political protection. Machiavelli clearly demonstrates that the Roman people were willing to side with the senate and the magistrates against personally ambitious economic redistributors when the republic safeguarded sufficient economic well-being; they would sacrifice no political liberty for the sake of the economic relief offered by Spurius, Maelius, and Manlius under relatively equitable economic conditions. But they recalculated that equation once the senate had thoroughly impoverished and effectively disenfranchised them, thus—as we will see below—making the appeals of Marius and Caesar increasingly attractive.

Economic Inequality and Civic Corruption

The inequality exacerbated by senatorially driven pursuit of empire, Machiavelli suggests, corrupted the civic quality of Rome's domestic politics in the following way: increasingly poor and vulnerable citizens—even the most "virtuous" among them—stopped openly questioning, criticizing and, when necessary, actively opposing candidacies and legislation pursued by increasingly rich, influential, and self-interested individuals (D I.18). Machiavelli details quite explicitly how Rome's modes and orders did not keep pace with the corruption generated by inequality in these two especially important spheres: magistrate appointments and legislation.

Machiavelli reports that, with respect to the elections of magistrates, in the beginning, only worthy citizens stood for "the consulship and other first ranks," presumably positions in the tribunate, as well (D I.18). As long as Rome remained uncorrupt, according to Machiavelli, citizens sought to be viewed worthy of high office and acted in an appropriately public-spirited fashion. Because citizens considered rejection in electoral contests to be ignominious, they avoided behavior that would have reflected poorly on their candidacies. But as Rome became corrupt, "not the virtuous but the powerful," increasingly and then exclusively, sought high office within the republic; citizens who were "virtuous" but not "powerful" eschewed competition for office because they feared their mighty adversaries (D I.18) (This statement suggests that Machiavelli considers it possible for a citizen to be virtuous but not necessarily powerful or even especially courageous.)

Machiavelli observes how, after the Punic Wars, Rome proceeded to conquer "Africa, Asia and most of Greece," thus eliminating all credible military threats to its existence (D I.18). This newfound security made the Romans complacent, and the Roman people began elevating "party hosts rather than conquerors" to the ranks of the consulate. However, Machiavelli's "bread and circuses" critique of this situation immediately gives way to a more sinister analysis: "good individuals" no longer held high office because consular appointments went instead to those who "bestowed favors upon those who wielded power." The principal agents of corruption in these circumstances were not primarily those who flattered the many, but rather those who intimidated the many with force and who cultivated the few with favors.

Earlier in the *Discourses*, Machiavelli noted how well the uncorrupted Roman Republic conducted consular elections: after the expulsion of the kings, "imperium," the authority to command, "was wielded by the consuls, who ascended to supreme magistracy not by birth, duplicity or violence but through free votes, and were thus invariably the most excellent men" (D I.20).[43] The potential for Rome's electoral orders to produce virtuous consuls was, in Machiavelli's estimation, unlimited:

> If two virtuous men in succession, like Philip of Macedon and Alexander the Great could acquire the world, then a republic should accomplish even more, through the mode of electing magistrates, for it potentially produces not only two in succession but an infinite number of virtuous princes as each other's successors. A virtuous mode of succession will be observed in every well-ordered republic (D I.20).[44]

But this potential is realized only under conditions of relative equality and not those associated with radical inequality.

The corruption of Rome's electoral orders soon infected its legislative orders as well (D I.18). According to Machiavelli, before Rome was corrupt, the tribunes—and, he claims, all citizens—freely proposed, discussed, and contested laws in assemblies, evaluating the extent to which they advanced the common good.[45] By contrast, once Rome succumbed to corruption, Machiavelli observes that public-spirited citizens no longer proposed or voiced their opinions on laws; only the "powerful" did so—not for the sake of "common freedom" but in pursuit of their own interests—and the rest of the citizenry was simply too afraid to oppose them. "Thus were the people either deceived" through entertainment or favors or "forced" through intimidation "to decide their own ruin" in assemblies.

Whatever hesitation or equivocation Machiavelli exhibits early on, by the end of Book I, chapter 37, he places the blame squarely on the nobles for creating such circumstances and for causing the demise of the republic: "so enormous is the ambition of the nobles that it rapidly ruins a city if it is not subjugated by *various ways and modes*" (D I.37, emphasis added). The nobles' aspirations are more damaging to a republic than that of the plebs, and the latter need more than one means, such as the tribunate, to hold back the insolence of the great. "Rome may have been subjugated after three hundred years of contestation over the Agrarian Laws, but it likely would have been made subservient far more quickly if the plebs had not always obstructed the nobles' ambition with both this legislation and other appetites" (D I.37). That is, in addition to the tribunate, the plebs were correct in seeking to reduce the nobility's material advantages through the Agrarian Laws and by seeking to share in offices such as the consulship (D I.60).

As the quote above suggests, Machiavelli understands the obstinance of the *grandi* to be responsible for the "scandals" that eventually destroy Rome; these scandals were not in truth generated by the Agrarian Laws promulgated by the Gracchi, which, by that time, were largely a much needed response to oligarchic greed and intransigence. Machiavelli insists that the *grandi* would have ruined the republic much earlier had they not been constrained both by laws precisely like the Agrarian Laws and by the plebeian appetite not to be dominated that demanded the passage of such laws (D I.37). On this basis, economic inequality should not be dismissed or minimized as a key factor in Machiavelli's analysis of civic corruption and republican decline. Ultimately, the ambition of the *grandi* and the avarice of the senate, in Machiavelli's estimation, made possible the brothers' popular appeal and set in motion the republic's collapse. The bulk of the Agrarian Laws chapter is devoted to a wholesale demonstration of how the nobility intensified inequitable conditions in Rome, and to a detailed description of how steadfastly they refused to ameliorate these conditions by sharing the republic's wealth with the people.

Conclusion: The Gracchi's Prudence and Intentions

What exactly does Machiavelli mean when, he expresses sympathy with the Gracchi's "intentions, if not their prudence" (D I.37)? As I demonstrated above, he clearly does not besmirch the Gracchan cause. Therefore, he must reproach their methods. Machiavelli does not denounce the Gracchi for pursuing redistributive policies; again, he seems only to criticize them for their timing in reviving these laws. But perhaps Machiavelli has something else entirely in mind here: rather than reviving what he describes as "a very old law," Machiavelli intimates that the Gracchi ought to have instituted a thoroughly new law. Like lawgivers or founders such as Lycurgus, to make the public rich and the citizens poor, they should have created their own laws—those that bore their own names. In order to do so without any compromise of their political vision, the Gracchi, in all likelihood, would have been compelled to intimidate, coerce or neutralize the most intransigent obstacle to their designs, namely, the Roman senate.

Historically, the Gracchi merely pleaded with senators to acquiesce to their policies: they essentially asked the nobles for permission to distribute to the plebeians lands that enriched the former; and they followed fairly strict procedural avenues in doing so. In response, the senate liquidated the brothers. Again, Machiavelli insists that the nobility were willing to negotiate with the plebs the sharing of honors and offices; but reforms aimed at economic equality require sterner measures and more compelling leverage. Perhaps, then, the "defect" in the Agrarian Laws that Machiavelli mentions is actually the defect in the Gracchi's prudence that he explicitly criticizes, if less than fully explains: they attempted to legislate—to seek lawful compliance on the part of the nobility—a matter where straightforward compulsion is necessary. In *The Prince*, Machiavelli criticizes the Gracchi for failing to avail themselves of a militarily organized people (P 9). But in the *Discourses*, he attributes their demise to the imprudent, that is, fundamentally humane, course by which they pursued a domestic agenda against the nobles.

The two modes of proceeding are not, of course, mutually exclusive. Machiavelli seems to suggest that the Gracchi had neither the inclination to coerce the senate, *nor*, even if they did, the command of armed citizens necessary to do so (P 9). As tribunes, the Gracchi presided over the people collected in their assemblies; but they lacked the formal, legal authority to command the people enrolled in legions. Machiavelli emphasizes on several occasions how such authority can be wielded effectively to eliminate an entire senate: most notably, by Agathocles the Sicilian (P 8) and Clearchus of Heraclea (D I.16). Consuls of Rome and praetors of other Italian republics— supreme magistrates publicly authorized with imperium and command of armed citizenries—can more successfully institute proplebeian reforms than can tribunes, who are merely civic magistrates. Or, at least, Machiavelli hints, supreme military magistrates can more successfully institute controversial reforms than can tribunes who are faithfully—perhaps too faithfully—committed to observing established legal conventions, as were the Gracchi.

If I am correct that Machiavelli insinuates that the Gracchi, in pursuit of their redistributive agenda, should have violently eliminated the senate rather than allow themselves to be violently eliminated by it, then the following becomes an inconvenient fact for Machiavelli's constitutional model. While Machiavelli insists, against his antagonists among the aristocratic literati, that the plebeian tribunate made Rome "more perfect" (D I.3), it could not solve the fundamental problem that led to the republic's collapse. The episode of the Gracchi and the socioeconomic circumstances surrounding the Agrarian

Laws demonstrate that the tribunate was a necessary but ultimately insufficient institutional means of protecting Rome's liberty. To be sure, Machiavelli declares that without tribunes constantly promoting agrarian reform and exercising their other institutional powers on behalf of the plebeians, the Roman republic would have become corrupt and would have collapsed much sooner. But the tribunate could not definitively solve the problem of economic inequality and, thereby, indefinitely forestall the republic's decline and fall.

There is another obvious problem with my interpretation of Machiavelli's ultimate judgment of the Gracchi. Had the Gracchi indeed violently neutralized the senate, what would have separated them from the republic-destroying warlords, whose very rise the successful passage of agrarian reforms was supposed to have prevented in the first place? Would not the Gracchi have become the moral and factual equivalent of the successful tyrants that followed them— those who did, in fact, destroy Roman liberty? Would not the Gracchi have hastened rather than delayed the republic's demise? Since Machiavelli emphasizes "intentions" in his account of the Gracchi, we should examine his invocation of intentions elsewhere in the *Discourses*, when he discusses the need to reform a republic in danger of becoming irredeemably corrupt.

In Book I, chapter 18, Machiavelli states: "One supposes that a good man is required to reorder a city for the political way of life, and that only a bad man becomes prince of a republic through violence; therefore only very rarely does someone good wish to become prince through recourse to evil, even if his end is good" (D I.18). In other words, there exist real, albeit very rare, instances where a good individual who wishes to reform a corrupt republic will resort to extralegal violence to do so. The Gracchi, on Machiavelli's account, were oriented by intention, if not by prudence, to fulfill such a role. Their intentions were good but their prudence was deficient. Had it occurred to them to resort to evil means in support of their good ends, there is little chance, according to Machiavelli, they would have established a tyranny.[46]

Moreover, not only were the Gracchi internally disinclined to be tyrants, they faced external circumstances not yet conducive to tyranny: at the moment when the Gracchi confronted the opportunity to crush the senate, the Roman people were not yet corrupted clients who fully depended on their military patrons for their economic well-being. Tiberius Gracchus, like Agathocles the Sicilian for instance, might have eliminated his republic's nobility, instituted robust economic-military reforms, and died in his bed, leaving behind him a more egalitarian and civically vibrant republic.[47] However, as the Spartan example mentioned before makes clear, to Machiavelli's mind, unilateral executive action aimed at instituting economic equality within a republic is a recurrent necessity, not a one-time proposition. Machiavelli notes how Lycurgus's laws, however successful at the beginning, required violent re-establishment by successors such as Agis and Cleomenes to be effective in the long term (D I.9). Moreover, the results in the Spartan case, according to Machiavelli's own account, were mixed. Even if the Gracchi had acted effectively, as Machiavelli hints they should have, other "Gracchi" would have had to emerge in the future to guarantee the perpetual success of their reforms. This occurred in neither the Spartan nor the Roman context.

There is another possible route to reforms that would minimize the threat to a republic's civic liberty posed by proliferating economic inequality. This one is less explicitly violent and less potentially threatening to civic liberty than one in which a supposedly well-intentioned magistrate violently eliminates the aristocratic opponents of his proplebeian reforms. It is, however, one for which there is even less support in Machiavelli's texts: a republic's wealthiest citizens could prudently avoid pursuing policies that increase inequality and therefore risk their own eventual political emasculation or economic expropriation by a tyrannical champion of the plebs.

Rather than murdering moderate economic reformers like the Gracchi, as did the Roman senate, a republic's wealthy citizens perhaps ought to give away a few golden eggs rather than allow a princely usurper to emerge and kill the goose that lays them. At several points in his writings, Machiavelli notes how the nobles of Rome and Florence might have been more accommodating to the people rather than pursuing courses that jeopardize their polity's free status and their own privilege and prestige within it. In particular, he demonstrates how Octavian and the Medici gained their respective principates by exploiting hubristic aristocratic overreaching in such circumstances (D I.52–53).

Despite underscoring these opportunities for prudent judgment on the part of a republic's wealthiest citizens, Machiavelli provides no examples where such nobles actually do pursue a wisely conciliatory strategy on the issue of economic inequality. Instead, the oligarchs invariably seek to maximize their economic advantages such that they inevitably undermine both the people's liberty and the very conditions on which their own status and privilege depend.

3

On the Myth of a Conservative
Turn in the *Florentine Histories*

THE NOTION THAT the later political writings of Niccolò Machiavelli, in particular the *Florentine Histories*, convey his newly developed conservatism has today become settled opinion.[1] Even many
scholars who tend to locate the former Florentine secretary's political
preferences, as reflected in *The Prince* and the *Discourses*,[2] on the
democratic rather than aristocratic side of the republican political
spectrum conclude that the more mature author of the *Histories*
transformed his views in several fundamental ways: most prominently, that Machiavelli became substantially more critical of common peoples and more admiring of elites than in his earlier writings;
that he moved from a bipartite to tripartite understanding of social
class; and that he abandoned the Roman Republic (or ancient democratic republics, generally) as a political-constitutional model worthy
of emulation in favor of an aristocratic republican model, best exemplified by Venice.[3]

In what follows, I question how far one can advance all three of
these assertions. I address the claim that the later Machiavelli developed a more pessimistic view of the people (and the plebs) as a political force, and I refute the argument that, after 1519, Machiavelli
abandoned both the neo-Roman democratic republican model that
he sets forth in the *Discourses* and the bipartite class analysis so central to his political magnum opus. I hope to demonstrate that the
details of Machiavelli's historical account of the respective actions of

the Florentine people and nobles within the *Histories* undermine any statements on Machiavelli's part that overtly criticize the people and that signal a newfound sympathy for the nobles. I suggest, therefore, that proponents of the "conservative-turn" thesis err when they rely overwhelmingly on the latter to the utter neglect of the former in their analyses of the *Histories*. They consistently ignore the blatant discontinuity between Machiavelli's demonstration of *how* peoples and nobles behave throughout the book and *what* he says about the behavior of these groups. I will argue that the former contravene the latter, and that the literary-rhetorical method deployed by Machiavelli in the *Histories*—a mode of writing through which, even more so than in *The Prince* and the *Discourses*, deeds trump words—reinforces rather than undermines Machiavelli's previously expressed democratic republicanism in his later, seemingly more conservative political writings.

Sometimes Machiavelli contradicts himself in the *Histories*, as when he insists that the Florentine people refused to share political offices with the nobles (FH III.1), only a few paragraphs after he describes in explicit detail how they had tried, in good faith, to do just that (FH II.39). At other times, Machiavelli establishes stark incongruities between his descriptions and his evaluations of actions and events: he often denounces popular or plebeian behavior as inappropriate, excessive or indecent, when, in fact, indications in the *Histories* and statements from previous works suggest that Machiavelli not only tolerates but countenances such conduct. For instance, Machiavelli criticizes the Florentine plebs for creating a commotion in the streets during an important council meeting at the height of the Ciompi Revolt (FH III.15). But by Machiavellian standards, which explicitly favor tumults as civically salutary events (or minimize them as harmless occurrences) (FH III.1; D I.4), this unruly behavior ought to be judged as either perfectly appropriate or morally neutral—especially since the plebs, in this instance, inflict no bodily harm on their political adversaries among the city's magistrates.

The evidence affirming Machiavelli's consistent view of social classes across the span of his political writings, I will demonstrate, is deeply embedded within the *Histories'* narrative, which I will be compelled to recapitulate at length. Moreover, I suggest they only be-come apparent—without explicit signaling on Machiavelli's part—when one compares Machiavelli's accounts of the people and the great in the *Histories* with those set forth in *The Prince* and the *Discourses*. After addressing the peculiar form of rhetorical exposition that Machiavelli uses throughout the *Histories*, I suggest that conservative-turn scholars fail to take seriously the immediate context of the book's composition—a context in which the addressees of the book, the Medici prelates who ruled Florence through their friends (*amici*) among the Florentine aristocracy, had come to view the city's common citizens as stalwart enemies, and the people had come to view Florence's rulers as illegitimate tyrants.

Machiavelli's answer to the central question posed in the *Histories*—why is the modern Florentine Republic so inferior to the ancient Roman one?—cannot be derived from any change in motivations or "humors" that he supposedly attributes to modern peoples or nobles. Rather, I argue, the answer to this question emerges from Machiavelli's analysis of the different "modes and orders" that characterize modern as opposed to ancient republics. According to the Florentine, modern and ancient republics exhibit vastly different institutional-constitutional frameworks within which historically constant popular and aristocratic appetites operate and interact.

A More Pessimistic View of the People?
A More Laudatory View of the Nobles?

The following frequently quoted passage from the *Florentine Histories* plays a central role in virtually every scholarly effort endeavoring to demonstrate that Machiavelli became more critical of the common people in the *Histories* and other works of the 1520s than he was in *The Prince* and the *Discourses*:

> While the Roman people desired to *share* supreme honors with the nobles, the Florentine people fought to govern Florence *all alone without the nobles' participation*. As the desire of the Roman people was *more reasonable*, the nobles came to view popular offenses as more bearable, and they conceded to them more readily,

without taking up arms. Therefore, after some disputes, [the Romans] came together to make laws that satisfied the people and permitted the nobles to *maintain their dignities*. On the contrary, because the desires of the Florentine people were so *harmful and unjust*, the nobility defended itself with greater force, which resulted in more bloodshed and exile for citizens. Moreover, the laws that were subsequently enacted [in Florence] *never corresponded* with the *common good*, but rather reflected *the advantage of whosoever prevailed* in any particular conflict. . . . Thus, the [Florentine] *nobles' military virtue and generosity* were entirely eliminated . . . such that Florence became more humble and servile. (FH III.1, emphases added)[4]

I will now focus on three episodes from the *Histories* where Machiavelli's account of popular behavior drastically (and I would say deliberately) repudiates the evaluative judgment that the Florentine himself levels in the above quoted passage: popular conciliation with the nobles after the overthrow of the Duke of Athens's tyranny (FH II.39–42); the people's relenting from destroying the nobles after the departure of popular champion Giano della Bella (FH II.14); and the supposedly evil and indecent behavior exhibited by the Florentine plebs during the Ciompi Revolt (FH III.12–15).

It is necessary and illuminating, I contend, to read such episodes from the *Histories* with the aim of assessing the extent to which Machiavelli's evaluative judgments prove compatible with the political circumstances he describes; that is, to put it somewhat crudely, it is worth asking whether Machiavelli's adjectives match his verbs when he discusses the political actions of the Florentine nobles and people. My intuition is that most of Machiavelli's evaluative judgments of the nobles and the people expressed in the *Histories* are consistently belied by his actual descriptions of each group's behavior. I suggest that, at almost every point when Machiavelli explicitly criticizes the people in the book, he places material within the details of the events and actions he describes that seriously mitigates those criticisms, especially when judged by the standards set by our author in *The Prince* and the *Discourses*.

Allow me now to explore at length the details of these three cases that bear directly on claims made by the now abundant number of scholars who insist that Machiavelli became much more critical of the lower classes of republics in his later, more Florence-focused works as opposed to his earlier, more overtly ancient-occupied writings.

The Nobles Cause Their Own Defeat and Disenfranchisement (1343)

The first episode that explicitly contradicts Machiavelli's claim regarding popular intransigence over sharing offices with the nobles occurs five paragraphs before he makes the oft-cited declaration at the outset of Book III, quoted above. In the aftermath of the expulsion of Florence's protector cum tyrant, Walter Brienne, the so-called Duke of Athens, Machiavelli shows at the conclusion of Book II, despite his claims just a few pages later (FH III.1), that the Florentine people reformed the republic's constitution precisely with the intention to "share" offices with the nobles. These constitutional revisions, as Machiavelli indicates, were intended to benefit the common good and not merely, as Machiavelli will soon declare at the opening of Book III, any particular political actor or group.

Furthermore, Machiavelli makes plain that the truce between the people and the nobles, who had cooperated in overthrowing Walter, is disrupted by the nobles, who resort to violence in their efforts to exert a preponderance of power within the *Signoria*, the supreme magistracy of the city, whose seats the people had reopened—quite reasonably and with an eye toward the common good and not partisan advantage—to the nobility. By using violence to intimidate members of the *popolo* in these circumstances, the nobles ignite the war that brings about their own military defeat and final political disenfranchisement at the hands of the people. The latter's initial impulse, on Machiavelli's straightforward description (if not his explicit assessment) was, again, to share magistracies with the nobles rather than deploy force to exclude them entirely from such offices.

As Machiavelli begins to recount these events, he reports that once the *grandi*, the ancient nobility, and the *popolani*, citizens enrolled in guilds, expelled Walter, both groups deliberated over constitutional reforms. They agreed that a third of the *Signoria* would go to the nobles, and, furthermore, that the nobles would hold half of all the positions in the republic's other magistracies (FH II.39). The Florentines proceed to change the division of the city from sixths to quarters and increase the number of priors in the *Signoria* from six to twelve to accommodate the inclusion of the nobles in the city's chief executive committee. Previously, the *Signoria* comprised one prior from each sixth of the city, none of whom could (officially) be nobles; under the new arrangement, there would be three priors (or, as Machiavelli prefers to call them, *Signori*) from each quarter, of which a third, total, would be nobles—a number that actually overrepresented the nobility given their smaller percentage among the citizenry overall.

These reforms make clear that Machiavelli is fully aware that the Florentine people, no less than their Roman antecedents, were willing to share the highest magistracies with their republic's nobility. It was not the people who initiated the circumstances under which the nobles would be entirely, and permanently, expelled from such offices (but not deprived of political influence). As Machiavelli himself observes at this juncture: "If the great had been inclined to comport themselves with the modesty requisite for a civil way of life, the city would have lived contentedly under this order of government. But the great could tolerate neither companions in private life nor colleagues in the magistracies—nay, they desired to be lords" (FH II.39). Just as he had in both *The Prince* and the *Discourses*, Machiavelli here attributes to the nobles an unquenchable appetite or humor for oppression—they desire undisputed distinction (status) and rule (power) over all others in the city (P 9, D I.3–5). Moreover, in contradistinction to what he declares at the outset of Book III of the *Histories*, Machiavelli, in this instance, shows that the nobles, not the people, behave "unreasonably" in wanting to rule the city "alone," without any "participation" from their class adversaries.

Machiavelli then recounts how daily outbursts of insolence and arrogance on the part of the great against the people thoroughly outraged the people, who lamented that they had merely swapped one tyrant, in the person of the duke, for a thousand tyrants, in the form of the recently re-enfranchised nobles (FH II.39). Machiavelli's description of the resulting circumstances—"insolent displays abounding on one side and indignant ones on the other"—fully comports with Machiavelli's assertion in the *Discourses* that insolence (*insolenzia*) is the most frequent expression of the aristocratic appetite to oppress, and that indignation or even rage (*rabbia*) over such insolence is the most common expression of the people's desire not to be dominated (D I.16).

The heads of the *popolani* soon complain to Archbishop Acciaiuoli (who had previously mediated, with mixed results, social conflict within the city) of the great's general indecency and their individual acts of incivility toward the people (FH II.39). The word that Machiavelli uses to describe the nobility's indecency in this instance, *disonestà*, calls to mind the opposite quality, *onestà*, that Machiavelli attributes to the people in *The Prince* when he attests to their superior goodness, decency, and justice over the nobles (P 9). Here, the popular leaders prevail upon the archbishop to once again grant "the people alone" exclusive tenure in the *Signoria*. But the people do not, in this instance, seek to shut the nobility out of the government altogether; instead, they attempt to preserve, in some part, the "dignities" of the great by upholding their eligibility to serve in the city's other major magistracies.[5]

Acciaiuoli attempts to justify this outcome to the nobility, enlisting "kind words" to do so and promising "peace" if they acquiesce to it (FH II.39). But the great, nevertheless, become furious, especially Ridolfo de'Bardi, who bitterly condemns the archbishop as a faithless and frivolous friend of all parties. He declares that the nobles would now happily risk the same mortal danger in defending their honors that they previously endured in reacquiring them during the struggle against the Duke of Athens. Machiavelli describes how the great arm themselves, and, in response the people do likewise, following the nobles to the *Palazzo della Signoria*. He reports that much shouting and tumult ensues at the *palazzo* as the two sides confront each other: the nobles vociferously support their fellow *grandi* within the *Signoria*, and the *popolo* publicly demand that the noble priors resign their offices. However, Machiavelli reports that many nobles did not, in fact, show up to defend their own magistrates, choosing instead to remain in their houses rather than dare to confront "the entire armed people" (FH II.39). So much for the nobles' "military virtue and generosity" famously invoked by Machiavelli at the start of the next book.

The sitting priors representing the people then take up the cause of the noble priors, at first trying to calm the people's animosity by insisting that the noble members of the *Signoria* were "men of modesty and goodness." But, failing in the effort to save the nobles' offices, they order their noble colleagues to be escorted safely home through the intensely hostile crowd. The popular priors do not turn on their noble colleagues (they abide by collegiality, a quality that, as Machiavelli mentioned previously, was not exhibited by the nobles), and the agitated Florentine people in the piazza do not attempt to harm or kill the noble members of the *Signoria* while the latter proceed to their homes.

In the armed conflict that then ensues, the people, who suffered heavy casualties attempting to cross the Ponte Vecchio, the Rubaconte, and the Carraia bridges, ingeniously attack the nobles through an undefended road to the rear of their fortifications. Machiavelli notes that the most intransigent noble family, the Bardi, who had publicly pledged to fight to the death, "lost their spirit," abandoned their defenses, and surrendered (FH II.41). The people, Machiavelli notes, had treated captured nobles, such as members of the Cavicciulli, Donati, and Pazzi families, humanely at the start of hostilities. However, the people, perhaps because of the massive losses that they incurred in the subsequent fighting, now treated the last holdouts among the nobility, the Bardi, with abject cruelty. Machiavelli remarks that even Florence's worst enemies would have been ashamed of their behavior: the people, especially "the most ignoble among them," thoroughly ravaged and burned to the ground all the houses and towers of the Bardi. From a different perspective, though, we might instead consider whether this is a less than fully unjust outcome since, as Machiavelli reported two chapters previously, Ridolfo de' Bardi initiated this conflict that brought the entire city to arms and cost the *popolo* such massive losses. Indeed, throughout Book II, Machiavelli identifies the Bardi as one of the noble families most guilty of disrupting the civic peace and of threating the people's liberty, not least of all by helping to facilitate the rise of the Duke of Athens (e.g., FH II.32–33, II.36).

Machiavelli describes how the people, having thoroughly conquered the great in open battle, then reorder the city according to three parts (corresponding with the division of guilds into major, middling, and minor groups): the powerful people (*potenti*) would hold two seats in the *Signoria*, the middling people (*mediocri*) three, and the minor people (*bassi*) three, and the Gonfalonier of Justice would rotate from among the three parts as the ninth member of the chief executive committee (FH II.42).[6] The Ordinances of Justice, which previously barred the nobles from all high office, were reinstated against the great, many of whom, to be made weaker, Machiavelli notes, were mixed among the multitude of the people—that is, they were compulsorily enrolled in guilds and thus rendered subject to the guilds' laws and judicial decisions. Later developments suggest that the people perhaps ought not to have mixed the nobles among themselves in this fashion, for in doing so, the people precipitate their own military (not to mention political) corruption. Without martial adversaries like the nobles within the city, Machiavelli avers, the people become increasingly "effeminate" militarily.

Machiavelli declares here that the nobles were so devastated by this defeat that they never again resorted to arms against the people, and that they became "more humane and miserable" (FH II.42). But his own later accounts of their machinations and behavior during "the War of the Eight Saints" and, as we will observe, during the Ciompi Revolt, raises serious questions about the veracity of this assessment. In particular, as captains of the still powerful Guelf Party, the nobles later nearly bring the city to civil war by conspiring once again to seize the *Signoria* by force and expel their adversaries from it (FH III.8); moreover, through their surreptitious prodding of the city's dissatisfied working class, they actually do instigate a full scale civil war in the form of the Ciompi insurrection (FH III.12–13).

Be that as it may, as a result of this popular victory over the great, Machiavelli declares, "Florence lost its arms and its generosity" (FH II.42). But this raises pressing questions: Why is this the case? Were not the people both sufficiently armed and tactically adept to beat the supposedly more militarily skilled and valorous nobles? Moreover, since Machiavelli peppers his account here and elsewhere with hints of cowardly behavior on the part of the nobles, just how "generous," in the sense of military spirit, does he actually consider them to be?[7] Finally, why did the victorious people not, from this point going forward, maintain and expand their arms for the good of the city? Machiavelli later reveals that by mixing with the nobles, increasingly at the latter's initiative, the people, especially the wealthiest *popolani* among the guilds, begin to take on all of the nobles' bad attributes—an appetite for domination—while losing the good attribute that they previously shared with them— military virtue.

The People Relent from Destroying the Nobility (1295)

I turn now to the second example from the *Florentine Histories*, which, I believe, demonstrates that Machiavelli does not fully endorse his own indictment of the Florentine people for harboring "unreasonable desires" and for committing "harmful and unjust" acts in their dealings with the city's nobility. This example occurs earlier in Book II of the *Histories*, after the people's champion, Giano della Bella, has left the city rather than employ violence to enforce the Ordinances of Justice, laws that he enacted to restrain the nobles from inflicting via legal and extralegal means harm on members of the *popolo*.

After Giano's departure, while the nobles and the people are poised to engage in open warfare, an informal committee of well-meaning members of the people, the nobles, and the clergy intervenes in the conflict (FH II.14). As a result of this intercession, Machiavelli shows that the people relent from oppressing—indeed, possibly destroying—the nobles when they have the opportunity to do so. The episodes seems to conform quite closely to Machiavelli's claims in the *Discourses* that the people usually can be dissuaded from behaving rashly and unjustly by the words of "a good man" (D I.2, I.5, I.59) or, in this case, good men. The trilateral commission begs the people not to press their numerical advantage against the nobles and instead to accept the political gains that they have already made. The people, in response, not only relent from armed conflict with the nobles, but they actually relax the legislative restrictions that they and Giano had previously imposed upon the great.

Machiavelli presents the details of this incident as follows. Once Giano exits the city, the nobles manage to put aside sectarian differences among themselves and delegate two from among their numbers (presumably, one Guelf, one Ghibelline) to petition the *Signoria*, which had a composition favorable to the great, on the matter of reducing the severity of the Ordinances (FH II.14). The people, still smarting from the effects of a conspiracy among the city's elite that forced Giano's exile, feared that the laws—however ineffective they were proving to be in practice—would now be completely eviscerated. Machiavelli recounts how the people and the nobles prepare to engage each other militarily as a result of this controversy. Thus, the violent conflict that Giano sought to avoid, and perhaps could have settled more effectively himself, is about to ensue despite his abdication. The nobles and the guildsmen take up positions against each other around the city, and the people assemble in very large numbers near the *Signoria*.

Machiavelli describes how, in the midst of this crisis, the aforementioned group of guildsmen, nobles, and clergy take up the role of mediators, attempting to quell the impending conflict by addressing each group directly (FH II.14). First approaching the great, the mediators insist that the nobility's "arrogance," "misgovernance," and "evil modes of proceeding" have brought them to these straits with the people and compelled them to strip the nobles of their honors and offices and to pass punitive legislation against them. They remind the nobles that the Ordinances were enacted against them in response to their own malevolent behavior, and that they themselves were responsible for their exclusion from the highest magistracy. To attempt to take back forcibly through evil what they had lost through the same, the commission insists, would be tantamount to desiring the ruin of the patria and of themselves.

But, presumably because Machiavelli elsewhere exhibits skepticism concerning the great's ability to be shamed into good behavior (e.g., D I.40, I.48), the mediators conclude their entreaty to the nobles with largely tactical considerations (FH II.14). The nobles, they pointed out, were clearly outnumbered, and the cowards among them would not fight in the face of "so many numbers, so much riches and so much hatred" on the popular side. The people, they insist, are on the verge of showing that the nobility are that in name only, for many will not fight, and those who do will be soundly beaten.

Turning to the people, the trilateral commission also addresses them with tactical concerns, but they more heavily emphasize moral considerations. They first suggest that it would be imprudent of the people to always seek to be victorious over the nobles (FH II.14). From the start, this is a rather strange injunction since Machiavelli has shown in the immediately preceding chapters that the Ordinances neither prevented nobles such as Corso Donati from inflicting physical, indeed fatal, harm upon members of the *popolo*, nor from getting away scot-free with such crimes (FH II.13). Moreover, Machiavelli shows how the nobles successfully turned the *Signoria*, even without any members of the great serving as priors, against the people's patron, Giano, compelling his exit from the city (FH I.13).

Nevertheless, Machiavelli recounts how the mediators continue to argue in this manner, suggesting that the people would be unwise to make the nobles sufficiently desperate that the latter would have nothing to lose by fighting them to the death (FH II.14). After all, they point out, fortune does not always favor with victory those who enjoy greater numbers in battle. Turning to the moral concerns that predominate their entreaties to the people, the mediators insist that it was unfair that individual nobles could be so easily sent into exile under the Ordinances of Justice. They remind the people that the nobles had served the city well in war, and that it was "neither good nor just" to assault them with "such hatred." The nobles might tolerate their exclusion from the *Signoria* (a claim often contravened by Machiavelli's narration of events), but they will not endure continued legal vulnerability under the ordinances (specifically, the fact that they could be exiled from the patria or executed on the basis of undersubstantiated charges). Once again, this is a less than accurate account of recent events: Machiavelli has shown that the nobles get around their exclusion from the *Signoria* by gaining merely one sympathetic ear among the priors, and that they avoid criminal punishment under the ordinances by intimidating the foreign rector of judicial affairs, the people's *Capitano*, into rendering judgments favorable to them (FH II.13).

The people, according to Machiavelli, then debate the commission's proposal among themselves: some of them insist on commencing battle now while they have the nobles outnumbered; some suggest that the nobles might be made more content if the people moderated the terms of the ordinances; others declare that the nobles would never be satisfied unless they were made so through violent compulsion (FH II.14). Ultimately, Machiavelli recounts how the people of "milder and wiser spirit" prevailed upon the others, arguing that conciliation would prove less costly than war. Thus, the people laid down their arms and ordained that legal provisions for additional witnesses be added to the Ordinances of Justice.

The mediators appeal to necessity and morality in trying to keep both the nobles and people from going to war, but accentuate necessity much more in their deliberations with the nobles and morality much more in their pleadings with the people. This accords well with Machiavelli's suggestion in earlier works that "steel" is required to deter elites from incorrect behavior, while words on the part of good men are sufficient to persuade peoples, who are more inclined toward decency than are nobles, from deleterious courses of action (D I.58; P 9). As Machiavelli insists in the *Discourses*, insolent aristocrats, the "sons of Brutus," will not desist in their endeavors to undo institutional orders that both constrain them and empower the people unless their malevolent envy and insatiable appetite to oppress is met with mortal necessity, i.e., death (D III.3).

The lesson is precisely the same in the *Histories*, even if, here, Machiavelli never makes it explicitly. Machiavelli's descriptions of popular moderation and noble malice in the book conform precisely to Machiavelli's earlier accounts in *The Prince* and the *Discourses*. In the *Histories*, he simply fails to accentuate this distinction in his evaluations of the people and the nobles. The *Histories*, it would seem, provides much less direct guidance regarding the "effectual truth" of class politics than do either *The Prince* or the *Discourses*. Ultimately, the point is that Machiavelli's descriptions of popular behavior in the *Histories* consistently evinces a moderation that Machiavelli fails to explicitly attribute to the people in his general evaluations of them, most famously in the opening of Book III.

The "Evil" Nature and "Indecent" Behavior of the Florentine Plebs? (1378)

To support the argument that Machiavelli, in the *Florentine Histories*, altered his previously declared opinion of the people's fundamental goodness, scholars often emphasize: firstly, the infamous speech of the unnamed *ciompo* or woolworker during the Ciompi Revolt (FH III.13); and, secondly, Machiavelli's deeply derogatory references to the Florentine plebs throughout the *Histories*, denunciations that seem to reach a crescendo during his account of the woolworkers' uprising (FH III.10–14). Such scholars often draw a stark contrast between, on the one hand, the immoral attitudes that Machiavelli seems to be imputing to the people via the anonymous *ciompo*'s speech in the *Histories*, and, on the other, the "decent" or "good" nature that Machiavelli attributed to the people in *The Prince* and the *Discourses*. Two important, unprecedented aspects of the speech, they claim, are the blatant duplicity, cunning, and rapaciousness endorsed by the *ciompo* and the latter's insistence that the people and the nobles are constituted by the same nature; that is, his claim that underneath the filthy rags and fine robes that respectively clothe them, the plebs and the nobles are essentially the same.[8]

There is, however, one insurmountable problem with any attempt to use the anonymous *ciompo* as a proxy for Machiavelli's "new" view of the common people: his fellow *ciompi* do not ultimately follow his advice. The woolworkers and other plebs, despite the *ciompo*'s exhortations, do not use violence to completely overturn the sociopolitical order of the city, even though they secure the opportunity and power to do so. Therefore, Machiavelli demonstrates, without any explicit commentary on the fact, that the plebeians prove ultimately unwilling to fully engage in the immorality demanded of them by the nameless *ciompo*, or to fully engage in the oppressive behavior that Machiavelli, without reservation throughout the *Histories*, continually shows to be characteristic of the nobility.

As in the two episodes discussed above, while analyzing the *ciompo*'s speech and the subsequent behavior of the people (or, more specifically here, the lesser people and the plebs) during the first phase of the Ciompi Revolt, I demonstrate that readers ought to carefully compare Machiavelli's ostensible assessments of the people with the evidence that he adduces concerning their actions. Scholars of the "late-conservative" persuasion, here as elsewhere, exhibit little sensitivity to the contrast between words and deeds in Machiavelli's presentation. Machiavelli does indeed remark throughout the *Histories* that it is the nature of the Florentine plebeians to "revel in evil" (FH II.34); that they invariably throw in their lot with whomever is most "disgruntled" in the city (FH III.8); that they resort to "indecent" behavior (*disonestà*) during the riots of July 1378; and he expresses rather extravagant indignation over the plebeians' "dishonorable and grievous" demands during the first wave of the woolworkers' revolt (FH III.15). But Machiavelli's descriptions of their actions, I will suggest, belie such ostensibly harsh criticisms.

Indeed, as Machiavelli's historical account makes plain, when the plebs have the city by the throat, they propose a constitutional arrangement by which they, the majority of free, indigenous, adult males in the city, can be outvoted in the *Signoria* by their antagonists in the major and middling guilds (moreover, they also grant their inconstant allies in the minor guilds more seats than they claim for themselves) (FH III.15). As we will observe, Machiavelli shows that, on July 21, 1378, the plebs could rule the city alone—fully in keeping with the anonymous *ciompo*'s recommendation—should they wish to do so. However, their institutional demands reveal what they really want: inclusion in, not "usurpation" of, the guild republic that previously had excluded and oppressed them, and even their willingness to accept a disproportionately subordinate role within that regime.

Let us then turn to Machiavelli's account of the conditions under which the *ciompi* and other plebs worked in the years leading up to the Ciompi Revolt; let us examine the words that the Florentine places in the mouth of his anonymous woolworker during this now notorious speech; and, most importantly, we must analyze his descriptions, as well as his assessments, of the plebeians' subsequent behavior during July of 1378.

Machiavelli begins Book III, chapter 12, by addressing the state of mind of Florence's lower classes during July of 1378. The nobles and most powerful guildsmen affiliated with the Guelf Party had incited "the lowest plebs" to burn and pillage during the latest episode of social unrest in the city (FH III.12). According to Machiavelli, "the most audacious" among these plebs feared that, with peace being restored, *they* would now be punished for their offenses, and, "as always occurs," they would wind up betrayed and blamed by their social superiors who had, in fact, encouraged them to commit such crimes. Machiavelli had already shown that other prominent citizens, those who had been admonished rather unfairly as so-called Ghibellines by the party, had encouraged the lower *popolani* of the minor guilds to also engage in arson and riots on their behalf (FH III.10). For reasons that Machiavelli will soon make clear, these guildsmen are, however, less vulnerable to severe and arbitrary punishment than are members of the plebs who had performed the bidding of the Guelf nobility.

Machiavelli then moves from these particular, recent circumstances to explain more generally why, for quite some time, "the lesser people had hated the city's richest citizens and the princes of the guilds," and why the vast majority of the city's workers overwhelmingly considered themselves insufficiently compensated for their labors (FH III.12). Machiavelli recounts how, over the last century and a half, members of the Florentine people enrolled in commercial guilds (the *popolani*) ordered the republic's government to conform to the guilds' division into seven richer, "more honored" guilds and fourteen less wealthy and hence "less honored" ones (FH III.12). Two consequences resulted from these institutional developments.

Firstly, a new ruling class, comprised of the ancient nobility and the richest guildsmen, emerged in the republic. The nobility, who may have been excluded from the highest magistracies during various incarnations of the Ordinances of Justice, still wielded significant power through their prominence in the Guelph Party—notwithstanding Machiavelli's claims that they had been utterly destroyed by the *popolani* in armed conflict after the expulsion of the Duke of Athens. These "arrogant" nobles, according to Machiavelli, "began to bestow favors upon the *popolani* of the greater guilds" (FH III.12). Secondly, this new ruling class set about oppressing the city's lower classes: specifically, the ancient nobility and the new so-called popular nobles "persecuted members of the minor guilds, as well as [the plebs] with whom the lesser people were allied" (FH III.12). The minor guilds were, at various times, allied with prominent citizens identified anachronistically as "Ghibellines," who were often "admonished" (that is, disenfranchised or exiled) by their adversaries among the Guelfs, or with the plebs who stood below the guild community in social status and political-economic power.

Thus, according to Machiavelli, the consolidation of this new ruling class—comprising Guelph nobles and members of the richest guilds, which would be completed once the Ciompi Revolt was definitively suppressed (and once the popular government that emerged out of the revolt's ashes was overturned)—had actually begun many years before. Furthermore, not only was the military virtue of the warlike nobles being dissipated by their alliance with the commercial "princes of the guilds," as Machiavelli suggests at the start of Book III (FH III.1), but the princes, who previously had served as champions of the *popolo's* liberty in armed struggles with the great, were now being corrupted by the appetite for oppression characteristic of the nobility.

A crucial, related consequence resulting from the institutional arrangements of the guild republic was, in Machiavelli's account, the comprehensive subjugation of the city's working class:

According to the ordering of the guilds, several of the occupations in which the lesser people [*il popolo minuto*] and the lowest plebs [*la plebe infirma*] were employed were granted no guilds of their own. Instead, they were relegated to the subjection [*sottomissono*] of other guilds, corresponding with the nature of their occupations. Thus, when [the lesser people and plebs] were dissatisfied with the compensation that they received for their labors, or were oppressed in some other mode by their masters, they had no place to turn other than the guild magistracy which governed them. As a result, in their estimation, they never received from the latter the justice that they deserved. (FH III.12)

Thus, the guild republic confronted circumstances in which its richest citizens were colluding with the arrogant, disenfranchised, but still quite powerful nobility to oppress members of the minor guilds and others, and the majority of the city's laborers were being exploited by their socioeconomic superiors within the major guilds, with no recourse to an appellate process that they deemed to be fair. Although Machiavelli suggests that the plebs' belief that they were suffering exploitation was largely subjective, he provides no evidence that this oppression was not, in fact, a very real state of affairs.

Machiavelli's account here provides some retrospective context for why, in his earlier account, Walter, the Duke of Athens, was able to gain "the grace" of the plebs at the start of his tyranny by executing prominent *popolani*—one of whom, it so happens, was a Medici (FH II.33). These executions did not please the plebs so much because, as Machiavelli declares at that point, it is their "nature" to "revel in evil" (FH II.34). Instead, perhaps the plebs had good reason to view these wealthy guildsmen as their oppressors, and therefore to expect that some measure of justice would be served as a result of such executions. Moreover, we now understand better why the duke further endeared himself to the plebs by providing them with arms and banners (FH II.36): since the plebs were not organized in any guilds of their own, but rather only subjected to other guilds, they had no right to carry arms and bear standards in their own guild-organized militias until the duke bestowed these upon them for the short tenure of his tyranny.

As Machiavelli elaborates upon the conditions that made the woolworkers, in particular, so dissatisfied, he takes the opportunity to suggest that, despite all the Sturm und Drang of the impending Ciompi Revolt, in the end, this event—which the Florentine ruling class believed, up to Machiavelli's day, to be the worst thing to have ever occurred in the city—changed not a thing concerning the city's socioeconomic conditions. Note how Machiavelli merges past and present in the following passage: "Of all the guilds, the one which had, *and still has*, the largest number of workers [*sottoposti*] not enrolled in their own guilds, was, *and remains*, the wool manufacturers' guild. This guild, which was much more powerful and exercised greater authority than all the others, then employed, and *still now employs*, most of the plebs and the lesser people" (FH III.12, emphases added). The Ciompi Revolt, Machiavelli implies, did nothing to end the oppression of the city's working class by the rich *popolani* of the guild community.

These were the long term circumstances that serve as the backdrop for the infamous speech that Machiavelli attributes to the anonymous *ciompo* in chapter 13: a context in which the "plebeian men" (*uomini plebei*), both "the *sottoposti*" working for the wool manufacturers' guild and the plebs who were subordinated under other guilds, were, in Machiavelli's words, "fully indignant" (FH III.13). In the Spring of 1378, the plebs were, as Machiavelli reports, quite anxious as a result of the arson and robbery they had committed at the instigation of malcontents within the city's upper class. At one of the nightly meetings that the plebs were holding to discuss the "common danger" they all faced during these trying times, "one of the boldest and most experienced of their number," whom Machiavelli does not name, addresses his comrades. The anonymous *ciompo* serves, for many scholars, as an amoral, politically realist stand-in for Machiavelli himself in the *Histories*; a figure, moreover, that supposedly confirms Machiavelli's mature belief in the common people's inclination toward political evil.

The first point to notice within the speech is that the *ciompo* himself acknowledges that his fellow plebs are not inclined to persist in the evil that others had impelled them to commit. He states, "I am very much aggrieved to hear that many of you suffer a guilty conscience for committing these recent offenses, and therefore prefer to avoid undertaking more" (FH III.13). The second important point is that after the speech, as I will show, the plebs do not follow the *ciompo*'s advice all the way through. The *ciompo* begins his speech by stating that if necessity did not dictate it, he might be willing to advise that they all continue to live in "restful poverty" rather than risk "perilous gain" by perpetrating more crimes (FH III.13). However, in circumstances where "the whole city bubbles over with hatred" for the plebs and with a desire to punish them for their misdeeds, they need to go on the offensive to secure themselves. So, it is not any inclination toward evil that motivates the speaker or his audience, initially, in Machiavelli's account, but merely a desire for security under dire immediate circumstances.

However, the *ciompo* also looks to the future, insisting that the plebs must seek "to live in greater freedom, and with more satisfaction, than we have enjoyed in the past" (FH III.13). He advises an escalation of burning and robbery, a proliferation of violence that enlists ever more compatriots in such crimes, because "when many misbehave, none are punished; while petty crimes are often punished, great and grave ones are usually rewarded. . . . By multiplying our evils, therefore, we will surely gain an easy pardon." As for the future, if they seize the riches of their wealthy enemies, he insists, such resources will help them secure "our freedom" going forward. It is tempting to explore at length all of the Machiavellian principles apparently distilled within the *ciompo*'s speech. Some of his proclamations are as outrageous in their audacity as they are irresistible in their eloquence. For instance, the *ciompo* exclaims: "The faithful servant remains always a servant, and the good one remains always poor. No one escapes servitude except the faithless and the bold, and no one avoids poverty but through rapaciousness and duplicity" (FH III.13). Nevertheless, I will confine myself to those aspects of the speech that pertain to the central issues of this chapter.

Midway through the speech, the *ciompo* issues the statement on the equal nature of all men that many scholars take as Machiavelli's repudiation of his own previous declarations that all cities, all polities, are constituted by two different kinds of natures or humors: namely, the desire to oppress characteristic of the nobility, and the desire not to be oppressed characteristic of the people. On the contrary, the *ciompo* confidently declares here:

> Be not intimidated by the antiquity of blood with which they reprove us. All men originate from the same beginning; hence all are equally ancient, having been fashioned by nature in the same mode. If you strip us all naked, we are all alike; if we were to cloak ourselves in their garments and they in ours, we would appear

noble and they ignoble. What ultimately separates us is only poverty and riches. (FH III.13)

Few commentators, however, ask the following questions: Why must
the *ciompo* exert himself so strenuously in the effort to convince the
people of what is supposedly their true nature? Why must he instruct
the plebeians in ways of behaving that supposedly should come to
them as spontaneously, indeed, naturally, as it does to their social
antagonists? In fact, the *ciompo* himself raises the possibility that he
is mistaken in his estimation of his comrades' real nature, for, in discussing the pervasive guilt from which they presently suffer, he
claims: "if you are so susceptible to conscience and shame, then you
are not the men I take you to be" (FH III.13).

Put simply, the *ciompo* pleads with the plebs to forsake the very
"decency" (P 9) that Machiavelli had attributed to them in previous
works: "If you observe well the proceedings of men you will see that
all who acquire massive wealth or great power, do so by fraud or
force, and after having won them, whether by deception or violence,
cloak their ignominious gains under some falsely decent guise [*falso
titolo di guadagno adonestono*]" (FH III.13). With these entreaties, the
ciompo implores those to whom Machiavelli attributes natural decency to learn how to behave indecently, and then to retrospectively
camouflage such behavior with a false veil of decency. Again, if the
plebs "always revel in evil," why is such persuasion necessary?

The *ciompo* then sets out the following as the ultimate goals that
the plebs will achieve through the violence, fraud, rapacity, and generally evil means that he recommends: "We shall either become undisputed princes of the city, or, at the very least, gain such control
over a great proportion of it that not only will our previous offenses
be forgiven, but we will also wield sufficient authority and power to
threaten our adversaries with entirely new injuries" (FH III.13). In
this spirit, the *ciompo* exclaims near the conclusion of his speech:
"How many times I have heard you complain of your masters' arrogance and your magistrates' injustice! Now is the time, not merely to
free yourselves from them, but to subject them so entirely to your
power that they will have more cause to fear and to complain about
you, than you them" (FH III.13). The people's subsequent actions

must be judged precisely with these stated goals of complete authority over the city, or preponderant power within it, in mind.

Machiavelli reports that the *ciompo's* speech fanned the already "inflamed evil spirits" of the plebs, who all agreed to recommence their violence once they increase the number of their confederates. Moreover, he begins the next chapter by writing that the plebs, in response to the *ciompo's* speech, were setting out "to usurp the republic" (FH III.14). But I will show that the actions recounted by Machiavelli in this and subsequent chapters prove that the plebs want neither complete mastery over nor even a lion's share of power within the city.[9]

The *ciompi* and other plebs do not, however, enjoy the leisure of waiting until some more opportune moment arises to resume their insurrection, as the *Signoria* immediately learns of their plans and extracts through torture its details from one of their number (FH III.14). In consultation with representatives of the guilds, the *Signoria* decides to summon to the piazza the next morning all of the sixteen neighborhood standard-bearers, at the heads of their militias. However, alerted to these plans by an artisan who overheard them being made in the *Palazzo della Signoria*, thousands of plebs gathered at the squares of major churches throughout the city that very evening, with the intention of marching on the palazzo in the morning. Hearing that such forces were being amassed, none of the Gonfalonieres show up to defend the *Signoria*, which winds up protected by a mere eighty members of the neighborhood companies.

The "multitude," according to Machiavelli, descends on the *Signoria* in the morning, insisting that the priors release their prisoners, a demand that is refused until the plebs set ablaze the houses of the Gonfalonier of Justice, Luigi Guicciardini, who presently presides over the *Signoria* (FH III.14). Once the prisoners are released, the plebs seize the Gonfalonier's Standard of Justice, and under its authority, burn the houses of citizens who had offended them by either public or private means. Machiavelli recounts how in the heat of the moment certain citizens of higher social standing manage to turn the crowd against the houses of their own personal enemies.

But the plebs, by and large, follow their own agenda: unsurprisingly, they burn the records of the Wool Guild, which presumably contained information concerning past offenses and pending indict-ments of individual *ciompi* (FH III.14). They also elevate to the rank of knights the citizens whom they considered sympathetic to their plight, such as Salvestro de' Medici, Antonio Alberti, and Tommaso Strozzi—as well as some citizens, such as Luigi Guicciardini, whose houses they had burned earlier in the day (FH III.14). Machiavelli notes that the *Signoria* remained largely undefended by guild leaders and the militia heads; even the few standard-bearers who did finally appear during the day departed shortly thereafter.

Then, the multitude—the plebs and lower guildsmen—on Machi-avelli's account now numbering over six thousand, demand that the guilds surrender all of their standards, and they duly receive them (FH III.14). Under these banners and the Standard of Justice, Machiavelli reports, they march upon the *Podestà*'s palace the next morning, seizing it by force. There, "the heads of the plebs" conduct a meeting with "the syndics of the guilds, as well as other citizens" to articulate the terms that the plebs would soon present to the *Si-gnoria* (FH III.15). Whether the guild representatives and other prominent citizens came to the plebeian leaders on their own initia-tive or were summoned, Machiavelli does not say. However, he does report that the *Signoria*'s representatives, four members of the Colleges whom the priors sent to negotiate with the plebs, were surprised to find these guild leaders already there conferring with the plebs.

By the end of July 21, 1378, after extensive rioting and demonstra-tions, over six thousand *sottoposti* and lower guildsmen charge four individuals from among their ranks, along with the four representa-tives of the government, to formally present their peace terms to the *Signoria* (FH III.15). The plebs demanded the following concessions: that three new guilds be instituted to include workers and lesser people who previously had not been enrolled in guilds of their own; that these three new guilds together be represented by two priors in the *Signoria*; that the number of priors allotted to the minor guilds be restored from two to three;[10] that provisions be made for public space where the new guilds could conduct their meetings; that use of a foreign judge by the wool guild be banned; that prisoners pres-ently under indictment or recently convicted be pardoned; and that citizens who had been admonished as Ghibellines by the Guelfs have their honors and rights restored. The plebs also insisted upon a two-year amnesty for themselves from sentences for petty crimes and requested favorable fiscal policies from the city's authority overseeing the public debt, the *Monte*.

Machiavelli reacts to this proposal with the following declaration: "these demands were dishonorable and grave for the republic" (FH III.15). But just how egregious are they in reality? In assessing them, readers should keep in mind the following considerations: the previous, highly inequitable sociopolitical order of the city laid out by Machiavelli himself; the nameless *ciompo*'s declaration of what the plebs' ultimate, arguably immoderate goals should be; and the plebs' near absolute control over the city at this very moment.

In Florence's constitutional structure before the revolt, twenty-one guilds shared eight seats in the *Signoria*: Machiavelli's earlier account (FH II.42) suggests that the seven major guilds held two seats, and the minor fourteen guilds, split into groupings of middling and lower guilds, enjoyed, respectively, three and two apiece.[11] Once again, contradicting his own statements at the start of Book III, Machiavelli shows here that the plebs, who heretofore had been completely excluded from these arrangements, ask for the passage of laws that benefit the entire citizenry and not just themselves as the prevailing party. In this regard, it is worth emphasizing what the plebeians actually demand and what they do not demand: they leave the major and middling guilds their established seats in the *Signoria*; they restore the seats of the minor guilds from two to three; they do not call for the abolition of the Guelf Party, hence keeping intact the source of the ancient nobility's dignity and authority; and they call for an end to admonishments, thus attempting to do right by the dubiously identified "Ghibelline" citizens who had been persecuted by the party. The plebs ask for amnesty regarding their own crimes, of course, and they demand that the Monte be reorganized in a way that transferred the financial burden of the public debt from rank and file guildsmen to the wealthiest members of the guilds.

However, most importantly, by demanding for themselves only two seats in the *Signoria*, the plebs signal that they have no desire to deprive the major, middling, and minor guilds of their political preeminence, although the plebeians outnumber the members of these other three sets of guilds combined. In short, despite enjoying a position to impose their will on the city, and despite the nameless *ciompo*'s entreaty that they make the republic entirely their own (or at least allow themselves to dominate it), they ask for a subordinate role within its government.

In the two previous examples from the *Histories* that I examined above, Machiavelli had shown—through his recording of deeds, if not through his general assessments thereof—that the *popolani* of the guild community did not act in anything approaching an oppressive manner toward the Florentine nobles. Here, his extravagant criticisms of the plebs notwithstanding, Machiavelli demonstrates, through his account of their actions and demands, that the plebs desire neither "evil" for the whole republic nor its entire "usurpation" by making themselves "princes of the city"; rather, they seek a political outcome amenable to all of the city's various parts, including themselves and their most stalwart adversaries.

Returning to Machiavelli's account of the events of July 1378, he records the response of the city government to the plebs' demands: "from fear of worse, the *Signoria*, the Colleges, and the Council of the People each agreed to them all" (FH III.15). But, for the proposed reforms to pass, approval by the Council of the Commune was also necessary. According to the city's statutes, both the popular and the communal councils could not meet on the same day, so the vote in the latter assembly was postponed until the next day. The plebs conceivably could have insisted that statutory conventions be abrogated under these extraordinary circumstances, demanding that the final vote be commenced immediately, but they do not. Machiavelli concludes his account of the day's events by stating, "Since it seemed, for the moment, that both the guilds and the plebs were satisfied, the latter promised that all tumults would cease once the new laws were passed." However, popular indignation and elite cowardice combined on the next day to insure that the present tranquility would not be sustained.

Machiavelli writes that the next morning, while the Council of the Commune was deliberating, "the impatient and variable multitude returned to the piazza under the city's standards, with such loud and intimidating shouts that they frightened the entire Council and the *Signori*" (FH III.15). How much does Machiavelli—who, it is fair to say, likes his politics rough—really disapprove of such loud, intimidating, and frightening shouting and this public demonstration of popular solidarity? In the *Discourses*, Machiavelli downplays the extent to which a republic's elites ought to be worried by such commotions, citing the behavior of the Roman plebeians (D I.4). He declares that ruckus and outcry in the street should be "frightening" exclusively to those who have "only read about them in books" (D I.4). It is not the Florentine plebs who behave differently than their ancient Roman counterparts at this juncture of the *Histories*, but rather, as Machiavelli shows in what follows, it is the Florentine elites who do.

Machiavelli writes that, as a result of this commotion and yelling, "one of the priors, Guerriante Marignolli, motivated more by fear rather than by private interest, ran downstairs on the pretense of securing the door, and fled to his house. As he snuck outside, he proved unable to conceal his identity from the crowd" (FH III.15). The supposedly evil plebs, shouting in the piazza, do him no harm. But the sight of a magistrate exiting the palace for some undiscerned purpose aroused the suspicion of the plebs, and therefore "prompted the multitude to demand that unless all the other *Signori* also evacuated the palace, they would slaughter their children and raze their houses to the ground." Here, as later in the revolt, uncertainty over the motivations of magistrates (eventually, in particular, those of Michele di Lando) arouses distrust among the plebs who, as a result, resort to intimidation but not actual physical harm to insure that the concessions which were promised to them would actually be granted.

The Council of the Commune passes the new laws (FH III.15). However, in Machiavelli's account, the priors retire to the safety of their chambers, and the council members fear leaving the shelter of the palace. Apparently, among neither group is there a single Menenius, Valerius, Horatius, or Camillus willing to address the crowd with either conciliatory entreaties or chastising admonitions. Machiavelli writes that the officials were deeply anguished over the state of affairs: "Having seen both the multitude behave with such indecency [*disonestà*], and those who could have restrained or repressed them behave with such malignity or cowardice, [the magistrates] were in utter despair for the safety of the city" (FH III.15). Nevertheless, the plebs have not, at least by Roman standards, behaved indecently at all. They have threatened but not actually committed any harm to the persons of the city's leading citizens, despite enjoying more than ample opportunity to do so.

When Tommaso Strozzi and Benedetto Alberti, whose families were honored by the plebs the previous day, advise the priors to bow to "the popular impetus" and leave the palace, Machiavelli reports that two of the priors, deeply insulted by the idea and highly suspicious of Strozzi's and Alberti's favor with the people, adamantly refuse (FH III.15). However, each of the priors eventually exits the palace in safety, even those who had initially expressed reluctance; they proved, according to Machiavelli, "unwilling to risk being considered more bold than wise." Thus, the first wave of the Ciompi Revolt concludes with, all things being equal, highly moderate reforms instituted at the instigation of the plebs and with no physical harm inflicted on the leading citizens of the city.

We may conclude that Florence's plebeians, do not have "the same nature" as the nobles in Machiavelli's estimation; they do not desire to oppress, and when given the opportunity to do so, they do not engage in oppression. Rather, the plebeian reform proposal suggests that the *ciompi* merely want inclusion in the guild order; they seek institutional guarantees to insure that they will not continue to be oppressed—as Machiavelli, without any contravening evidence, shows that they had been—by the nobles and by "the princes of the guilds." Thus, Machiavelli's descriptions of plebeian behavior seriously undermine the notion that he actually believes what he says about them, either in his own words or in those he attributes to the nameless *ciompo*. In this light, there is more than a little retrospective irony, I think, in Machiavelli's rhetorical denunciations of the plebeians' supposedly "evil" motivations and of their purportedly "indecent," "grave," and "dishonorable" demands.

In fact, the behavior of the lower classes here actually seems to confirm, not qualify—and certainly not contradict—Machiavelli's description of the plebeians in his earlier writings. As Machiavelli often states and shows, the common people may lash out violently in response to circumstances of egregious oppression (P 19; D I.44, II.2), but if appropriate institutional and organizational resources are available to them, as Machiavelli demonstrates time and again, they are much more inclined to behave moderately (P 9; D I.4, I.40). For instance, the Roman plebeians claim to want to tear Coriolanus to pieces on the Senate steps, but they prove amenable to the prospect of trying him for his life in a formal assembly (D I.7). Furthermore, as Machiavelli was fond of pointing out, the Roman plebs secede from the city rather than burn it down to protest debt bondage and to negotiate the creation and subsequent restitution of the plebeian tribunate. He also describes how, in less dramatic instances, Rome's common people refuse to enlist for military service or resort to tumultuous demonstrations, rather than inflict bodily harm on any nobles to gain political concessions from the Roman senate.

According to the evidence presented by Machiavelli in the *Histories*, the Florentine plebs seem to want merely comparable civic-military arrangements enjoyed by their Roman counterparts; institutions through which they can air their political-economic grievances and gain future concessions without recourse to the riots, arson, and pillaging that they have recently committed in the absence of such institutions. Indeed, how differently would the Ciompi Revolt have unfolded if all of the common people—*popolani* and *sottoposti*, people and plebs alike—had enjoyed recourse to a magistracy like the Roman plebeian tribunate that would formally voice their complaints, and if the entire Florentine elite had been gathered together, like their Roman forbearers, in a Senate house?[12] As I have suggested, Machiavelli shows that the humors characteristic of both Rome and Florence are fundamentally the same; it is primarily the institutional modes and orders through which they are channeled that differ.

The Compositional Context of the Writings on Florence

I have shown that in the *Florentine Histories* much more than meets the eye occurs in Machiavelli's depiction of Florence's social classes and their interactions; much more at least than has been detected by scholars advancing the argument that Machiavelli's later political

works exhibit a conservative or aristocratic turn. But what accounts
for the fact that Machiavelli does indeed change the mode of presentation through which he conveys the unequivocal superiority of
peoples over nobles and of democratic over aristocratic republics?
Why is Machiavelli no longer the full-throated advocate of republics
where, rather than the nobility, the people—as a result of their overall decency, generally correct collective judgment, and humor not to
be oppressed—deserve to serve as "the guard of liberty" (D I.4–5)?[13]
After all, conservative-turn scholars are not wrong to detect palpable
changes of tone in Machiavelli's writings of the 1520s, even if they do
not interrogate these changes with adequate sensitivity and requisite
tenacity. Here, I offer some textual and contextual considerations to
help explain what might account for these changes, and to argue that
such changes are actually much more superficial than fundamental;
that is, more rhetorical than substantive.

The revived Florentine Republic (1494–1512), which Machiavelli
served as an administrative secretary, diplomatic emissary, and militia organizer for over a decade, was overthrown by an aristocratic
coup, foreign intervention, and Papal intrigue that returned the
Medici family to power in his native city. The now-unemployed
Machiavelli responded by writing to the restored princes, advising
them to betray their allies among the nobility and to align themselves
instead with the suddenly disempowered Florentine people.[14] As is
well known, Machiavelli was subsequently implicated in an anti-
Medici conspiracy, tortured, imprisoned, and confined to internal
exile.[15]

In 1520, Machiavelli, in an important memorandum on constitutional reforms solicited by the family, repeated his advice to the
Medici that they ultimately re-empower the Florentine people at the
expense of the family's aristocratic friends (*amici*).[16] However, in this
proposal, "The Discursus on Florentine Affairs," Machiavelli much
more tentatively recommends that the popular assembly, the Great
Council, which had been the heart of the 1494 popular government,
be given the preeminent institutional role in the restored republic.
Machiavelli carefully assures his Medici addressees that their clients
among the Florentine aristocracy would not be threatened by the
people assembled in the Great Council during the lifetimes of their

Medici patrons. Indeed, Machiavelli seems to embed this popular assembly within a Venetian-style mixed regime, a vaguely aristocratic republic in which elite citizens, *ottimati* of signorial rank and middling citizens of intermediate rank, hold the preponderance of power.

However, Machiavelli insists that once the Medici earn their fast approaching eternal reward, the Great Council should be re-empowered with preeminent legislative, electoral, and judicial authority within the republic. Furthermore, he proposes the creation of a plebeian magistracy, the *proposti*, through which the common people could affect these democratic reforms to the republic's constitution. What accounts for the change in Machiavelli's style from straightforward to circumspect popular advocacy in the years 1512 to 1519?

Compositional context, I suggest, is decisive here. When the Medici commissioned the "Discursus" and, almost simultaneously, the *Florentine Histories* from Machiavelli, the family was at the lowest point of their popularity with common Florentines since the expulsion of Piero de' Medici in 1494, and perhaps at the lowest point ever. When the Medici returned to the city in 1512, it was not yet entirely clear how much they would satisfy the *ottimati's* desire to suppress the people and shut down the Great Council. Their subsequent actions, however, would leave no doubt regarding that question, and, consequently, over time they incurred increasing animosity on the part of the Florentine *popolo*.

It would be imprudent for Machiavelli in these precarious circumstances to lavishly praise his patrons' steadfast sociopolitical antagonists, the people and the plebs, in the historical account of the city, the *Histories*, that the Medici are financing or to overtly empower those very antagonists in the constitutional proposal, the "Discursus," that the family solicited from Machiavelli as a possible basis for contemporary political reforms. Discretion was all the more necessary, since Machiavelli himself was so closely and personally associated with both the popular government of 1494–1512 and its chief magistrate, the staunch Medici rival Piero Soderini. Scholars who advance the conservative-turn argument either ignore or too readily dismiss this situation when they analyze the role of the common people in Machiavelli's later writings. Indeed, they completely overlook the incongruity between words and deeds that attend

Machiavelli's discussion of the people and the plebs in the *Histories*, and they unconscionably neglect the vibrant democratic potential that Machiavelli subtly builds into his constitutional proposal in the "Discursus."[17]

An Abandonment of the Roman Republican Model in the *Histories*?

With these contextual factors in mind, simply because Machiavelli does not mention the Roman Republic all that often in the *Histories*, and does not use his earlier reconstruction of Rome as a democratic republic to serve as an explicit constitutional model in the "Discursus," there is no reason to conclude that Machiavelli is not still implicitly drawing upon Roman lessons or still inviting comparisons with them from anyone reasonably familiar with *The Prince* and the *Discourses*. Without a specific injunction on Machiavelli's part to do so, why should readers assume that, in the *Histories*, Machiavelli no longer offers implicit comparisons between the "near perfect" Roman Republic of the *Discourses* and the "great and wretched" Florentine Republic discussed in his writings from the 1520s (D I.3; FH II.25)? As I sketched in the introduction to this book, Machiavelli's account of Florence's origins, its constitutional forms, its relations with foreign powers, and the conduct of its leaders in the *Histories* bear direct contrast with his description of republican Rome in *The Prince* and the *Discourses*. Implicit references to ancient Rome and ancient Romans can be found throughout the *Histories*, if one bothers to look for them, whether or not they are mentioned by name at any particular instance.

Yet there is one salient difference between Machiavelli's writings where ancient polities serve as his primary frame of reference and those where modern republics are his principal focus: an apparent move from two to three social classes. For instance, why does Machiavelli speak of a split between the plebeians and the people in the *Histories* when he discusses them as a unified social class in *The Prince* and the *Discourses*? In the latter two works, he uses the terms plebs, plebeians, people, and multitude interchangeably, while in the *Histories* he often separates the *popolo*, or the *popolani*, from the *popolo minuto*, the *sottoposti*, or the *plebe*. In the *Histories*, Machiavelli traces the development of three political classes in Florence: how they emerged out of the guild community's decision to divide themselves into three groupings to be represented in the *Signoria*. The upper guilds eventually merged with the ancient nobility to create a new elite class of "popular nobles" or *ottimati*, while the middling and minor guilds, after the Ciompi Revolt, returned to their practice of excluding the city's plebs from the guild community. In the "Discursus," Machiavelli duly proposes a constitutional model that accommodates this tripartite historical division of Florentine citizens, which are the socioeconomic facts on the ground confronting Machiavelli at the time. But conservative-turn scholars insist on taking this treatment of reigning social convention as a newfound normative preference on Machiavelli's part for a Florentine three-class as opposed to a Roman two-class system.[18] This is, I believe, unwarranted for a number of reasons bearing on Machiavelli's lifelong understanding of what constitutes a republic's civic and military well-being.

Machiavelli makes it clear that, unlike Rome, Florence suffered corrupt beginnings that adversely influenced much of its subsequent political development, including its class divisions. Rather than a proper founder like Romulus—who ordered the city of Rome with a publicly unified, armed common citizenry and a senate composed of the richest and most prominent citizens—Florence was a politically disorganized colony that eventually became a disarmed commercial republic, one that consistently permitted social strife to spill over from natural class animosities to what Machiavelli considers artificial family, guild, party, and religious conflicts.

Whether one believes that Catiline, Sulla, or Caesar founded Florence, Machiavelli demonstrates in the *Histories* that none of these republican usurpers properly ordered the city in a healthy civic manner (FH II.2).[19] Hence, all future social conflict between the nobles and people in Florence played out in ways that undermined the natural division of the great and the people—social classes who respectively oppress and resist oppression, and who are bound only by one fundamental, civically salutary commonality: military virtue. Florence's natural, potentially beneficial division of two social classes fragmented over time into the multiple, insufficiently, or inappropriately armed commercial classes that conservative-turn scholars take to be Machiavelli's newly preferred class arrangements.

It is difficult to argue that Machiavelli ceased to favor Roman constitutional and class arrangements over Florentine ones, since he continued to demonstrate that the latter prove less stable and less conducive to military prowess than did the former. As Machiavelli makes plain throughout the *Histories*, the people in Florence enjoyed only limited institutional means to minimize the abusive behavior visited upon them by the nobles—again, Florence lacked both a tribunate and a senate. Machiavelli criticizes the Florentine people for totally excluding the nobles from the highest magistracies, but, as we have observed, Machiavelli's account of actual events suggests that they ultimately had no choice. Unlike the civically armed Roman plebeians who could negotiate with a nobility formally assembled in a proper senate to create a magistracy, the tribunes, which would effectively protect them, the Florentine people were offered no alternative but to use public offices, once they gained them (and initially tried to share with the great), to expel the nobles from eligibility for high office. When faced with what Machiavelli describes (again, through the facts and events he relates, if not always through the rhetoric he uses to describe them) as consistent recidivist acts of violence and oppression by the nobility, the Florentine people feel compelled to disenfranchise the nobles completely.

In response, as Machiavelli describes, the Florentine nobles made themselves appear popular by enrolling in trade guilds and by abandoning positions of military leadership, from which, as in Rome, even the common people benefit and learn (FH III.1). Machiavelli's Roman bipartite class model allowed socially mobile members of the *popolo* to integrate upward into the nobility without causing the demise of a republic's military virtue; Florence's tripartite class model results from the fact that its deficient initial ordering encouraged the aristocracy to give up its military prowess as it attempted to integrate downward into the elite guilds constituting the wealthiest commercial strata of the *popolo* (FH III.1).[20]

Moreover, the guild structure of Florence permanently left the plebeians out of the political organization of the city—the temporary gains that they won during the Ciompi Revolt notwithstanding. No founder or reformer in Florence, as did Romulus in Rome, created a senate into which socially mobile members of the people could ascend via displays of military virtue; nor did anyone organize the entire class of common citizens, both richer and poorer, into a unified, public military force (the two princes who made overtures in this direction, the Duke of Athens and Michele di Lando, ultimately relented in these endeavors). Out of the military legions that Romulus created emerged the popular assemblies that came to vie with the Roman senate for political power and gave the entire people the leverage to demand the creation of the plebeian tribunes.

There is little evidence in his later writings that Machiavelli abandoned the belief that a Roman two-class political sociology is preferable to a Florentine three-class one. In fact, Machiavelli continues to call the two-class arrangement "natural," and treats the three-class order as historical, circumstantial, and inherently defective. More importantly, for Machiavelli's lifelong civic-military priorities, the former is conducive to a martially empowered citizenry, while the latter reflects a more variegated, vulnerable, and unarmed commercial citizenry. Modern and ancient republics, in Machiavelli's view, exhibit vastly different institutional-constitutional frameworks within which historically constant popular and aristocratic appetites operate and interact. The differences between Florence's defective "modes and orders" and Rome's more vigorous ones, Machiavelli indicates, are attributable to three interrelated factors: the different political dispositions of modern as opposed to ancient founders or reformers (and the diverse kinds of institutions they create or revitalize); the pernicious influence of Christianity over contemporary princely and republican virtue; and the proliferation of artificial versus "natural" types of social division within modern republics.

Given the staunchly held preferences of the Florentine *ottimati* for a Venetian as opposed to a Roman style republic,[21] it is little wonder that Machiavelli, when undertaking writings directed exclusively to an elite Florentine audience (especially writings that are intended to have an immediate political impact) would downplay the neo-Roman nature of his republicanism. Put simply, his preferred form of democratic republicanism prioritizes a militarily armed and organized citi-

zenry that is fundamentally anathema to his audience's political inclinations. Needless to say, Machiavelli's aristocratic audience also
disliked the Roman tribunate and Rome's fully empowered large
popular assemblies.[22]

The question of institutional means that further populist resistance and democratic rule leads us to conservative-turn scholars'
discussion of Machiavelli's "Discursus."[23] Because Machiavelli accommodates the three classes of Florentine citizens (rather than reduce them to two), because he seems to empower the very highest
class of *ottimati* with apparently unassailable authority, and since he
is willing to accept (at least provisionally) a less powerful popular
assembly, the revised Great Council, such scholars conclude that
Machiavelli has moved toward a more Venetian constitutional ideal.
Such scholars read the "Discursus" as a proposal for a mildly or thoroughly aristocratic republic, but they all neglect to take seriously or
even mention a crucial institutional element that moves the proposal
away from Venetian appearances in the present to potential Roman
possibilities in the future: the *proposti*.

Toward the end of the proposal, Machiavelli suggests that a magistracy for which the Florentine elite is ineligible, the *proposti*, must
be appended to the two highest councils of the republic, inhabited
by its highest and middling citizens. These *proposti* will be selected
by lottery from the Companies of the People and assigned on short
notice to the republic's executive and senatorial councils for very
short tenures. Machiavelli empowers the *proposti* to appeal decisions
reached in the upper councils to the Great Council for ultimate arbi-
tration, hence giving the latter, the republic's most populous body,
final judgment over public policy. The random selection of the *proposti*, their quick notice assignments, and short terms within the
higher bodies minimize opportunities for them to be intimidated,
corrupted, and coopted by the elite citizens with whom they will sit
in such councils. As to the reduced authority of the more populous
assembly to which they will refer ultimate policy decisions: Machiavelli's previous, famous remarks in both *The Prince* and the *Discourses*
concerning the memory of liberty in republics, and the people's unquenchable thirst for regaining it, as well as hints within the "Discursus" itself, suggest that he expects the Great Council to reassume its

traditional powers (and perhaps add more) after the death of the Medici pope.

Machiavelli famously praises Rome's founding over Sparta's early in the *Discourses*: rather than establishing each of its institutions all at once as Lycurgus did in Sparta, Romulus set institutions in place that allowed Rome to evolve from a monarchy to an aristocratic republic to a more democratic republic. By arming the plebs and establishing the senate, Romulus created the possibility that plebeians could extract from senators an office like the tribunes, who in turn conducted policy in Rome's popular assemblies in an increasingly democratic fashion. One need not read too closely to observe similar intentions on Machiavelli's part in the "Discursus": his Florentine tribunes over time will work in concert with the city's not quite yet fully empowered popular assembly, the Great Council, to transform an ostensibly Venetian republic dominated by the upper classes into a quasi-Roman one ultimately governed by common citizens.

Conclusion: A Consistent View of Class Politics

In the dedicatory letters of both *The Prince* and the *Discourses*, Machiavelli declares that each work contained "everything" he knew, most relevant to our purposes, everything he knew concerning politics. Machiavelli neither explicitly repudiates these claims anywhere in subsequent writings, nor asserts that later works such as the *Florentine Histories* deserve to occupy a similarly comprehensive epistemological status within his oeuvre. Therefore, I have been operating under the assumption that the two earlier works continue to serve as authoritative guides for any attempt to understand the arguments of all of Machiavelli's political writings, including later ones such as the *Histories*. On these grounds, I find it discouraging that scholars associated with the conservative-turn thesis so rarely read with requisite care the actions of modern political actors—individual and collective agents—as Machiavelli conveys them in the *Histories*, in more direct connection with his depictions and assessments of ancient (and modern) political actors presented in *The Prince* and the *Discourses*.

Machiavelli never declares in his later writings that he had changed his mind with respect to the proper functioning of principalities and republics. He never states in any programmatic terms that he had fundamentally reconceptualized how he thinks princes, founders, reformers, and magistrates ought to behave generally, or, especially, how they ought to act vis-à-vis the nobles and the peoples of principalities and republics. His previous assessments, elaborated in *The Prince* and the *Discourses*, must, I argue, be brought to bear with at least equal force as are those that sometimes seem to contradict them within the *Histories* themselves. There is no reason to assume, as conservative-turn scholars consistently do, that Machiavelli had forgotten or abandoned the political principles that he set forth in his earlier works. It is a profound mistake to read the *Florentine Histories* as if he had. Too much of importance that operates below the level of mere words in this complicated, magnificent work is missed if we do.

PART II

4

Rousseau's Repudiation of Machiavelli's Democratic Roman Republic

JEAN-JACQUES ROUSSEAU'S writings have inspired democratic theorists and activists for centuries. Yet, at crucial if neglected junctures of his political magnum opus, the *Social Contract*,[1] Rousseau prescribes institutions that inhibit political participation by common citizens and that enable rather than constrain the prerogative of elites within republics and popular governments. This chapter demonstrates that large portions of the *Social Contract* devoted to the Roman Republic promote institutions that obstruct popular efforts: to participate as free and equal citizens within republics, to keep the wealthy from dominating society, and to keep magistrates from exercising excessive political discretion. Like Niccolò Machiavelli before him, Rousseau expounds his theory of liberty, equality, and well-ordered government through an extensive discussion of republican Rome's political institutions and practices. However, while the Genevan citizen famously champions the republican bona fides of the author of *The Prince* (SC III 6, 95), he directly repudiates specific aspects of the Florentine secretary's democratic reconstruction of Roman republicanism in the *Discourses*.[2]

In what follows, I argue that Rousseau's analysis and appropriation of the Roman Republic deliberately undermines Machiavelli's efforts to reconstruct and promote institutions that both maximize the participation of poor citizens in popular governments and facilitate their efforts to control or contain economic and political elites.

Rousseau's radical revision of Machiavelli's appropriation of the ancient Roman Republic, I suggest, historically served to foreclose the possibility of an alternative, popularly participatory, and anti-elitist strand of modern republicanism that in subsequent centuries would have better served democratic theory and practice. Through the promulgation of sociologically anonymous principles like generality and popular sovereignty, and by confining elite accountability to elections alone, Rousseau's institutional analyses and proposals allow, nay encourage, wealthier citizens and magistrates to dominate the politics of popular governments in surreptitious and unassailable ways.[3]

To sketch the contrast that I pose in this chapter between Machiavelli's and Rousseau's respective appropriations of the Roman Republic: Machiavelli democratizes Rome's assemblies, intimating that they functioned via majority rule and insisting that they granted plebeian citizens equal voice with patricians in assemblies where both attended; furthermore, that he countenanced the exclusion of wealthy citizens from certain assemblies to maximize popular influence over the laws and policies of a republic and to qualify the influence exerted by economic and political elites. To the contrary, Rousseau emphasizes the timocratic voting structure of the republic's primary assembly, the *comitia centuriata*, an arrangement by which wealthy citizens effectively disenfranchised poorer ones.

Moreover, Machiavelli singled out the "tribunes of the plebs" as the domestic institution above all others that preserved Rome's liberty. Machiavelli's tribunate was a standing magistracy reserved for plebeian citizens that enabled them to contest the power and privilege of Rome's senatorial class. For his part, Rousseau blames the demise of the republic and the rise of the emperors on the Roman tribunate, and, in his own reconstruction of the magistracy, he demotes it to temporary status and neutralizes its usefulness to common citizens. Finally, Machiavelli accentuates the extent to which clientelism, intensified by growing socioeconomic inequality, contributed to the eventual collapse of the ancient Roman Republic and rendered the medieval Florentine Republic almost irredeemably corrupt. Rousseau, in stark contrast, praises patron-client relations in ancient Rome, through which wealthy and wise patrician citizens

influenced, indeed manipulated, the voting of poorer, dependent plebeian citizens in ways that, in Rousseau's estimation, promoted "the
common good." On the basis of his advocacy of these Roman institutions and customs, I will venture the following conclusion: two and
a half centuries of mostly laudatory commentary on the Genevan's
egalitarianism notwithstanding, Rousseau distrusts the poor much
more than he despises inequality.

Whereas Machiavelli insisted on plebeian-specific and extraelectoral techniques of magistrate appointment or sanction to keep a
republic from degenerating into a mere oligarchy, Rousseau promotes a formally egalitarian but substantively inequitable aristocracy
that confines popular contestation of elites to electoral procedures
biased toward the wealthiest citizens. Central to Machiavelli's democratic republicanism was a strenuous attempt to undermine and mitigate the state of affairs described above; at the core of Rousseau's
aristocratic republicanism is a subtle, elaborate effort to ratify and
preserve precisely such a state of affairs. I suggest that a substantive,
contemporary theory of democracy requires reforms inspired by
Machiavelli's class-specific, Rome-inspired model of popular government rather than Rousseau's already too influential model of formal
political homogeneity. Circumstances in which wealth inequality
proliferates and political unaccountability runs rampant within contemporary democracy demand institutional means through which
economic and political elites are actively contested rather than allowed to conceal and sustain the entrenchment of their privilege and
prerogative.[4]

Commentators on the *Social Contract* tend to underestimate or
ignore the extent to which Rousseau intended to teach his general
theory of republican sovereignty and government through the specific example of Rome in Book IV of that resplendent work.[5] This is
unfortunate in at least two respects: firstly, scholars who attribute to
Rousseau's formulations of the general will or popular sovereignty
the intellectual origin of modern democracy, or who appropriate
Rousseau's institutional prescriptions in the service of more robust
models of democratic politics, do so in uninformed ways; and, secondly, many philosophical puzzlements and controversies over
Rousseauian political principles (e.g., legitimacy, majority rule, au-

tonomy) that pervade the secondary literature could be clarified or perhaps even settled through simple consultation with Rousseau's own efforts to concretize his abstract theorizing in Book IV of the *Social Contract*.

If scholars engage to any extent the multiple chapters devoted to ancient Rome in Book IV, they usually treat Rousseau's institutional analysis as a descriptive and not a prescriptive endeavor; i.e., he is merely reflecting on the way politics was organized in Rome, but he is not necessarily recommending the republic as a model for emulation. And yet, Book IV, dedicated almost exclusively to Rome's political institutions and practices, is the longest book of the *Social Contract*; chapter 4 of that fourth book, in which Rousseau discusses and endorses the timocratic organization of Rome's centuriate assembly, is likewise longer than any other chapter in the entire *Social Contract*. I heartily doubt that Rousseau would have devoted so much time, space and energy to the minute details of Roman institutions, and to such meticulous exposition of their functioning, if he did not intend for his reconstructed Roman Republic to serve, in a profound sense, as a practicable political exemplum. In fact, as I will demonstrate, Rousseau himself sometimes intimates, sometimes insists, as much.[6]

Rousseau and Democracy

The central question of this chapter is not whether Rousseau is a good democrat, but rather, based on his interpretation of the Roman Republic, whether Rousseau's political thought is a worthy resource for democratic theory and practice.[7] In the *Social Contract*, Rousseau never claims to be a democrat. In fact, he is harshly critical of regimes called "democracies" and deeply skeptical of whether democracy is practicable at all. Rousseau famously insists that "a genuine democracy never has existed and never will exist" because the people cannot remain assembled to decide all of the matters that good government constantly requires (SC III 4, 91). According to Rousseau, administrative necessity always undermines rule by the many because government requires smaller bodies that irresistibly accumulate more and more power for themselves (SC III 4, 91).[8] If democracy were to be approximated in reality, Rousseau insists that it would require rare circumstances: a small polity where citizens can easily know one another personally and readily assemble for civic purposes (SC III 4, 91). But even under such conditions, Rousseau is reluctant to endorse democracy since such "popular governments" are more prone to "intestine turmoil" than are all other regimes (SC III 4, 92).

To be sure, Rousseau is no democrat. He is a "republican," even if this, too, is hardly an unproblematic attribution. After all, Rousseau's most general definition of what constitutes a republic does not delineate a specific regime type or particular institutional form. Rousseau avers that any regime, even a monarchy, is a republic so long as it adheres to the rule of law and governs in the common interest—i.e., if it is "legitimate" (SC II 6, 67). But just as Machiavelli sets out a very broad, general definition of the kinds of regimes that might be identified as republics,[9] within which he intimates more particular socioinstitutional preferences, so too does Rousseau set forth criteria for the institutional form of what we would properly recognize as a republic. For each author, the more a republic, or at least a large republic, conforms to the model of ancient Rome, the more that entity approximates the best form of republic. But before turning to Rousseau's and Machiavelli's respective reconstructions of the Roman Republic, I discuss a few aspects of Rousseau's theory of generality to help explain why certain inegalitarian characteristics of Roman politics that he praises do not necessarily violate the standard of equality promulgated by this most celebrated of egalitarian theorists.[10]

Generality, Aristocracy, and Elections

I will not recite here the intricacies of Rousseau's theory of the general will.[11] Instead, I briefly describe some of Rousseau's requirements for determining whether institutional arrangements can facilitate expression of the general will. First and foremost, the general will abides no exclusion of citizens: no one may be excluded from attending the sovereign assembly, no one's votes may ever be discarded and no citizen may be declared ineligible for a specific privilege or an individual magistracy on any particularist grounds (SC II 2, 58 n).

Contrary to some interpretations, Rousseau does not insist on unanimity as an expression of the general will; a majority vote will suffice so long as all citizens participate in the vote (SC II 2, 58 n) but not necessarily on equal terms, as we will see. Rousseau's antipathy to public discussion in advance of voting—his communicationless deliberation—is notorious (SC II 3, 60) and comports quite well with the voting, not speaking, quality of Rome's legislative and electoral assemblies.[12]

Ultimately, however, formal requirements as such do not guarantee realization of the general will. A specific quality that inheres within the will, for Rousseau, whatever way it is formulated, is the factor that properly "generalizes the will" (SC II 4, 62). For instance, some stipulation that a certain number of citizens participate in will-formation is not what generalizes the will, and Rousseau's anxiety over the dangers of majority rule are well known (e.g., SC II 11; IV 1; and IV 4). Rather, Rousseau insists, "the common interest that unites" the citizens is what generalizes the will (SC II 4, 62). It is not until readers encounter Rousseau's subtle endorsement of Rome's timocratically organized assembly, the *comitia centuriata*, that they can begin to comprehend how this precept might operate in practical reality. If some number among the sovereign better understand the common interest of all, in Rousseauian terms, then the republic may downgrade the votes of those who are less perceptive regarding the common interest—so long as it does not completely exclude them from the assembly in which votes are counted. Rousseau remains adamant throughout the *Social Contract* that the "whole people" must be included in the promulgation of laws (SC II 6, 67). However, it turns out that by privileging, in the law-making process, those citizens who are most likely to understand the common good, a republic may better guarantee full realization of the general will, which is indistinguishable from the common good. In Rome, as Rousseau explains in Book IV, this was achieved by weighting votes according to wealth in the republic's most important assembly.

As we will observe in the next section, this logic allows Rousseau to praise Rome's centuriate assembly for performing precisely those tasks that he admonishes the Athenian assembly, the *ekklêsia*, for undertaking. Rousseau criticizes the Athenian assembly for acting without requisite generality when it honored or ostracized particular citizens—even if such measures passed by overwhelming majorities (SC II 4, 62). Rousseau is suspicious of a democratic people's capacity to act both generally as sovereign and particularly as the government. While the Athenian demos, gathered in assembly, might pass laws appropriately, according to Rousseau's notion of separating sovereignty from government, the demos ought not render particular judgments like assigning honors or deciding political trials. Yet, why does he not reproach the Roman *comitia centuriata* for exercising both sovereign and governmental functions by legislating, on the one hand, and trying cases or conducting private business, on the other (SC III 12, 110; IV 4, 136)? I will suggest that Rousseau prefers the inequitably structured Roman assembly to the equitably structured Athenian one; the former might successfully function as both sovereign and magistrate, in his estimation, while the latter most certainly cannot.[13]

If this is so, then equality may possess two dimensions for Rousseau: one, strictly formal, the other, deeply, almost illusorily, substantive. Formal equality is satisfied by general inclusion; substantive equality might be realized by inequitable procedures that are intended to guarantee everybody's good. The *comitia centuriata* best exemplifies both dimensions for Rousseau: all Roman citizens are included in the assembly but the wealthiest ones have more votes. In such a case, the general will is divined by those, through greater patriotism or prudence, who have better access to it; it is not secured through strict adherence to egalitarian procedures like majority rule and one man/one vote as was the case in the Athenian assembly. This notion of a more profound substantive equality that is achieved through inequitable institutional arrangements justifies Rousseau's rationale for deeming aristocracy, albeit elective aristocracy, to be the best form of government in the passages examined here. According to Rousseau, elective aristocracy gives preeminence to the wise, who, in turn, govern with the common interest in mind: "the best and most natural order is to have the wisest govern the multitude, so long as it is certain that they will govern for [the multitude's] advantage and not their own" (SC III 5, 93).[14]

Rousseau's argument in favor of election seems, at first blush, to be based on a genuine faith in the multitude's ability to choose magistrates who will serve the common good. In the passages devoted to election generally—that is, before his specific discussion of the Roman centuriate assembly in the next book—Rousseau never raises the possibility that voting should be structured such that rich citizens have greater say in the election of magistrates. Electoral outcomes seem to be fully in the hands of the multitude, which presumably appoints magistrates on the basis of simple majority rule. In this context, Rousseau declares that election is "a means by which probity, enlightenment, experience, and all the other reasons for public preferment and esteem are so many further guarantees of being well governed" (SC III 5, 93).

Rousseau's explicit preference for elected aristocracy—or, aristocracy "properly so called"—over hereditary aristocracy suggests that electorates *make* individuals aristocrats *through* the electoral process (SC III 5, 93). As opposed to hereditary systems where aristocratic designations are conferred prior to the political process, from birth, elective aristocracy presumably opens the ranks of magistracies to anyone. On this account, one might assume that election creates aristocrats; it does not merely ratify those who already exist. However, matters are not quite so simple. Rousseau equivocates over the purported equal opportunity offered by elective aristocracy before ultimately conceding that elections *do* bias the magistrate appointment process, and hence his own republican model, in favor of the wealthiest citizens—whether or not voting procedures are structured in their favor, as in Rome.

At first, Rousseau seems to merely tolerate economic inequality in his aristocratic republic. Such a regime requires "moderation among the rich and contentment among the poor" (SC III 5, 94). But he immediately reveals that elective aristocracy, aristocracy proper, relies on significant inequality: "it seems that a rigorous equality would be out of place in aristocracy; it was not even observed in Sparta" (SC III 5, 94). Presumably a "rigorous" equality among citizens would make it difficult or impossible for the electorate to identify who among the citizenry are the best and therefore who should be elevated to office. Rousseau never entertains the notion that everyone might be more or less equally virtuous, competent or public spirited in such a regime. Instead, Rousseau's statement permits wealth, the attribute most rewarded in electoral contests from time immemorial, to be the preeminent marker of political worthiness.[15] For elections to function properly, some distinctions must prevail among citizens, and without serious institutional adjustments, wealth is too easily associated with or mistaken for virtue under such circumstances.

After all, wealth enables citizens from the "best" families to improve their reputation, appearance, and speaking skills such that voters almost inevitably choose them in electoral contests. As discussed before, democratic Athens minimized the oligarchic biases of elections by distributing most magistracies through a lottery among the entire citizenry, and Italian republics guaranteed positions in executive councils and committees to members of middling and lower guilds.[16] Furthermore, Rousseau's inability or unwillingness to distinguish virtue from wealth in the context of electoral politics raises unpleasant ramifications for his endorsement, to be discussed below, of hierarchical patron-client relations in the Roman Republic: money allows wealthy citizens to fund, groom, or bribe nonwealthy candidates in order to serve their own interests at the expense of the wider citizenry.

Perhaps uncomfortable with the inegalitarian implications of his argument for unqualified election, Rousseau quickly attempts to banish any appearance that he accepts any affiliation of wealth and virtue and, in fact, he attempts to attribute that affiliation to another author. Rousseau insists that it is not he himself, but Aristotle, who favors a "certain inequality of fortune" so that the rich should rule; Rousseau, for his part, merely favors material inequality so that those with leisure time might assume the magistracies (SC III 5, 94). However, unless public provisions enable all citizens to hold political office, as many democracies and democratic republics afforded their poorer citizens, wealth and spare time will be irrevocably linked. Therefore, whether Rousseau's motivation is to ensure that either those with wealth or those with spare time should rule, the fact is, in each case, that the rich shall rule in government. Rousseau admits that magistrates will be drawn mostly from the ranks of the wealthy in his aristocratic republic, but he insists that this is not why they rule (SC III 5, 94). Rather, they monopolize offices because they are the most meritorious of citizens. Unfortunately, Rousseau's argument here is as unfalsifiable as it is potentially ideological; he offers his readers no way to distinguish candidates or magistrates who are merely wealthy from those who are truly virtuous.[17]

So what, in the end, is the difference between hereditary and elective aristocracy? Both generally facilitate rule by the wealthy—except, Rousseau suggests, that the elective aristocracy provides for the instance, "occasionally," when a token nonwealthy citizen will assume office (SC III 5, 94). How and why? Rousseau suggests that such tokenism serves to "teach the people that men's merit offers more important reasons for preference than do riches" (SC III 5, 94). But who does the teaching, if it is the electorate itself that places a nonwealthy citizen in office? Why do the people need a lesson in something that they have already undertaken? Perhaps Rousseau means that the people can learn from their own electoral decisions or that a subsequent electorate can learn from the choices of an earlier one. Still, the idea that elections can "teach the people" if it is they who do the electing is rather strange.[18] The statement makes more sense in light of Rousseau's reflections on Roman assemblies: if the election of magistrates is firmly in the hands of the few, then they can decide to elect a common citizen now and again to "teach the people" that a republic like Rousseau's Rome is a meritocratic aristocracy and not merely a plutocratic oligarchy.

Rousseau and the Roman Assemblies

Rousseau declares that the concrete example of ancient Rome is the key to a proper understanding of his abstract theory of political right, and that the voting arrangements of the Roman assemblies, especially the *comitia centuriata*, will guide "the judicious reader" on how to order a large republic (SC IV 3, 127).[19] I quote Rousseau at length here since, again, most scholars have been insufficiently attentive to the role that ancient Rome plays in the *Social Contract*, especially with respect to the inequitable organization of voting in the republic's primary assembly. The following passage, which occurs where Rousseau begins to embark upon a discussion of the proper place of popular assemblies in his own political theory, raises serious questions about interpretations that neglect the chapters devoted to the Roman Republic:

> It remains for me to speak about the way votes *should* be cast and collected in the assembly of the people; but perhaps the historical sketch of Roman administration in this matter will explain *more concretely* all the maxims that I might establish. It is not unworthy of a *judicious reader* to consider in some detail how [both] *public and particular business* was conducted in a Council of *two hundred thousand men.* (SC IV 3, 126–27, emphases added)

I will refer back to this passage often throughout this chapter since it reminds the reader that Rousseau uses Rome prescriptively rather than merely descriptively, and that he enjoins his readers to pay careful attention to his account of Roman institutions. In particular, Rousseau emphasizes Rome's voting procedures, which, as we will see, are highly inequitable since the voting conducted through them is heavily weighted in favor of wealthy citizens.

In addition, Rousseau instructs readers to pay careful attention to the minute details of Roman institutions like the centuriate assembly because, as I demonstrate below, he often lets the details speak for themselves rather than elaborating at length on their ramifications for power relations within a republic. The reference to the conduct of both "public and particular business" in a large assembly further supports a claim that I have already advanced but will substantiate further in this section: In the abstract, Rousseau disapproves of popular assemblies performing the tasks of both sovereign and government, as demonstrated by his severe criticisms of the Athenian *ekklêsia*. Yet he condones the Roman *comitia centuriata*'s exercise of both "public and particular" functions, when, respectively, it makes laws, on the one hand, and elects magistrates and tries judicial cases, on the other (SC IV 4, 136). While Rousseau never says so explicitly, I suggest that he expects his judicious reader to conclude that the resolution of this apparent inconsistency is attributable to the Roman assembly's peculiar voting structure, where citizens with the most wealth cast the most votes in the presence of poorer citizens who may not even enjoy the opportunity to vote at all.

Finally, in remarking on the enormous scale of the *comitia centuriata* in the passage cited above, Rousseau makes a case for the viability of large republics. As he goes on to write, Rome illustrates that "the bounds of the possible" in republican politics are not so narrow as many tend to think; through Rome's example, Rousseau demonstrates "what can be done in the light of what has been done" (SC III 12, 110). Democracy may require a small regime in which citizens know one another. Rome, a city of "four hundred thousand citizens bearing arms," on the contrary, serves as inspiration to those who imagine a republic of large territorial expanse.[20] By adhering faithfully to the sovereign (general), electoral, and timocratic aspects of the Roman Republic, and by jettisoning the plebeian-specific, popularly contestatory elements that Machiavelli praised in his *Discourses*, *The Social Contract* opens the possibility of republics whose success, from Rousseau's perspective, surpass even that of Rome.

Rousseau's Rome is ostensibly the republic of the Roman *populus*, of all the people, plebeian and patrician alike, the Rome concerned first and foremost with the *res publica*, the "public thing," the business of every citizen. Rousseauian Rome is not the republic as in "SPQR" (*Senatus Populusque Romanus*), in other words, a republic composed of both a distinctly senatorial Rome and a distinctly plebeian polity, the republic that Machiavelli praises for its class conflict or "tumults" (D I.4; D I.5). Rousseau's admiration for the unitary, politically homogenous, sovereign republic is evident in statements such as the following: "Few weeks went by when the Roman people was not assembled. . . . It exercised not only the rights of sovereignty, but a part of those of government as well" (SC III 12, 110). Rousseau's disposition is less than critical when he remarks on the fact that the Roman people, assembled as sovereign, passed laws and also "dealt with some business" and "tried some cases"; indeed, in "the public square this entire people was nearly as often magistrate as it was citizen" (SC III 12, 110). Again, this description begs the question: why does Rousseau elsewhere criticize the smaller Athenian demos gathered in assembly for deciding matters both general and particular, when he praises the larger, assembled Roman people for doing precisely the same thing here? Rousseau buttresses the argument that the Roman people at its best was sovereign, and that Rome's popular assemblies expressed a general will, with his insistence that Roman magistrates were not representatives (SC III 14, 112).[21] Only the assemblies expressed the common good; the magistrates neither personify nor embody the sovereign people's general will. According to Rousseau, when the *comitiae* assembled, the chief magistrates, the consuls, were mere presiders or conveners, the tribunes of the plebs were simply speakers, and the senate was "nothing at all" (SC III 12, 110). For Rousseau, the people's magistrates are not their representatives but rather their agents:

> In ancient republics . . . the people never had representatives; the very word was unknown. It is quite striking that in Rome where the tribunes were so sacred, no one ever so much as imagined that they might usurp the functions of the people, and that in the midst of such a great multitude they never attempted to pass a single plebiscite on their own authority alone. (SC III 15, 114)

In a seemingly robust Athenian voice, Rousseau asserts that "assemblies of the people" like Rome's have always been "the dread of chiefs," the scourge of tyrants, and deterrents to magistrates who would pretend to speak for the sovereign people (SC III 12, 110). However, Roman assemblies are something other than democratic assemblies.[22] They are organized much differently than Athenian-style assemblies where majorities rule and one-man, one-vote prevails. Tellingly, Rousseau, the renowned proponent of formal political equality and generality, begins his discussion of assemblies with praise for the imposition of sociopolitical stratification in early Rome.

Rousseau is much more forthright than was Machiavelli about the sketchiness of information pertaining to Rome under the kings and during the early republic. He concedes that most accounts of "the first times of Rome" amount to little more than "fables" (SC IV 4, 127). Nevertheless, Rousseau proceeds to commend Servius, the king reputed to have reformed Rome's social order and ensured its future success. Rousseau praises Servius for protecting the social prominence of the patricians: he reformed the racial cum residential tribes of Rome in response to an influx of foreigners that threatened to overwhelm the tribes populated by the leading families (SC IV 4, 128–29). Servius created six classes of Horsemen between the lower and upper classes and gave the rural tribes, dominated by patricians, preeminence over the urban ones composed of plebeians, proletarians, and freedmen (SC IV 4, 128–29).

Without fully explaining how, Rousseau links these reforms to the republic's success at insulating high political office from foreign contamination or lower class infiltration: for instance, he celebrates the fact that because of these arrangements, no freedman ever became a magistrate (SC IV 4, 129).[23] However, he does blame the patricians ("the great and the powerful") for abusing these divisions for their own advantage through the office of the censors, who were responsible for managing the place of individuals within the social hierarchy (SC IV 4, 129–30). These excesses provoked "the rabble" of the urban tribes to start selling their votes in response (SC IV 4, 129–30). But this insight does not prompt Rousseau to question whether the very idea that some better, wealthier, more prominent citizens should have more say in determining the common good necessarily invites such corruption independent of the abuses associated with the censors.

Bracketing these residential, class divisions that had an indirect political impact, Rousseau reserves his greatest praise for Servius' second effort at social organization: the partitioning of the Roman citizenry into voting classes, weighted by wealth, in the *comitia centuriata* or "comitia by centuries" (SC IV 4, 130). These classifications vastly minimized the political impact of votes by poorer citizens:

> Servius distributed the whole Roman people into six classes, which he distinguished neither by district nor by persons, but by goods: So that the first classes were filled with the rich, the last with the poor, and the middle ones with those who enjoyed a moderate fortune. These six classes were subdivided into a hundred and ninety-three other bodies called centuries, and these bodies were so distributed that the first class alone contained more than half of them, and the last formed a single one. Thus it

came about that the class with the smallest number of men had the largest number of centuries, and that the entire last class counted only as one subdivision although it alone contained more than half the inhabitants of Rome. (SC IV 4, 130)

As a result of this arrangement where votes were weighted according to property possession, the richest citizens could enact a law, elect a consul, or decide a trial before the poor even had a chance to cast a vote:

> Since of the hundred and ninety-three centuries which formed the six classes of the entire Roman people, the first class comprised ninety-eight, and the votes were only counted by centuries, this first class by itself alone prevailed over all the others by the number of its votes. When all of its centuries were in agreement they did not even go on collecting ballots; what the smallest number had decided passed for a decision of the multitude, and in the comitia by centuries majorities of cash more often than votes can be said to have settled affairs. (SC IV 4, 133)

Note that Rousseau does not lament the state of affairs described in the last clause of this passage. I suggest that this passage needs to be read in light of two earlier discussions: Rousseau's largely positive correlation between election and rule by the rich, and his considerable doubts over the ability of popular assemblies to decide the common good or realize the general will. Since the *comitia centuriata* elected the consuls and initially passed all major legislation, Rousseau is instructing his "judicious reader," through the example of this assembly, both how to appoint the best magistrates and to pass laws reflecting the general will: that is, how to establish an assembly that allows the wealthiest citizens to perform both functions themselves through perhaps less than transparent means. The penultimate clause of the above-cited passage is what I take to be the core of Rousseau's republicanism applied to large polities, and, indeed, the guiding spirit of modern mass democracy. It bears repeating: "what the smallest number had decided passed for a decision of the multitude" (SC IV 4, 133), with "pass" ambiguously connoting both a formal enactment and a false appearance.

When discussing Rome's more plebeian assemblies, Rousseau seems to conflate two bodies that are generally understood to be separate, the *concilium plebis* and the *comitia tributa*: "The comitia by tribes were properly the council of the Roman people. They could only be convened by the tribunes" (SC IV 4, 134). Rousseau claims that the tribunes not only presided over this comitia but also, in fact, had founded it (SC IV 4, 132). However, the *comitia tributa* was a formal, legitimate assembly, and thus it is unlikely that the tribunes, who began as unofficial, informal magistrates, would have wielded sufficient authority to establish it early in the republic. On the contrary, the *concilium* shared the same early "illegitimate" status with the tribunes. It was the *concilium*, and not the *comitia tributa*, as Rousseau suggests, that likely "elected the tribunes and passed their plebiscites" (SC IV 4, 134). The *concilium* probably excluded patricians and may in fact have been founded by the tribunes. The *comitia tributa*, on the other hand, may have included patricians, but since it was subdivided by tribes rather than centuries, plebeians and poorer citizens would have had the numerical superiority to outvote their social betters.[24] It seems to be the *concilium* that Rousseau conjures when he states the following regarding the *comitia tributa*:

> Not only had the Senate no standing in them, it had not even the right to attend them, and the Senators, forced to obey laws on which they could not vote, were in this respect less free than the last of citizens. This injustice was altogether ill conceived, and it alone was enough to invalidate the decrees of a body to which not all of its members were admitted. (SC IV 4, 134)

Thus, more important than Rousseau's confusion (perhaps understandable in light of the available historical evidence) over these two plebeian-dominated assemblies is his reaction to the fact that at least one of them formally excluded patricians. He cannot contain his indignation at the thought that the most prominent citizens were not eligible to attend this plebeian assembly and yet were subject to its legislation.

Observe how Rousseau denies to the assemblies that tended toward "popular government" the praise that he lavishes on the *comitia* by centuries because the former "lacked the Senate and the patricians": Rousseau pronounces that "the whole majesty of the Roman people resided" in the *comitia centuriata* because no one was excluded from it, even though, as Rousseau understates the matter, it tended toward aristocracy in its voting procedures (SC IV 4, 134–35). Within the framework of conventional interpretations, one could attribute Rousseau's indignation to his vaunted commitment to egalitarianism and preference for generality: nobody should be subject to laws that they did not participate in formulating. However, on the basis of the analysis that I have been developing here, one may also detect a certain class elitism: how dare the plebeians bar patricians, the best citizens, from a political body of such consequence.

As we have observed, Rousseau voices no such complaints over the de facto exclusion of the poorest citizens from suffrage and legislation in the *comitia centuriata*. He certainly does not fret that they were "less free in this respect." At least, Rousseau might protest, poor citizens did attend such assemblies and enjoyed the de jure right to vote within them—in fact, their votes did have genuine impact when the wealthier classes of citizens were in sufficient disagreement that balloting descended into the lowest voting classes. In other words, when the wealthiest citizens agree on candidates or policy, matters should be so. When they do not, the lower classes may be permitted to participate in making the decision. However, from the plebeian perspective—in many respects adopted by Machiavelli—Rousseau has things backward: the patricians and the wealthy possess so much privilege and wield so much power within a republic—freedom, after all, favors wolves over sheep—that it is more legitimate, more just, to exclude them completely from certain assemblies or offices so that common citizens might have some direct impact on law- and policy-making. It is simply ridiculous for Rousseau to declare that the senatorial class is "less free" than common citizens in any respect, when he then proceeds to recommend institutions that formally include plebeians and the poor in all assemblies, while exacerbating their power disadvantages within them by empowering the wealthy to outvote them.

Therefore, neither inequality nor even exclusion so perturbs Rousseau in this instance; rather it is plausible that the plebeian assembly's violation of the Rousseauian principle of aristocratic affirmative action—weighted voting for the rich—most provokes his ire.

This passage reminds us that Rousseauian popular sovereignty is a sovereignty of inclusion but not one of equality; the political holism of Rousseau's model citizenry does not entail equality of each individual citizen in any meaningful sense.[25] And here we observe most clearly how much Rousseau disdains Athenianesque, one-man/one-vote, majoritarian procedures:

> Even if patricians had attended the comitia [by tribes] as, in their capacity as citizens they had the right to do, they would have been counted as simple particulars, and would therefore have had scarcely any impact on a form of voting which consists in counting heads and in which the least proletarian counts for as much as does the prince of the Senate. (SC IV 4, 134)

Rousseau's principle of republican citizenship is simple: each citizen must be eligible for every assembly or office, must qualify for every privilege or immunity, but some persons are entitled to enjoy decidedly more of such eligibility and qualification than others. Some citizens need to count as more than "simple particulars." Substantive equality and majority rule are not necessary, and, in fact, the egalitarian practice of merely "counting heads" should be avoided. Of course, Rousseau attempts to downplay the extent to which inequity characterizes his preferred voting procedures in the centuriate assembly by speaking of all the Roman assemblies together: "since there was not a single citizen who was not enrolled in a curia, a century or a tribe, it follows that no citizen was excluded from the right to vote, and that the Roman people was genuinely sovereign both by right and fact" (SC IV 4, 132). However, not all citizens were "genuinely sovereign" in exactly the same way within the most important assembly, the *comitia centuriata*, which elected the highest magistrates and passed major legislation.

At this point Rousseau may be accused of wading fully into the pool of perversity. He seems to justify the Roman practice of weighted voting for the wealthy by suggesting that it was actually unnecessary: even if patrician privilege had not been formally enshrined in the procedures of the *comitia centuriata*, the social practice of clientage, Rousseau avers, would have guaranteed the same policy outcomes anyway. The socioeconomic indebtedness of plebeians to patricians and poor to rich allowed the rich to guide the poor's political behavior toward the common good. Loans, jobs, and favorable marriage arrangements provided to poor clients by rich patrons insured that voting would never depart too far from the interests of the patricians and, hence, to Rousseau's mind, from the general interest of the republic. Rousseau, the great denouncer of servitude and dependence, a philosopher who compares parliamentary representation to slavery (SC III 15, 115), deems the Roman clientelist system of hierarchy and manipulation "admirable" and "humane" (SC IV 4, 133).

These assertions, again, seem to indicate that Rousseau distrusts the poor more than he loathes poverty: the poor's faulty political judgment is more potentially pernicious to the common good than the inequitable socioeconomic conditions that impact their judgment—through either impairment or compulsion—in the first place. Machiavelli, of course, had nothing good to say about clientelism, "private modes of benefiting various private individuals" in either ancient or modern contexts (D III.28). He denounced the following private modes as the most malevolent practices afflicting republics: "lending money, arranging marriages, providing defense from the magistrates, and bestowing similar private favors that accrue partisans for patrons and encourage clients to corrupt the public and abrogate the laws" (D III.28; see also FH VII.1). As I discussed in chapters 2 and 3 of this study, Machiavelli documents the secular trends operating in both the Roman and the Florentine republics whereby elites exploited socioeconomic inequality to seduce or compel poorer citizens into clientelist relations that eventually generated, in these respective republics, the rise of the Roman emperors and the Medici principate.[26]

Rousseau admits that the Roman patriciate behaved in a manner contrary to the civic spirit of the republic when status was inherited as opposed to when it was conferred by election (SC IV 4, 133). However, even when the patriciate was hereditary, he praises its success at preserving itself through the "honorable" and "fine example" of patronage. Patron-client relations "never led to any abuse" in Rousseau's estimation, unless one considers vote buying to be abusive (SC IV 4, 133). Indeed, this assertion appears to conflict with Rousseau's criticisms, raised both previously and later (SC IV 4, 129–30, 135), of vote selling on the part of poorer citizens. On the basis of the preferences that Rousseau has been signaling throughout these chapters, one may resolve this inconsistency in the following way: presumably, the vote-buying that patricians orchestrated in the early republic is acceptable to Rousseau because it resulted in the realization of the common good by facilitating an expression of the general will in the *comitia centuriata*. But when populist politicians like the Gracchi or Gaius Marius (about whom more below) exploited the practice for the advantage of plebeians and (undoubtedly) themselves in the later republic, Rousseau deems it unacceptable because the practice threatens the expropriation of wealthy citizens rather than the furthering of their preeminence, which better coincides with the common good. Rousseau himself, however, does not elaborate at this juncture.

Yet, just when Rousseau suggests that the "extreme authority" of the patricians within the *comitia centuriata*—whether procedurally enabled through weighted voting or socioculturally guaranteed through clientelism—was unavoidable and irresistible, he almost completely reverses himself. Rousseau ruminates along the following lines: "The division by centuries favored aristocracy to such an extent that one is at first left to wonder why the Senate did not always prevail in the comitia which bore that name and which elected the consuls, censors and other curule magistrates" (SC IV 4, 133–34). At first, Rousseau gestures to the influence of the tribunes, whom I will discuss below, and the possibility that rich plebeians who entered the ranks of the highest voting classes may have counterbalanced the social biases of the patricians (SC IV 4, 133–34).

Rousseau then settles on a procedural convention that purportedly kept centuries from simply voting in the socioeconomic interest of their own class: random selection of the "prerogative century" (SC IV 4, 133–34). The selection, through lottery, of the particular century that would cast the first vote established a religiously legitimated precedent that subsequent centuries were meant to follow when casting their own votes. In other words, when a poor plebeian century was designated at random as prerogative, and hence was entrusted with casting the first vote, any departure from that vote by succeeding centuries, whatever their class biases, would be perceived as impious. "In this way," Rousseau avows, "the authority of example was withdrawn from rank and given to lot in conformity with the principle of democracy" (SC IV 4, 133–34).[27] Lottery—the alternative to election as an appointment method, by which the unruly Athenian demos undermined oligarchic domination of most magistracies,[28]—emerges here, with religious implications, to seemingly democratize Roman election practices. However, as Rousseau explained previously, the richer census classes possess a disproportionately large number of centuries (SC IV 4, 130): the single wealthiest voting class, which contains the fewest number of citizens, enjoys a majority of the total one-hundred and ninety-three centuries— ninety-eight, to be precise—while the lowest voting class, containing the majority of Roman citizens, is allotted one single century. Therefore, even a random selection of the particular prerogative century that initiates voting still affords the voting class, dominated by the wealthy or by patricians, an overwhelming probability of setting the agenda on any vote.[29] If Rousseau expects his "judicious readers" to do the math, they would easily learn that, given the inequitable distribution of centuries, the richest voting class has a 51 percent chance of casting the first vote; the poorest class has a .5 percent chance of setting the voting agenda.[30] This is a "principle of democracy" that Rousseau deems worth upholding. The Athenians employed genuine lottery to avoid oligarchy; Rousseau, for his part, advocates a sham lottery to conceal it.

Even if readers were to believe that this passage shows Rousseau relenting in his preference for a large republic where the few enact decisions that merely appear to have been made by the many, they should consider the following observation: "what is incredible is that thanks to its ancient regulations this immense people, in the midst of so many abuses, did not cease to elect magistrates, pass laws, try cases, dispatch public and private business almost as readily as the Senate itself might have done" (SC IV 4, 136). One might interpret this statement as a comment on the efficiency of the comitia centuriata, a marveling at its ability to decide issues as expeditiously as would a smaller council like the Roman senate. However, it occurs in the midst of a passage dealing with the quality of the assembly's decisions; that is, how the republic's "ancient regulations" encouraged the people assembled in the *comitia centuriata* to make good judgments until the final days when "ambition eluded" all procedural prohibitions against corruption. What seems most commendable for Rousseau about the assembly by centuries, in the context of this passage—and in light of the ancient regulations that gave the assembly both a popular appearance and a timocratic structure—is its capacity to generate the same outcomes that the Senate would have enacted unilaterally. Presumably, public order and the appearance of legitimacy are better served for Rousseau by a generally inclusive but internally hierarchical assembly governing the republic than by a blatantly oligarchic and exclusionary council. The centuriate assembly affords the Roman Republic the benefits of rule—in the sense of both sovereignty and government—by an aristocracy through the equally beneficial façade of popular government.

In this sense, senators enjoy a dual role in Rousseau's Rome: when seated in the Senate house, they serve as visible members of a council of elders with mere consultative authority; but, when voting within a structured popular assembly weighted by votes toward the wealthy, they act as the invisible prime movers of appointments, legislation, and trials. As we will observe in the next section, according to Machiavelli, if a republic is to have a senate and tolerate the immense aristocratic power that inheres within it, that republic also requires popular assemblies that are proto- and not pseudodemocratic in nature to offset, counteract, and perhaps even overcome such power.

However, first let me offer a final consideration on Rousseau's advocacy for popular assemblies modeled on Rome's timocratically structured *comitia centuriata*: does Rousseau believe that the Roman plebeians were deceived into thinking that they participated in the centuriate assembly as fully free and equal citizens—especially since it is so obvious that most of the time, while they attend such an assembly, they do not enjoy the opportunity to cast votes within it? The answer is probably no; plebeians are poor but they are not necessarily ignorant. With this in mind, I would like to take the opportunity to mention a way that dominance by the wealthy in the centuriate assembly is potentially mitigated in Rousseau's account: namely, the fact that wealthy citizens cast their votes in full view of the assembled poor multitude of citizens. It is quite possible that Rousseau believes this to impose a conditioning or disciplining effect on how the wealthy cast their votes. One might surmise that if the richest citizens were to consistently cast their weighted votes in ways that flagrantly disregard or outrageously violate the interests of the mass of common citizens, the latter would, at some point, erupt in violent insurrection on the spot.

Rousseau admits that poorer citizens in the *comitia centuriata* seldom enjoyed the opportunity to cast their (less consequential) votes unless tallies among the wealthiest census classes proved inconclusive. Moreover, the poorest citizens gathered in the lowest census group, the majority of Romans, could only on the rarest occasion cast the influential first vote: that is, only if they beat the vast mathematical odds stacked against them and their single century was chosen at random as the prerogative century. Nevertheless, given the total inclusion of all citizens within the assembly, as Rousseau presents it, the wealthiest citizens may be informally encouraged to take into account the interests of the underenfranchised citizens in whose physical presence they are voting.[31] Rousseau's reconstruction of the centuriate assembly leaves open the possibility that legislative decisions made by wealthy citizens could reflect the general will rather than serve merely as enactments of a particularist will by a privileged few—that is, if the republic's wealthiest citizens are in fact also the most wise, prudent, and public-spirited citizens.

As a consequence of such arrangements, in blatant violation of Rousseau's earlier articulated stipulations for the formation of the general will, rich citizens in Rousseau's version of the *comitia centuriata* may be said to be the principal authors of legislation passed in the assembly, while poorer citizens serve overwhelmingly as mere objects of the law.[32] One can only speculate why Rousseau significantly relaxes the universally egalitarian standards that he establishes for his ideal sovereign assembly in the early, highly theoretical chapters of the *Social Contract* once he attempts to concretely apply such principles to large scale republics in Book IV. Perhaps he doubts the extent to which a lawgiver of the kind he extols in Book II, chapter 7 could ever impose sufficient unity upon a people in polities as large as Rome (or most modern nations), and thus he seeks out other means to insure that the people's judgment in such republics will prove conducive to the common good.

Machiavelli on Roman Assemblies and the Plebeian Tribunate

By way of contrast with Rousseau, I would like to emphasize two aspects of Machiavelli's treatment of Rome's popular assemblies in the *Discourses*. In Machiavelli's narrative they function more like the Athenian assembly than the *comitia centuriata* of historical fact because, he suggests (1) that one-man/one-vote, majority rule obtained within them, and (2) that they permitted public deliberation and were not strictly confined to voting. The point is that for Machiavelli, a republic, a mixed regime, must be *properly* mixed; that is, there must be institutions monopolized by wealthy and poorer citizens. The wealthy must not be allowed to dominate all of them, either overtly or covertly, if every kind of citizen is to exercise and enjoy the liberty promised by a republican way of life.

Machiavelli seems to acknowledge a distinction between the *comitia centuriata* and the *concilium plebis*. He calls the former the *comizi consolari* (D I.14), or simply the *comizi* (D II.28) and describes it as the assembly that elected magistrates wielding consular authority. Alternatively, Machiavelli seems to refer explicitly to the *concilium* when he juxtaposes the *publico consiglio* to the senate (D III.30), and he probably makes reference to it namelessly when he mentions the assembly where tribunes proposed laws on which the people deliberate and vote(D I.18).[33] Why do I assume that Machiavelli is either oblivious to the historical reality of weighted voting for the wealthy in the *comitia centuriata* or explicitly rejects it as an aspect of his reconstructed version of the assembly? For this reason: in the course of describing the ongoing conflict between the *popolo* and *grandi* in Rome, Machiavelli recounts a scenario that only makes sense if the lower classes, the common people as such, have the opportunity, via majority rule, to determine outcomes in this assembly.

As an example of the power of what Bernard Manin dubs "the aristocratic effect" of elections, Machiavelli demonstrates how the Roman plebeians, after relentlessly clamoring for eligibility to gain

the consulship, continued to elect patricians as magistrates as soon
as the plebs themselves were finally granted eligibility for the office
(D I.48; cf. also I.47). Unless plebeians have it within their power to
elect one of their own to the office—unless they can, by sheer force
of numbers, and without obstructionist provisions that inflate the
voting prowess of patricians or the wealthy—the example makes no
sense at all. (One of the lessons of the episode is to reinforce the
necessity of a plebeian-specific magistracy, like the tribunate, within
republics; general eligibility for an office, under conditions of even
the widest suffrage, will most often result in the election of wealthy
and prominent citizens—even without the special weighting of rich
voters that Rousseau favors.[34] I continue this line of reasoning in my
discussion of the tribunes below.) Machiavelli also makes it a point
to praise the Roman people, that is, the people identified with plebeians at the exclusion of the *grandi* or patricians, for consistently
electing, via "free votes"(D I.20), the best candidates to offices
throughout the life of the republic. This praise would be misplaced
if the electoral system were weighted, in Machiavelli's model, such
that the *grandi* could effectively elect whomever they liked with bal-
lot counting seldom or never reaching the ranks of common citizens
(D I.58).

An ambiguity concerning Machiavelli's version of Rome's assemblies is whether his *concilium*—that is, his plebeian-dominated assembly—excludes patricians. He writes concerning the assembly
presided over by the tribunes: "A tribune, or any citizen whatsoever,
could propose a law to the people, against or in favor of which every
citizen was entitled to speak before a decision was reached" (D I.18).
The sentence is vague. Is the "any citizen whatsoever" mentioned
confined to plebeians participating in the *concilium*, as would have
been the case historically? Or, does it mean literally any citizen such
that this description must include patricians, and therefore it implies
that they too participate in the *concilium*?

Or, does Machiavelli's statement refer to any one assembly at all?
Perhaps Machiavelli suggests that tribunes propose laws in the *concilium*, while "any citizen," including patricians, can propose laws in
the *comitia centuriata*. Maybe the discussion and disputes over laws
that Machiavelli mentions take place not in the plebeian-specific

environment of the *concilium*, but in the informal assemblies reserved for public deliberation, the *contiones* or *concioni* that Machiavelli mentions elsewhere (D I.4–5, III.34) but does not invoke here. However, if it is in fact the *concilium* to which Machiavelli refers in this instance, it is unlikely to include patricians, for this reason: since Machiavelli's social antagonists are even more class-conscious than were their actual historical antecedents (if that is possible), it is hard to believe that the proud and insolent *grandi*, patricians or *ottimati* would have deigned to participate in an assembly presided over by "tribunes of the plebs."[35]

Thankfully, Machiavelli is unambiguous about the place of deliberation in Rome's assemblies. In the passage just cited, Machiavelli gives reasons why, contra both Francesco Guicciardini in his own day and Rousseau centuries later, public deliberation in advance of voting on laws is healthy for a republic: "It was good that anyone who cared for the public good could propose laws, and that everyone could speak their mind on them so that the people could subsequently choose what was best" (D I.18). Machiavelli uses the same rationale for justifying discussion in advance of the election of magistrates— discussion if not in the *comizi* then certainly in the *concioni*: "good orderers of republics, when establishing the means by which the people make appointments to the city's highest offices . . . permit every citizen, in a manner accentuating his glory, to publicly accentuate in assemblies [*concioni*] a candidate's deficiencies, such that the people, having better knowledge of him, can better judge him" (D III.34). Historically, the presiding magistrates of *concioni* had the discretion to recognize whomever they liked as speakers, a practice that invariably favored prominent individuals. But Machiavelli is insistent here, as elsewhere, when discoursing on public deliberation: anyone entitled to attend an assembly—from a senator in the senate to a plebeian in a *concione*—must be entitled to speak within it.[36]

In short, Machiavelli's view of republican assemblies is more differentiated than Rousseau's and provides a genuine voice for common citizens. The patricians and the wealthy populate the senate; all citizens attend his *comizi*, which favors the wealthy through the aristocratic effect of (unweighted) elections; and the plebeians attend their own assembly—the *publico consiglio*, presided over by their own magistrates, the tribunes—that generates real laws, the plebiscites. Every citizen who is eligible to attend each of these assemblies enjoys free speech within them, just as all of them do in the informal *concioni*. The proceedings of no Machiavellian assembly are disproportionately weighted toward privilege. Plebeians and the poor, and patricians and the wealthy, may be excluded from a particular assembly, but no one is treated inequitably within any specific assembly. Rousseau believes that each citizen should be eligible for every assembly but can be treated differently within them. Machiavelli advises the establishment of separate assemblies for citizens of different social classes. Rousseau's theory of assemblies is egalitarian in principle but not practice; Machiavelli's is explicitly inegalitarian in a way that, counterintuitively, is intended to produce more egalitarian outcomes, or at least those that are more contestatory of power and privilege, more empowering of the poor and vulnerable.

However much he admires Rome's assemblies, Machiavelli reserves his highest praise for the tribunes, the republic's magistracy of the common people, for holding back the "insolence" of the patricians or *grandi* (D I.3). According to Machiavelli, the *grandi*'s insolence and the appetite for domination from which it arises are threats to the liberty of citizens and to the stability of republican regimes. The *grandi* will eventually raise up a prince or enlist a foreign power to further their inexhaustible efforts at oppressing the people, or the people will resort to such measures themselves for protection from or in retaliation to persistent abuse.

Over the course of the Roman Republic's history, two to five to a dozen plebs would serve as tribunes for one-year terms. Plebeians elected the tribunes in one of their assemblies, likely the *concilium plebis*, since it probably excluded patrician citizens. The tribunes conducted deliberation over the passage of plebiscites in the *concilium*. Their bodies were "sacrosanct," that is, patricians could not touch them physically, and the plebs pledged to kill any number of them who dared try. Moreover, tribunes wielded a power akin to habeas corpus (the *provocatio*): they could demand the release of plebs who had been seized (usually in situations of debt bondage) by patrician citizens or magistrates and appealed to the tribunes. Furthermore, the tribunes could veto laws favored by the senate, and about to be enacted by their agents, the consuls. Finally, the tribunes wielded the authority to accuse magistrates or powerful citizens of political crimes and try them before one of the assemblies.

On the basis of Machiavelli's discussion of Roman assemblies and, especially, the plebeian tribunate, it is striking just how much his reconstruction of Rome differs from Rousseau's socially holistic vision of the republic, or how much Rousseau seems to deliberately repudiate the former. Machiavelli's Rome is a tale of two cities: within the one republic there is a poorer, popular polity that shadows an elite, more wealthy one. The poor thereby serve as the elite's mirror, its negative image. The *grandi* deliberate policy in the senate, the plebs in the *concilium* (D I.18) (and both in *concioni*). The senate influences the consuls to enact laws that it favors; if the people dissent, they press the tribunes to veto them. The consuls wield the power of life and death, but the tribunes can deliver plebeians from just such a threat through the *provocatio*. Indeed, it seems that the formal separation of these two polities within one allowed the less dangerous one—the plebeian polity that, according to Machiavelli, desires only to avoid domination, to patrol the one that Machiavelli explicitly claims is more dangerous, a patrician polity or city of *grandi* that seeks perpetual oppression over others.

It cannot be overstated how difficult it is to sell the patricians or *grandi* on the establishment of a tribunate, or some functional equivalent thereof.[37] Common citizens have leveraged magistrate selection methods involving lottery fairly regularly in the premodern history of republics.[38] Council seats and even whole assemblies reserved exclusively for poorer citizens are not unusual.[39] But a popular magistracy for which the wealthiest and most notable are ineligible is a rarity in the history of republican constitutions. Yet Machiavelli considers an institution modeled on the Roman tribunate indispensable to a free regime. Popular government requires, almost paradoxically, both the participation and loyalty of the *grandi*, and the establishment of an institution that they inherently detest. As mentioned before, this is confirmed by Machiavelli's constitutional proposal for a re-established republican constitution in Florence: he insists on including, albeit subtly and almost surreptitiously, a tribunician institution, the provosts (*proposti*), into the plan.[40]

Tribunates, Roman and Rousseauian

While obviously not the great enthusiast of the plebeian tribunate that Machiavelli was, Rousseau is not completely dismissive of the Roman magistracy. Nevertheless, he believes that its authority should have been confined to its negative functions (the veto, *provocatio*, and accusations) rather than its positive ones (i.e., promoting laws), both of which Machiavelli praised. According to Rousseau, the tribunate should "do nothing" proactively in the legislative or executive spheres, but merely have the power to "prevent everything" in both (SC IV 5, 137). Only when it operates within such parameters does the tribunate deserve to be "sacred and revered as the defender of the laws," as in those cases in Rome when "those proud patricians, who always despised the entire people, were forced to yield before a plain officer of the people wielding neither patronage nor jurisdiction" (SC IV 5, 137). The tribunes should only serve as a check on patrician self-aggrandizement that threatened the liberty of plebeians; they should not attempt to change the shape of the republic by proposing to influence its policies or reform its constitution.

While "a wisely tempered tribunate is the firmest bulwark of a good constitution," Rousseau insists, in a decidedly anti-Machiavellian way, "if it has even a little too much force it overthrows everything" (SC IV 5, 137). I discuss below what Rousseau means by a tribunate "wisely tempered." Here I try to gauge his sense of what it means for tribunes to exert "too much force." Rousseau never provides concrete examples of the tribunate functioning as a bulwark of Rome's constitution, when healthy; rather, he seems singularly preoccupied with its purported excesses. This is the context in which to consider Rousseau's intermittent swipes at the brothers Gracchus along with Marius, the bêtes noire of all apologists for oligarchy, Roman or otherwise. Rousseau contends that the republic was only plagued by harmful "commotions" when magistrates, like these tribunes, forgot that they did not speak for the people (SC III 12, 110). As tribunes, the Gracchi, to Rousseau's consternation, passed their proplebeian legislative agenda by purportedly enjoining a portion of the people to "cast its vote from the rooftops"—i.e., by threatening the patricians and the senate with violence (SC III 15, 115). Echoing his critique of Greek democratic assemblies, Rousseau contends that in such instances the Roman people transgressed the boundaries of lawmaking and magistrate-appointment to "usurp [the] most important functions of the government" (SC IV 4, 132). In these cases, Rousseau insists that the tribunes took it upon themselves to represent the people by usurping the rights of the senate (SC III 15, 115). He fails to mention that the senate responded by usurping, in much less legal and much more violent ways, whatever authority the Gracchi legitimately wielded as tribunes.[41]

Contrary to Machiavelli, in whose estimation Rome was made "more perfect" by the tribunes, Rousseau blames the tribunes for the fall of Rome through their inappropriate appropriation of executive and legislative authority: "the excessive power that the tribunes had gradually usurped, served—with the help of the laws that had been made for the sake of freedom—as a safeguard to the emperors, who destroyed freedom" (SC IV 5, 137). The tribunate and its legal functions that were intended to defend the people wound up, in Rousseau's eyes, empowering the Caesars. Rousseau never even entertains the notion intimated by Machiavelli (D I.37; I.39; D III.24), and quite evident in the histories of Sallust, Appian, and Plutarch,[42] that the senate ruined the republic by impoverishing the plebeians by seizing their land while sending them away in ever distant wars, failing to alleviate their debts and insuring that they would become more loyal to the generals on whom their material welfare depended than the republic itself. As noted in chapter 2, this is the dire situation that the Gracchi unsuccessfully attempted to redress as tribunes and that Julius Caesar successfully exploited as Rome's dictator for life. However, for the author of "The Discourse on Inequality," the problem runs only as deep as the fact that Augustus Caesar partially legitimated his imperium by assuming the mantle of tribunician authority as defender of the people (SC IV 5, 137).[43]

Although rather fixated on the political abuses to which the tribunate could be put, Rousseau seems quite confident in the myriad means available to the Senate for constraining the plebeian magistracy's range of action. Indeed, Rousseau looks with favor on many limitations of the tribunate that Machiavelli basically reported as mere facts (D I.13; I.39; III.11). For instance, both authors note how the patricians used religion to keep the tribunes from advancing leg-islation favorable to the plebeians, and exploited the fact that the tribunate was a collegial magistracy which required concerted action to be effective. In the first instance, by manipulating the interpreta-tion of auguries, Rousseau remarks, "the Senate held in check a proud and restless people and, when necessary, tempered the ardor of the seditious tribunes" (SC IV 4, 132). In the second regard, the greater the number of tribunes who were elected at any time, the more easily the senate could bribe, intimidate, or delude one tribune among them into vetoing the proplebeian actions of another (SC IV 5, 137). The plebeians preferred having more tribunes available in the city so they might be more accessible to citizens needing protection from patricians; but this proliferation of their numbers undermined the tribunes' ability to pursue a proplebeian legislative agenda—it in-creased the number of tribunes who could veto their own colleagues' initiatives and actions.

However, Machiavelli never stooped to the classic oligarchic dis-paragement of the tribunes' authority or motivations to which Rous-seau consistently resorts. Rousseau insinuates that the tribunes were merely the wealthiest plebs and hence aspiring patricians who were clearly out only for themselves; he refers to tribunes as "well-to-do" citizens who were really only nominally plebeians (SC IV 4, 133). Certainly, the tribunate was an elected, not lottery-distributed, mag-istracy. The wealthiest or most notable citizens among the plebs would be expected to become tribunes most of the time. Neverthe-less, since plebs selected tribunes from their own ranks, the class specificity of the office minimized the extent of election's aristocratic effect (D I.4, I.6, I.37).[44]

Turning now to Rousseau's own reconstruction of the tribunate: his reformed magistracy is not a permanent institution through which common citizens surveille, contain, or repel better resourced and more powerful wealthy citizens within a republic. On the con-trary, Rousseau envisions a tribunician magistracy to be one that oc-casionally restores balance, equilibrium or "exact proportion be-tween the constitutive parts of state" (SC IV 5, 136). Whereas Machiavelli wished to further empower tribune-like institutions and encourage their spread, Rousseau proposes their emasculation by rendering them occasional and not standing offices (SC IV 5, 137). Because most republics are oligarchically organized and do not contain functional equivalents of the tribunes, Machiavelli thought that such polities needed to devise ways of establishing them. Rousseau, on the contrary, remarks that republics should consider ways of making tribunician institutions less prone to usurpation, adding the curious phrase "a means that has so far not occurred to any government" (SC IV 5, 137). One would think that the rarity of such institutions, especially in their proplebeian form, is itself a sufficient check on its usurpation.

Rousseau's remark suggests, unlike Machiavelli, that the Genevan is largely unconcerned with the basic fact that the wealthy enjoy persistent power advantages over commoners, and therefore that they neither need nor deserve to possess an institution of their own that continually challenges patricians, *grandi, ottimati,* etc. On the contrary, according to Rousseau's formulation, a tribunate should serve all and any branches of government when they are threatened with oppression: a tribunate should act "sometimes to protect the sovereign against the government, as the tribunes of the people did in Rome, sometimes to uphold the government against the people, as the Council of Ten now does in Venice, and sometimes to maintain the balance between the two, as the Ephors did in Sparta" (SC IV 5, 136). Rousseau conceives of the tribunate as much more of an intermittent, floating ombudsman than an ever-vigilant, robust defender of the people.

Note how Rousseau is particularly concerned that government elites have recourse, from time to time, to a tribunician institution against the people, when the latter become potentially oppressive. Based on the discussions above, we might have cause to suspect that behind this attempt to insulate government officials from popular assault is a concomitant desire to protect socioeconomic elites. It is certainly intriguing that Rousseau discusses the particular actors who ought to have access to an antipopulist tribunate as a government institution and not as an ascendant socioeconomic class who were, according to Machiavelli, largely the targets of the tribunes in Rome. Perhaps Rousseau demurs from describing his reform-as-reversal proposal for a tribunate in terms of a conflict between patricians and plebeians out of fear of too readily exposing his preference that the patricians be better protected from the plebeians. Whatever the case, by making the tribunate an institution that at various times serves multiple competing actors—sometimes the people, sometimes the government—rather than as a magistracy that exclusively serves the people in resistance against hierarchical class oppression, Rousseau effectively neuters it. As such, he is responsible along with other ochlophobic contributors to modern constitutional thought—Guicciardini, Harrington, Montesquieu, and the Federalist Madison—for insuring that post-eighteenth century republican constitutions contain no such plebeian magistracy.

Conclusion

Scholars have tied themselves into knots attempting to decipher the intricacies of Rousseau's conception of republican politics—especially his abstract theory of legislation intended to insure that majority votes reflect not the mere will of all (the simple counting of heads) but rather the general will (the common good). In this chapter, following Rousseau's own directions, I have pursued a less complicated route and examined his assessment of a concrete republic, arguably history's greatest, ancient Rome. Rousseau's chapters on the Roman Republic, I have argued, solve paradoxes and perplexities for political philosophy and democratic theory left open in the first three books of the *Social Contract*—and not necessarily in ways that would please scholars who cast Rousseau as a heroic figure in the history of democratic and egalitarian theory and practice. Rousseau denounces and neuters Rome's plebeian-serving institution of elite accountability, the tribunate; and he praises and elevates to exemplary status the republic's most inegalitarian institutional feature, its timocratically organized assemblies, where wealthy citizens outvote poorer ones. The contrast with Machiavelli's assessment of Rome's tribunate and assemblies better positions democratic theorists to analyze the elected aristocracy recommended by the purported intellectual father of modern democracy.[45]

When not asserting a fundamental agreement between the two theorists,[46] conventional interpreters often juxtapose Rousseau and

Machiavelli in a strange way. Rousseau is credited with founding modern democratic theory, while Machiavelli is, at best, considered the champion of an antiquated republicanism that casts in relief the deficiencies of contemporary liberalism. (Or, less generously, of course, he is still depicted as the adviser of oligarchs and tyrants in the art of manipulating the people). This is odd indeed. If equality and elite accountability are crucial components of modern democratic theory and practice, it is Machiavelli who more intensively explores ways to advance these goals, while it is less than clear whether Rousseau considers these to be desirable pursuits at all. Machiavelli exposes and criticizes "the few" in the midst of a plea for more fully empowered and broadly democratic institutions; Rousseau celebrates an oligarchy cloaked as a popular government as both the best state of affairs in Rome at its height and as an example to be followed by all large republics in general.

Notwithstanding the highly abstract philosophical gymnastics that Rousseau performs to explain sovereignty and the general will in other parts of the *Social Contract*, his Roman Republic reveals his political theory to be not all that different from the aristocratic "republicanism" of Aristotle, Cicero, Bruni, Guicciardini, Harrington, and Madison, among others. According to this tradition, a republic is a collegial regime that governs in favor of the common good, the people's welfare, or the public interest, but the substance of these ideals are determined and realized by the best, most notable, or wealthiest citizens. Consequently, institutions must be arranged to enable them to do so. The people should participate merely to the extent that they are deluded into thinking either that they rule or that they are consulted in the workings of government. Only in cases of last resort, when the best citizens disagree on such matters, should the people be genuinely empowered to decide anything; in the normal course of events, the wealthiest citizens, the senatorial class, must hold sway.

As a dissenter from this dominant strand of republicanism, Machiavelli insisted that plebeian institutions are necessary to protect the people from oligarchic domination and to facilitate their participation in law- and policy-making so as to preserve the liberty of republics. Were he afforded the opportunity to comment upon Rousseau's

Social Contract, Machiavelli likely would insist that the establishment of a single, sociologically anonymous constitutional framework—with or without the privileges for the wealthy that Rousseau explicitly builds into the model—only allows the *grandi* to manipulate and oppress the people in an unchallenged fashion. Even a less than fully judicious reader of Rousseau's account of the Roman Republic would have a fairly clear sense of what his response to that charge would be.

5

Leo Strauss's Machiavelli and the *Querelle* between the Few and the Many

THIS CHAPTER EXAMINES Leo Strauss's engagement with the democratic elements of Niccolò Machiavelli's political thought; specifically, Machiavelli's self-avowed departure from the ancients in favoring the political judgment and participation of the many over the few and in recommending the people, rather than the nobles, as the ultimate foundation for political authority.[1] I identify several of Strauss's misinterpretations of Machiavelli's democratic, anti-elitist republicanism and explore tensions and discrepancies within Strauss's reconstruction of Machiavelli's political-philosophical project.[2] In the staggeringly impressive and ceaselessly provocative *Thoughts on Machiavelli*, Strauss argues that Machiavelli, while seeming to praise the people's political role in a democratic republic, actually levels an "unsparing analysis of the defects of the common people,"[3] thus implicitly, but deliberately and definitively, undermining his otherwise explicit praise. To make this case, I argue that Strauss exaggerates Machiavelli's criticisms of peoples and underplays his criticisms of the nobilities within republics. Strauss marshals instances of elite-popular interactions in the *Discourses* that purportedly demonstrate Machiavelli's preference for elite intervention and manipulation over popular participation and judgment. Strauss insists that Machiavelli actually endorses this kind of elite initiative precisely because it circumvents the ostensibly democratic institutions and practices that the Florentine's writings otherwise recommend, and that Machiavelli's rhetorical strategy subtly signals his lack of genuine commitment to popular government. In rebuttal, I will highlight some of the fallacious assumptions, questionable interpretive moves, and tendentious conclusions operating within or exhibited by Strauss's approach to Machiavelli's political thought.

My motivation, of course, is not merely to show that Strauss was wrong about a particular if crucially significant facet of Machiavelli's political thought. I hope to better illuminate the fundamental philosophical-political commitments driving Strauss's critique of modernity. In his earliest books, Strauss, the young devotee of Martin Heidegger, excavated the prerational foundations of the ostensibly rationalist philosophical systems of Baruch Spinoza and Thomas Hobbes: Strauss endeavors to uncover the "basic and ineradicable interest springing from [Spinoza's] heart" and to uproot Hobbes's "fundamental moral attitude."[4] In these writings, Strauss unearthed the psychological, affective, and ethical motivations that drove the intellectual projects of these illustrious founders of what Strauss considered the hopelessly misnamed "Age of Reason."[5]

I deem it apposite, then, to delineate and identify the nonobjective, prerational, moral commitments of Strauss's own intellectual project through a similar reading of his masterful study of Machiavelli—commitments inherited, wittingly or unwittingly, by his many disciples. Strauss, as we know, came somewhat late in his career to the view that Machiavelli, and not Hobbes or Spinoza, was the legitimate founder of modernity and the true initiator of the Enlightenment.[6] A painstaking comparison of what Machiavelli actually wrote about elites and the people, about aristocracy and popular government, with what Strauss claims that the Florentine wrote about them proves to be, I believe, illuminating of Strauss's own moral attitude and, indeed, his entire philosophical-political project.

The Democratic "Surface" of Machiavelli's Texts

Contrary to those who believe that Strauss gratuitously fetishized the esoteric, subterranean layers of texts and discounted or underestimated what political philosophers expressed on the exoteric level of their writings, in *Thoughts on Machiavelli* Strauss affirmed the indispensable importance of "the surface of things," including the surfaces of political texts:

> Not the contempt for the simple opinion, nor the disregard of it, but the *considerate* ascent from it leads to the core of Machiavelli's thought. There is no surer protection against the understanding of anything than taking for granted or otherwise despising the obvious and the surface. The problem inherent in the surface of things, and only in the surface of things, is the heart of things.[7]

Throughout his study of the Florentine's political thought, Strauss acknowledges the democratic Machiavelli that resides on the surface of things, that is, the advocate of "democratic" republics who speaks at an easily accessible layer of texts such as *The Prince*, the *Discourses*, and, to some extent, the *Florentine Histories*.[8]

As I have indicated to some extent elsewhere, when subsequent generations of Strauss's disciples are not altogether disregarding the democratic surface of Machiavelli's text, they seldom manage to conceal their outright contempt for it.[9] By Strauss's own hermeneutic standards, such disciples thereby jeopardize the possibility of penetrating to the core of the Florentine's political philosophy. A more serious question, however, is how faithfully Strauss adheres to his own declared hermeneutic standard; is Strauss himself sufficiently considerate of the democratic surface of Machiavelli's texts before he ascends philosophically to purportedly greater wisdom?

At the most general level, Strauss is remarkably attuned to the surface, democratic, layer of Machiavelli's political writings. He writes, for example: "It may easily appear that Machiavelli was the first philosopher who questioned in the name of the multitude or of democracy the aristocratic prejudice or the aristocratic premise which informed classical philosophy."[10] Furthermore, he notes, "when indicating the character of the ruling class in *The Discourses*, Machiavelli views the ruling class from the plebeian point of view."[11] Strauss even entertains the notion that Machiavelli himself was the first plebeian philosopher, an unprecedented "man of the people" among philosophers and historians.[12]

Indeed, Strauss cannot deny that Machiavelli outspokenly inverts "the traditional [philosophic] contempt for the multitude. This may incline us to believe that he was the philosopher who originated the democratic tradition. . . . The unmasking of the alleged aristocracy of the classics as oligarchy leads necessarily to a somewhat more favorable judgment of the common people."[13] To be sure, Strauss often articulates these assessments in the subjunctive, he qualifies them in various ways, and he almost invariably follows them up with alternative statements that significantly undermine the force of his original observations.[14] Nevertheless, one cannot dispute that Strauss, to a significant extent, permits the democratic surfaces of Machiavelli's texts, at least tentatively, to speak for themselves. However, at particular interpretive moments, Strauss often stifles and inverts Machiavelli's democratic voice before he has fully considered the latter's intensity and import. In such instances, Strauss compulsively leaps from the surface to some other level of meaning to disclose, unconceal, reveal the true antidemocratic motivations that, he presupposes and insists, must be operating within the Florentine's philosophic agenda.

Machiavelli's Purported Critique
of the People's Morality

Strauss is too sensitive a reader of texts to ignore the fact that Machiavelli explicitly attributes a superior moral quality, specifically, a certain *onestà*, to the common people rather than to the nobility within polities (see P 9). Strauss declares that Machiavelli considered "the purpose of the people" to be "more honest, or more just, than the purpose of the great."[15] Strauss furthermore acknowledges that Machiavelli's advocacy of the people's well-being necessarily transforms traditional notions of the common good into something dramatically utilitarian: "since the common good requires that innocent individuals be sacrificed for its sake, the common good is rather the good of the large majority, perhaps even the good of the common people as distinguished from the good of the nobles."[16] In the absence of harmony between the well-being of the many and the few, Strauss continues, "the good of the many takes precedence over the good of the few" in Machiavelli's considerations.[17]

From the aristocratic standpoint of the classical tradition, Strauss intimates that Machiavelli's utilitarian transformation of the common good is fundamentally unjust. However, Strauss does not consider in this context the fact that Machiavelli provides sufficient grounds for suggesting that his democratic utilitarianism coincides with a novel conception of justice: because Machiavelli attributes to the nobles, individually and collectively, an inherent, unquenchable desire to oppress, they are never fully innocent within his moral framework. Hence, in Machiavelli's estimation, the nobles of republics deserve to be treated in a disproportionately severe manner by public authority on behalf of the people.

A few pages after Strauss seems to accept as sincere Machiavelli's attribution of superior morality to the people, he abruptly takes back his provisional acquiescence: simply because "peoples are the repository of morality," for Machiavelli, this "does not mean that the peoples always or even mostly act morally or even that they are fundamentally moral" within the Florentine's framework; after all, Strauss avers, "belief in morality is not yet morality."[18] Strauss adds that "while the end of the many is most respectable," according to Machiavelli, "the many themselves are not."[19] While Machiavelli seems to posit "goodness" as the "peculiar kind of virtue" characteristic of, for instance, the Roman plebs, he actually demonstrates, in Strauss's estimation, something else entirely.

In particular, Strauss suggests that Machiavelli undermines his own depiction of the moral "innocence" of his seemingly "perfect" Roman plebs by recounting the latter's desire to burn alive members of the Decemvirate after the people had overthrown their tyranny (D I.44).[20] In a similar spirit, but without either discussing or even citing specific examples, Strauss insists that Machiavelli's *Florentine Histories* is "full of accounts of atrocious actions of the Florentine plebs."[21] Strauss may have in mind here one of the most graphically violent episodes in the entire *Histories*: the violence and cruelty that the Florentine people display toward supporters of the Duke of Athens, eating the flesh and drinking the blood of one of the duke's henchmen and his young son (FH II.37). As unsettling as this display of popular rage may be, Machiavelli makes it clear that the father had served as one of the duke's ruthless foreign rectors—one of the tyrant's ministers who had egregiously brutalized both citizens in the city and subjects in the countryside through rampant "fines, killings, and novel modes of torture" (FH II.36). On the basis of such at-best ambiguous evidence, Strauss concludes that for Machiavelli, "the goodness of the people consists less in its inability to *commit* impious or atrocious actions . . . than in its inability to color its wicked actions."[22] In other words, while the nobility artfully conceals its unjust motivations beneath the trappings of dignity and justice, the people nakedly evince their own injustice and immorality through their behavior.

The instances described above occur during episodes in which the Roman and Florentine peoples throw off tyrannies and re-establish republics. Machiavelli never casts as indecent or unjust the ferocity with which, he explicitly declares, the people reclaim their liberty, especially the violence that they inflict upon their erstwhile oppressors when doing so. In *The Prince*, Machiavelli famously states, "in republics there is more life, deeper hatred and greater desire for vengeance" against those who deprive the people of liberty (P 5). In the *Discourses*, Machiavelli declares that "there is nothing marvelous about the fact that peoples visit extraordinary acts of revenge upon those who have deprived them of their liberty" (D II.2); and, more generally, that the people are much more vicious in recovering their liberty than in either establishing or maintaining it (D I.28). Machiavelli apologizes for the apparently harsh ingratitude often attributed to the Athenian demos in its treatment of prominent citizens, characterizing such behavior as fiercely suspicious but entirely understandable reactions to the frequent and particularly intense instances of tyranny that they endured (D I.28). From Machiavelli's standpoint, there is nothing inappropriate or immoral about this kind of behavior. Strauss simply provides no evidence that such examples contravene Machiavelli's conception of goodness or justice, as much as they do Strauss's own.

Strauss also exaggerates the extent to which Machiavelli considered the people to be guilty of exhibiting the morally culpable character of insolence. Strauss invokes Machiavelli's supposed claim that a prince must "contend with the ambition of the great and the *insolence* of the people."[23] "Insolence," *insolenzia*, is the word that

Machiavelli uses to describe those who refuse to obey the laws or abide by civil modes; those who engage in oppression of others through either legal or extralegal means. But Machiavelli attributes insolence to the people, without qualification, on only two occasions: once in *The Prince* (P 19) and once in the *Florentine Histories* (FH IV.9).[24] In fact, when analyzing the social classes that characterize all republics or polities, Machiavelli applies this term of severe moral disapprobation overwhelmingly to the great, the nobles, the aristocrats—no less than sixteen times.[25] Perhaps most characteristic of Machiavelli's view is a quote from *Discourses*, Book I, chapter 16—a sentence that seems to serve as the basis of Strauss's mischaracterization (or mistranslation) quoted above: Machiavelli refers not to the ambition of the nobles and the insolence of the people, but rather to "the insolence of the aristocrats" (*la insolenzia degli ottimati*) and "the rage of the people" (*la rabbia de' popolari*). This distinction is crucial: by almost any standard of morality, expressions of insolence are seldom justifiable, while exhibitions of rage most certainly can be.

In sum, Strauss inappropriately undermines the admirable Ciceronian-aristocratic quality of *onestà* (goodness) that Machiavelli attributes to the people, and he applies to the people, either carelessly or disingenuously, the disreputable quality of *insolenzia* (insolence) that Machiavelli almost invariably attributes to the nobles. If Strauss merely commits a lazy mistake in these instances, then he reveals himself to be less than the unassailably meticulous reader of texts that his disciples repute him to be. Alternatively, if he cynically distorts the evidence in such cases, then Strauss's hermeneutic enterprise of considerately examining the surface of texts as guides to their ultimate meaning becomes deeply suspect. After all, once an interpreter is exposed for manipulating the surface of a text to predetermine what the content of its purportedly more comprehensive meaning will be, then the interpreter's entire enterprise is compromised.

While Strauss observes, as noted above, that Machiavelli views "the ruling class from the plebeian point of view," he also insists, more contentiously, that "with equal right he views the plebs to some extent from the patrician point of view."[26] The key phrases are "with equal right" and "to some extent"; Strauss asserts the "equal right" without textual support and significantly overstates the magnitude of the "extent" that he invokes. In the first instance, Machiavelli demonstrates time and again that the Roman patricians hold the plebs in abject contempt, which the Florentine himself never does. The patricians, as described by Machiavelli, would never concur with his attribution of greater honesty and justness to the people (cited on the previous page by Strauss). Moreover, in the second, if, as Strauss claims, "Machiavelli does not mean to say that the people is *by nature* good,"[27] then it would be incumbent upon Strauss to consider at some length why the Florentine defined the respective moral-empirical motivations of the people and the nobles with the highly naturalistic term "humors"; specifically, the more decent humor of the people "not to be oppressed" and the insolent humor of the nobles "to oppress the people" (P 9; D I. 4–5).

To demonstrate more conclusively that these views regarding the people's purported immorality are Strauss's and not Machiavelli's, allow me to briefly evaluate these claims in a text where Machiavelli seems most critical, even denunciatory, of the people and the plebs, the *Florentine Histories*. Drawing upon my analysis from chapter 3 of the present work, I suggest that Machiavelli's hermeneutical approach to presenting his evaluations of the people and the nobles is precisely the opposite of what Strauss describes. Rather than merely appearing to praise the people and condemn the nobles (while supposedly communicating the reverse), as Strauss insists, Machiavelli actually undertakes an entirely contrary rhetorical strategy in the *Histories*. There, Machiavelli indeed criticizes the Florentine people for, unlike their ancient Roman counterpart, refusing to share offices with the nobles. He furthermore exclaims that the Florentine plebs "always revel in evil" (FH III.1, II.34)—negative assessments that seem to contradict the positive ones that Machiavelli sets forth in the *Discourses*, and that seem to lend credence to Strauss's evaluation of Machiavelli's actual views of all peoples. Yet Machiavelli's words in these instances belie his description in the book of the people's and plebs' respective actions.

Again, in the concluding pages of Book II of the *Histories*, not long before he denounces the Florentine people at the start of Book III for unreasonably desiring to exclude the nobles from offices, Machiavelli recounts how the people restructured the republic's chief magistracy, the *Signoria*, precisely to accommodate inclusion of the nobles in that office. It is only after the nobles soon resort to violence to exclude all members of the people from this very magistracy that the people henceforth bar them from holding signorial offices—after defeating the nobles in open battle on the city's streets. In other words, Machiavelli demonstrates that the Florentine nobles compel the people to exclude them from offices that the nobles themselves refuse to share with the people; the latter do not, on the basis of the inherently selfish or oppressive nature that Strauss attributes to them, do so without provocation.

Moreover, in Book III of the *Histories*, the Florentine plebs, to whom Machiavelli apparently attributes evil motivations, behave in the following way according to Machiavelli's account: after seizing control of the entire city for themselves during the Ciompi Revolt, the Florentine plebs propose constitutional reforms whereby they themselves, newly enrolled in minor guilds, could be outvoted by their erstwhile adversaries in the middle and upper guilds. In other words, the plebs desire to enjoy inclusion in civic offices rather than to exercise domination through them. Machiavelli's description of actions in the *Histories*, not his surface evaluations of them, demonstrate that the people and the plebs—in ways perfectly consistent with Machiavelli's other political writings—merely desire not to be politically oppressed by their socioeconomic superiors in republics. Strauss proves to be less attentive to deeds than to words, to particulars than to generalities, in Machiavelli's writings when mere words conveniently support his own basic and ineradicable moral attitude in favor of the few over the many.

As I will discuss at some length below, Strauss seeks to shake the foundation of Machiavelli's professed faith in the judgment of the people by suggesting that, despite what the Florentine says otherwise, an inability to understand generalities compromises the supposed ability to judge particulars that Machiavelli attributes to the people (D I.47).[28] In his misapprehension of the relationship of particular deeds to general words in the *Histories*, Strauss himself proves susceptible to a similar charge. Strauss moves from the general to the particular less adeptly than do Machiavelli's vulgar; that is, unlike the plebeians, whose proficiency in this regard Machiavelli explicitly affirms (D I.47, I.58), Strauss apparently judges less adroitly than they do when moving from generalities to particulars.

Be that as it may, the civic-military deficiencies of the Florentine Republic laid bare by Machiavelli in the *Histories* lead Strauss to accurately depict Machiavelli's assessment of the proper role of an armed populace in a well-ordered republic. Strauss does not hesitate to cite as Machiavelli's "greatest truth" his recommendation that princes and republics extensively arm the common people.[29] For Machiavelli, Rome's greatness is due in no small part to "the virility of her plebs" in military affairs,[30] on which basis, Strauss notes, the Roman people demand a significant share of power in the republic:

> It is in the best interest of the people that it be confronted and led by a virtuous and warlike nobility with which it shares power in due proportion. Only if political power is shared by the great and the people in due proportion, or in other words if there is a proper proportion between the force of the great and the force of the people will there be public liberty and proper consideration for the common good.... [An] armed and virile plebs will naturally demand a considerable share in political power and in the fruits of conquest, and will not hesitate to support those demands with indecorous, disorderly and even illegal actions.... [An] imperial republic must give its plebs a greater share in political power than a non-imperial republic.[31]

But is this due or proper proportion the same for Strauss and Machiavelli? In what proportion does each author think that the nobles and the people should share power in a well-ordered republic? And in what respects does popular power translate into popular rule, for each of the thinkers?

The People's Supposed Inability to Participate in Rule

According to Strauss, Machiavelli's view on popular rule may be summed up as follows: the many "are unable to rule themselves or others";[32] "the majority cannot rule ... [f]or the multitude is ignorant, lacks judgment, and is easily deceived; it is helpless without leaders who persuade or force it to act prudently."[33] Consequently, for Strauss, to whatever extent Machiavelli exhibited a genuine "bias in favor of the multitude," this popular bias does not entail the conclusion that Machiavelli favored "the rule of the multitude."[34]

If by "rule" Strauss means the exercise of office—that is, the carrying out of executive duties such as applying general rules to specific circumstances, or exercising prerogative in time-sensitive and precedent-free circumstances—then his claim amounts to a truism that no democrat would deny: individuals or small bodies of individuals, not multitudes, populaces, or citizenries best exercise such authority. Athens, after all, appointed magistrates; the assembly did not perform all political functions within its democratic constitution. If, however, rule for Machiavelli also entails electoral, legislative, and judicial action—including decisions over capital crimes in political cases—then Strauss's claim is simply incorrect. Only exercise of magistracies, of command, constitute rule for Strauss, while for Machiavelli it also entails legislative and judicial judgment exercised collectively in assembly, as well as ultimate judgment over the appointment of magistrates. This is what permits Machiavelli to say that, in republics, "peoples are princes" (D I.58) rather than simply the individual "princes" of republics who hold offices or gather in senates, which primarily occupy Strauss's attention.

Machiavelli insists that the people exercise appropriate judgment when appointing magistrates, making laws, and deciding political trials (respectively, D 48; I.16, I.58; and I.7–8). Machiavelli makes clear that popular judgment is often less than perfect, but, in most cases, not as imperfect as judgment rendered by princes or nobles. Strauss devotes extensive attention to Machiavelli's examples of popular misjudgment, but very little to his many examples of poor decisions rendered by nobilities. To properly adjudicate this issue, let us first examine the place of collective popular judgment in Machiavelli's notion of rule, and then examine how this interacts with the kind of rule represented by individual action in Strauss's treatment of the Florentine's political thought.

How does Strauss evaluate Machiavelli's argument in favor of the people's superior judgment as a justification for their participation in rule? Strauss focuses on what appear to him to be obvious semantic cum logical contradictions in Machiavelli's account, contradictions that purportedly discredit the Florentine's explicit endorsement of popular judgment. At an important juncture, Strauss resorts to a peculiar semantic argument in his attempt to undermine Machiavelli's claim that the multitude's judgment "is likely to be right" in making political decisions.[35] Machiavelli famously declares in *Discourses*, Book I, chapter 58, that he departs from the common or universal opinion that criticizes the people for being poor judges of political matters. Strauss argues that Machiavelli's refutation of the "common" or "universal" opinion here concerning the inferiority of the people's judgment necessarily entails an indictment of judgments made by the commonality, by the universal—that is, by the people themselves. In other words, Machiavelli composes his defense of the people's judgment in such a way as to undermine, rhetorically or logically, the force of that very defense. Strauss formulates the argument as follows:

> [Machiavelli] attacks "the common opinion" according to which the multitude is inferior in wisdom to princes, and he contends that the voice of the multitude, "a universal opinion," is likely to be right. But is not "the common opinion" about the wisdom of the multitude "a universal opinion"? And does not "universal opinion" assert that "universal opinion" is likely to be wrong? Does not then the oracular voice of the multitude deny wisdom to the multitude? Must Machiavelli not question the authority of universal opinion in order to establish the authority of universal opinion? Must he not say that universal opinion must be wrong so that universal opinion can be right and that universal opinion must be right so that universal opinion can be wrong?[36]

I submit that the problem Strauss here presses rather pedantically, one might even say perversely, evaporates if we assume the following: in this instance, Machiavelli refers specifically to the common or universal opinion among the writers (and among nobilities) rather than to the common or universal opinion of the people. That is, Machiavelli is criticizing the common or universal opinion among the few here, rather than the common or universal opinion of the many. This interpretation is, I believe, what the surface of the text dictates.

Strauss addresses this possible, indeed more plausible, reading, and seems willing to engage it in a forthright manner: "Against this one might try to argue as follows: 'the common opinion' of 'all writers' is not 'a universal opinion,' i.e., an opinion of the multitude or of the people." If this retort to Strauss is correct, then when Machiavelli impugns the common opinion of many writers who argue that the many, qua common people, exercise poor political judgment, he is not thereby also impugning the latter's "common" opinion. But Strauss does not follow through on this commonsensical line of thought here; in fact, he attempts to dispel this more likely interpretation by constructing a straw man. Turning to Machiavelli's argument, expressed elsewhere in the *Discourses* (D I.47–48), that the people may be deceived by generalities but that they judge well when deciding on particulars, Strauss exaggerates Machiavelli's claims: Strauss insists that Machiavelli demonstrates that the people are "*likely*" to be wrong regarding generalities," indeed, that they are entirely "*incompetent*" when judging them.[37]

Strauss accentuates the people's supposed total incapacity to apprehend generalities in order to show that Machiavelli fundamentally undermines his own expressed praise of the soundness of the people's common or universal opinion. Basically, Strauss argues that if the people are incapable of deciding generalities, then they are also necessarily incapable of deciding particulars, since the two spheres of judgment are interdependent.[38] However, in the passages cited by Strauss, Machiavelli never attributes such absolute inability to apprehend generalities to the people; he merely claims that to whatever extent the people are deceived about generalities, they are less likely to be so deceived when judging particular cases. Machiavelli never declares that the people are incapable of deciding generalities and exclusively capable of deciding particulars; merely that they are better at judging particulars. For instance, Machiavelli states in the heading of this particular chapter: "However Much Men Are Deceived Over Generalities, They Are Not So Deceived in Particulars" (D I.47). More importantly, Machiavelli suggests that judgment over particulars can and do in fact enlighten the people regarding generalities.

Machiavelli discusses four cases in D I.47–48 pertaining to popular judgment, generalities, and particulars. Three involve the appointments of magistrates, two of which include institutional reforms enacted by elites to induce the people to elect nobles rather than plebeians to office and one of which entails acts of corruption on the part of the nobility to attain the same end. In the two cases involving institutional changes (D I.47): (a) the Roman nobles increase the number and change the name of the republic's supreme magistracy to permit the plebs to free themselves of resentment over the nobility's monopoly of the consulship and to simply elect whomever they consider the most qualified men for the chief magistracy—all of whom at the time turn out to be nobles; and (b) a Capuan leader permits the people to vent their anger over aristocratic oppression by offering them the opportunity to kill any noble whom they can replace in the senate with a worthy member of the plebeians. With Hannibal in the vicinity, threatening to conquer the city, the Capuan people decide to stick with the experienced senators that they already have. In both cases, decisions over individual appointments compel the people to liberate themselves of one false generality— that they should replace the nobles presently holding the supreme magistracies—and supplant it with a more true generality, the most qualified candidates should hold the highest offices, especially during time of war (which applies in both cases). Machiavelli, however, quite explicitly declares, as we shall see below, that there is a time in a republic's history when plebeians should indeed ascend to consular offices.

The effectual truth of the third episode, where the Roman nobles resort in part to corruption in order to secure the election of nobles, seems to concern primarily aristocratic and not popular judgment (D I.48). Machiavelli reports that the Roman nobles often bribed unworthy plebs to run for office, which shamed the people into rejecting their candidacies, or the senate encouraged the most reputable nobles to run for office, which induced the plebs to elect them. One is led to wonder the following: if the nobles had been previously nominating the very best citizens for office all along (instead of those who presumably were merely satisfying their humor to oppress the people) would the plebs have clamored to hold offices at all?[39] It would seem that the tumults between the people and the great, here spilling over into electoral affairs, induced the nobility to act in a public-spirited fashion that they were not otherwise inclined to do.

In the fourth case pertaining to generalities and particulars (D I.47), Machiavelli cites no instance of elite initiation or manipulation at all: Machiavelli notes how, when the Medici were expelled from Florence in 1494, members of the Florentine citizenry who had never held high office attributed, through gossip in the piazza, the city's mismanagement to corruption on the part of the elites who presently governed. When such *popolani* themselves did ascend to offices in the palazzo, however, now confronted with the specific responsibilities and difficulties of governing the republic, they realized that their previous opinions held little if any water (D I.47).[40] Thus does Machiavelli illustrate the educative effect facilitated by the particulars of governing upon the general notions of those who previously did not do so, an effect through which arises a new enlightened generality, or what amounts to the same thing, an apprehension of effectual truth.[41]

In his ruminations on particulars, generalities, and popular judgment, Strauss leads his readers far away from his original assertion: that by criticizing the general or common opinion of the writers regarding the people, Machiavelli is actually criticizing the general or common opinion as such; that is, the people's opinion. Ultimately, I believe, the dubious character of Strauss's claim here is underscored by the fact that throughout *Thoughts on Machiavelli*, Strauss himself often takes Machiavelli's use of "the opinion of many" or "the common opinion" to apply to writers exclusively rather than to the multitude or to the people generally.[42] I count at least twenty-six such instances where Strauss treats the universal or common opinion in Machiavelli's writings as the opinion of actors other than the people, most often the opinion of the writers. Is it not then safe to say that this mode of discussing the "common opinion" among the writers is precisely what Machiavelli is doing as well; that is, straightforwardly referring to the opinion of the writers, and not that of the people, in such instances?

Popular versus Aristocratic Misjudgment

Strauss attempts to bolster his case against the laudatory surface of Machiavelli's considerations on the people's judgment by discussing a number of cases where Machiavelli shows that the people misjudge circumstances or are deceived by appearances. Strauss argues that Machiavelli undermines his own positive assessment of popular judgment by citing specific instances of bad choices made by the peoples of republics. For instance, when the Roman plebs elect nobles to offices that the people claimed to have wanted for themselves, Strauss suggests, "in defending the virtue of the Roman people against its own opinion, Machiavelli questions the wisdom of the Roman people."[43] However, given Machiavelli's many examples of nobilities and senates who themselves misjudge or are deceived at critical moments, which I will document below, these examples of popular misjudgment do not remotely prove that Machiavelli does not believe that the multitude's judgment "is likely to be right" in most circumstances.

Throughout the vast literature inspired by Strauss's writings on Machiavelli, scholars emphasize the Florentine's criticisms of the Roman people for agitating military confrontation with Hannibal at Cannae or of the Athenian demos for voting to invade Sicily. Few if any of Strauss's disciples ever mention Machiavelli's potentially harsher indictments of similar decisions rendered by the senates of republics, including the Roman one.[44] Indeed, Strauss himself never reconciles the fact that Machiavelli blames the avarice of "his admired Roman nobility" for causing, as Strauss concedes, the ultimate collapse of the Roman Republic with: on the one hand, his claim that Machiavelli attributes perfect prudence to the very same nobles, and on the other, his assertion that the nobles pursue, in Machiavelli's view, *not* material gain but rather "glory in this world" above all things.[45]

Admittedly, the Roman and Athenian cases of poor popular judgment result in devastating military defeats for their polities (D I.53, III.16). Yet Machiavelli shows in no uncertain terms how strategic misjudgment and diplomatic mismanagement by the Carthaginian nobles after the victory at Cannae effectively set in motion the eclipse of their entire civilization (D II.27). Furthermore, while Strauss extensively discusses Machiavelli's criticisms of Sparta and Venice vis-à-vis Rome on the issue of imperial expansion, he never factors these criticisms into his scorekeeping over Machiavelli's relative favor of the people versus the nobles. After all, it was the senators of the aristocratic Lacedaemonian and Adriatic republics, who, according to Machiavelli, unwisely pursued territorial expansion when their respective polities were not suitably prepared for it, and thus caused the "total ruin" or the "complete loss" of their states (D I.6, III.31). In sum, according to Machiavelli, it appeared to the Spartan, Venetian, and Carthaginian senates that their republics could win wars in pursuit of imperial expansion, only, in all three cases, to lose entirely whatever empire they already possessed, and, in the third case, to suffer utter extinction. Neither Strauss nor his students acknowledge this line of argument in Machiavelli's texts.

Strauss insists that Machiavelli's specific examples of popular misjudgment demonstrate that "the multitude is frequently more moved by things which seem to be than by things which are."[46] But the same thing can be said with equal or greater force concerning instances of senatorial misjudgment throughout Machiavelli's writings. In Machiavelli's telling, at various junctures it seemed to the Syracusan, Heraclean, and Roman senates that bestowing supreme authority upon certain individuals would best serve their own efforts to maintain aristocratic republics that oppress the people. Ultimately, as Machiavelli demonstrates, each one of these senates winds up being neutered or thoroughly destroyed by these very individuals—respectively, by the tyrants Agathocles, Clearchus, and Octavian (P 8, D I.16, and D I.29).

In these instances, like the others noted above, faulty senatorial opinion proves more dangerous, in Machiavelli's estimation, than imperfect popular judgment. Yet Strauss confidently declares "the multitude does not desire public liberty in all cases; in case it does not, to use fraud and force against the multitude itself for the sake of public liberty is unobjectionable."[47] In light of a truly comprehensive reading of Machiavelli's writings, the appropriate response to this point is: So what? Machiavelli's corpus is filled with examples where nobles and senators too must often be compelled by necessity or by virtuous individuals to do what "public liberty" requires. For instance, Machiavelli notes how Cincinnatus prevents the Roman senate from extending the terms of consular office, a senatorial practice that later would contribute to the loss of Rome's liberty (D III.24). Machiavelli consistently shows that both nobilities and peoples rely on the guidance of individual leaders to maintain public liberty (see e.g., D I.30); and yet, as we will observe more clearly in the next section, Strauss exclusively marshals this fact to argue against the possibility of popular rule and never to ameliorate his own commitment to senatorial rule.

Put simply, the evidence that Strauss adduces to emphasize the people's deficient judgment proves insufficient to support Strauss's insistence that Machiavelli would actually deny the people a prominent share in ruling a republic—indeed, a predominant one in matters elective, legislative, and judicial. To convincingly support such a claim, Strauss ought to have analyzed just as closely, carefully, and indeed cynically Machiavelli's criticisms of the nobles as he analyzes the Florentine's supposedly negative depictions of the people. As matters stand, Strauss simply fails to consider Machiavelli's criticisms of nobles, both in and out of Rome, with a fidelity and intensity comparable to his emphasis on Machiavelli's criticisms of the people.

Again, Strauss argues that Machiavelli's examples of deference, credulity, and poor judgment on the part of the people discredit the force of his general claims in favor of their judgment. In making such a claim, Strauss must operate under the assumption that some political actors in Machiavelli's framework—especially the nobles—are more fully enlightened about their own level of enlightenment than are the people. What other evaluative standard could Strauss employ by which to judge the people's wisdom or ignorance? However, it seems to me that it is simply impossible to demonstrate that any actor in the *Discourses* possesses the absolute self-knowledge (qualified "Socratically," perhaps) that Strauss consistently attributes to Machiavelli's nobles.[48] After all, Machiavelli blatantly rejects the ideal of philosopher kings whose perfect judgment might be even remotely approximated by the educated, wealthy, and prominent nobles of worldly cities (P 15). By declaration and example, Machiavelli insists that there exists no group of few best individuals whose wisdom, prudence, or love of the common good can be counted on to settle with impartial justice, or solve with consistent acuity, political controversies and crises. On the basis of his critical assessment of the nobilities of republics, Machiavelli makes more defensible than any political thinker before him a claim for the people's good political judgment—or at least political judgment comparably better than the kind exercised by the few or by a prince (D I.58).

In spite of this, Strauss and his disciples fixate disproportionately on Machiavelli's isolated expressions of hesitation over the people's political capacities while they significantly underplay his incessant indictments of the elite's designs and behavior—indeed, as I will suggest below, they often go so far as to rehabilitate the elite's moral and cognitive capacities far beyond what texts such as the *Discourses* warrant.[49] For now, the preceding should begin to cast serious doubt over the extent to which Strauss successfully undermines Machiavelli's positive endorsement of popular judgment and the people's participation in the governing of a republic.

Is Leadership Anathema or Ancillary to Machiavellian Popular Government?

Strauss attempts to undercut Machiavelli's favorable assessment of substantive participation by the people in a republic by showing that Machiavelli's multitude is dependent on the intervention of individual leaders in developing and exercising their good judgment. However, no serious scholar who has ever put forth the view that Machiavelli is an advocate of democratic republics, or a partisan of the many over the few, has ever ignored or denied examples where individuals, noble or otherwise, dissuade or enjoin the people from a deleterious or toward a salutary course of action: for instance, Machiavelli argues that a "good man" must often persuade the people to make an appropriate decision in assembly (D I.4); that senatorial intransigence is sometimes necessary to dissuade the people from a disastrous course of action (D I.53); and even that naked force at times must be deployed to ensure that the people, enlisted as citizen-soldiers, act correctly in adverse circumstances (D I.11). The more pressing question is, *how much* individual, even elite, intervention within Machiavelli's writings must Strauss emphasize to show successfully that the Florentine believes that the people, by themselves, are fundamentally and consistently incapable of good judgment, and that, for Machiavelli, a democratic republic is a façade for an oligarchic regime?

As Machiavelli famously declares, "the multitude is wiser than a prince" (D I.58). However, he also insists that a people "without a head is useless" (D I.44). Strauss cannot disprove Machiavelli's commitment to the first statement. Here, I will argue that he therefore proceeds to overemphasize the second: for instance, when Strauss claims that Machiavelli believes the people "cannot find the truth by itself. By itself, it is ignorant."[50] Strauss wishes to demonstrate that the Roman people always and at every moment "must be compelled or persuaded by prudent citizens to act sensibly," with "the Roman Senate" serving as the principle "body of such prudent citizens."[51] This claim, however, is problematic, especially when read in light of Machiavelli's account of popular-senatorial differences of opinion; for instance, over the invasion of Africa to draw Hannibal out of Italy, over the ill-advised expansion of Rome's empire throughout the Mediterranean after the Punic War, and, especially, over the necessity of the Agrarian Laws (D I.53, D III.24, D I.37).

Strauss suggests further that even if the senate as a whole is not necessary to guide the people's judgment, then certainly individual princes, "the leading men in a republic," must do so in its place.[52] Machiavelli of course acknowledges the benefits often afforded a republic by elite advisement of its common citizens: following Cicero in this respect, Machiavelli claims that "a good man"—perhaps a citizen of wealth and good name—may effectively persuade the assembled people when they verge toward committing serious political errors (DI.4, D I.58).[53] But unlike Cicero and many contributors to the "republican tradition," Machiavelli also insists that "any citizen whatsoever" (D I.18) retains the ability to advise the people in assemblies. Furthermore, Machiavelli's view that the people ought to be advised by outstanding leaders does not preclude the common people deliberating and deciding over legislation in public assemblies. In Machiavelli's Rome, once individual citizens speak out for or against a law, "the people as a whole decided what was correct" (D I.18).

Moreover, according to Machiavelli, the Roman plebeians demonstrate, in the two episodes of plebeian secession from the city, that a people can act on its own initiative. The people without heads, therefore, would seem to be not entirely useless. In this spirit, Machiavelli shows that the Roman plebeians themselves lobby for both the establishment of the tribunate (D I.3) and for early enactment of agrarian legislation that would have kept "the public rich and the citizens poor" in a civically beneficial way (D I.37). Strauss, however, dismisses the relevance of such examples by insisting that prominent plebeians act as "heads" of the plebs and hence as elites in such circumstances. Machiavelli certainly provides multiple examples of plebeians such as Virginius in Rome and the infamous nameless *ciompo* in Florence, who step forward to influence the opinions and behavior of their fellow common citizens. However, to Strauss's mind, when such individuals act in politically significant ways, they necessarily shed their vulgar origins. Strauss insists on identifying such figures primarily as *leaders* rather than as *plebeians*—the two significations are mutually exclusive.

In Strauss's estimation, anyone who emerges from the ranks of the people to speak in an assembly—or to take initiative in any capacity whatever—must be considered a member of the elite, whatever their social origins. According to his conception of leadership, all individual intervention into politics necessarily constitutes elite intervention that, by definition, contravenes democratic rule. Strauss thereby applies something deeply reminiscent of the so-called iron law of oligarchy to Machiavelli's conception of popular government: "every so-called democracy is in fact an oligarchy unless it verges on anarchy."[54] On this view, the possibility that individual plebeians qua common citizens actually participate in politics is ruled out, tout court; moreover, the assumption that all individual speech and action is fundamentally "elitist" becomes an unfalsifiable proposition.[55]

Consider Strauss's depiction of the nameless *ciompo* from the *Florentine Histories*, discussed in chapter 3, who notoriously exhorts his fellow plebeians to escalate their arsons and riots at the start of the Ciompi Revolt (FH III.13). Strauss notes the Machiavellian character of the speech delivered by this "plebeian leader,"[56] and he closely affiliates certain aspects of it with Machiavelli's own political prescriptions and (im)moral agenda. But Strauss refuses to associate this nameless *ciompo*—a poor woolworker, who has never before been permitted to participate formally in civic politics—with the people themselves. Strauss quips: "a plebeian leader is not simply a plebeian, and a leader of the plebs is not necessarily himself a plebeian."[57] A plebeian leader, for Strauss, is always much more a leader than, if at all, a plebeian. I submit that Strauss judges too hastily in this instance. Resorting to iron law logic, Strauss rushes to classify such an individual as a member of a preexisting, presumably natural, class of elites. In doing so, Strauss frees himself from the necessity of problematizing the passive and credulous nature that he (and later his followers) consistently attributes to the people—in a manner often very much at odds with Machiavelli's writings (e.g., P 19; D I.4; FH III.12). In fact, Strauss puts himself in a peculiar logical bind here. Recall that Strauss asserted that Machiavelli's *Histories* is "full of accounts of atrocious actions of the Florentine plebs."[58] This suggests that Machiavelli's peoples are capable of self-motivated, collective action, but that Strauss is only prepared to acknowledge it as such when he deems their behavior to be morally reprehensible. When Machiavelli's peoples act in ways that may be considered civically spirited, even virtuous, Strauss insists that leaders must have been the true agents of the people's behavior.

Moreover, precisely what kind of a "leader" is this unidentified *ciompo*? He is a speaker, to be sure, but not necessarily a leader in any formal sense: Machiavelli merely notes that he was "one of the boldest and most experienced" among his comrades—not even the most brave or experienced (FH III.13). This *ciompo* certainly did not earn, either before or after his speech, sufficient prominence to insure that his name would be recognized by his contemporaries or remembered by posterity. Furthermore, as I have suggested before, it is less than clear how far, ultimately, the other *ciompi* are willing to follow his advice. On these grounds, it seems to me that one needs to explore this episode further before one draws the rather inconsiderate conclusion that anyone, like the *ciompo*, who publicly speaks is a leader in Strauss's overexpansively elitist sense; that is, an individual who may no longer be classified as a member of the *popolo*. Strauss's mode of interpretation here consigns the people to be a passive, reactive mass, which does not reflect Machiavelli's depiction and assessment of the *popolo* within his three major political works.[59]

There is another figure from Machiavelli's writings whom Strauss identifies as a "plebeian leader" to illustrate the point that leaders lead and peoples follow: Strauss invokes the example of Virginius, the plebeian centurion, from the *Discourses* to prove that the people are incapable of governing.[60] Virginius slays his daughter to prevent her from being civically degraded and sexually defiled by the tyrant Appius Claudius; he orders the election of military tribunes among the plebeians during their second secession from Rome; and he denies Appius the right of appeal to the people after the overthrow of the Decemvirate (D I.40, D I.44, D I.45). In the first instance, Virginius has no idea that killing his daughter will spark the riot that initiates the plebs' second secession from the city, which sets in motion the Decemvirate's demise. The people themselves undertake both the riot and the secession spontaneously. In the second instance, Virginius certainly exercises leadership by insuring that the plebs establish officials who can maintain order and receive emissaries from the senate. But in the third, Virginius actually oversteps the implicit boundaries of his role as leader, unilaterally denying Appius the right to appeal his incarceration to the people—a move that, Machiavelli suggests, puts an end to Virginius' political career, as he appears to the people to have put the satisfaction of a personal grudge ahead of legal procedures that empower popular judgment.[61]

Therefore, in some sense, the example of Virginius proves both that sometimes the people do not need a head (as when the plebs spontaneously evacuate Rome, for the second time) and sometimes they do (as when Virginius recognizes before the plebs do that they need to elect tribunes to serve as their commanders and representatives during the secession). Virginius also proves another significant point that cuts against Strauss's "iron law" reading of Machiavelli: the people will abandon a head when that leader inappropriately and self-servingly accrues to himself political functions that such leaders themselves previously declared to rightfully belong to the people.

The two secessions of the plebs and the original creation of the plebeian tribunes seem to confirm one of Machiavelli's central lessons that qualifies his claim that the people are useless without a head: that is, a militarily organized *popolo* can, at times, act as its own head or create heads from out of itself. Machiavelli demonstrates that the people, organized in military legions and civic assemblies, are capable of salutary judgment and action. The Roman armies make tribunes out of themselves in the absence of their noble commanders, and the Roman assemblies, "shackled by laws," both legislate public policy and adjudicate political offenses with appropriate acuity. This, of course, begs the question of who created the military and civic institutions through which the people often act on their own behalf and participate in ruling the republic. Machiavelli is clear that founders such as Moses or Romulus, rather than peoples, do so. A militarily organized *popolo*, especially, depends on a founder sufficiently prudent to have armed the plebs (D I.43; P 20), as Romulus did in Rome (D I. 1–2, D I.9). Once organized in such a fashion the Roman people can quit the city in an orderly fashion on their own accord, negotiate the creation of the plebeian tribunate, and, when collective initiative is lacking during the second secession, acknowledge individuals among themselves, such as Virginius, with requisite leadership experience.[62]

Strauss manages to exaggerate the influence exerted by elites over the people in Machiavelli's writings by consistently blurring the distinction between founders of extraordinary virtue and nobles of ordinary capabilities; that is, the distinction between those who establish republics and those who subsequently seek to exercise political influence within them.[63] Strauss renders the difference between these two very different kinds of elites invisible when he equates the wisdom of founder-princes with that of senatorial-princes. Strauss writes that, for Machiavelli, political guidance "is supplied ordinarily by laws and orders which, if they are to be of any value, of necessity originate in superior minds, in the minds of founders *or* of princes."[64] These superior minds are confined not only to the original founder-princes of republics, but also include the continuous founders-nobles of republics, whose superiority may approach "superhuman" ability. As Strauss remarks in one of the most Nietzschean-Heideggerian utterances in *Thoughts on Machiavelli*: "We suspect that Machiavelli sometimes uses 'princes' in order to designate superhuman powers."[65]

Strauss obscures the fundamental distinction between these two kinds of princes: one is the founders, on whom the people are certainly dependent (individuals, who more often than not are traitors to the patrician class); and the other is members of the nobility, the great, who, according to Machiavelli, often pursue either their own selfish personal interests or their own oppressive class agenda against the people, doing in the process more harm than good for republics, peoples, and themselves. Founders are certainly superior to the common people politically, in Machiavelli's estimation; *ottimati* are not necessarily so.[66] The "superhuman" knowledge, which takes on increasing importance over the course of Strauss's study,[67] would seem to apply much more to founder-princes than to noble-princes. Strauss, however, transforms the latter into the former when he declares that ordinary nobles become quasi-founders in Machiavelli's Rome: the people, Strauss declares, are dependent on "the series of first rate men who were responsible for the continuous foundation of Rome . . . to establish new laws and orders."[68] Strauss, however, neglects to mention that the people themselves initiate the establishment of the institution that above all others made the republic "more perfect": the tribunes of the plebs (D I.5–6).

To put an abrupt end to what could be an interminable disquisition: the issue of leaders and peoples in Machiavelli's political writings is simply irresolvable within the terms that Strauss himself sets out for analyzing it.

Machiavelli's "Young": Enlightened Elites
or Treacherous Sons of Brutus?

Strauss puts great store in the central role that the young play in Machiavelli's philosophical-political project. According to Strauss, in *The Prince* and the *Discourses*, Machiavelli is "anxious to establish . . . intimacy . . . with a certain kind of reader whom he calls 'the young.'" This intimacy, Strauss suggests, serves to further Machiavelli's "subtle corruption or seduction" of the young,[69] whom he enlists in "a potential conspiracy" to inaugurate modernity.[70] The enactment and longevity of Machiavelli's philosophical-political enterprise "depends upon the cooperation of 'the young'"; more specifically, "those young men or potential princes or . . . conspirators proper who might put into practice [Machiavelli's] new modes and orders."[71]

Strauss's obsession with youth, and his attribution of a similar fawning fixation on the young to Machiavelli, convey, at best, only one side of the story. Youth is not an unmitigated good in Machiavelli's political thought. Strauss entirely leaves out of his account an enormously important aspect of Machiavelli's political teaching: namely, Machiavelli's concern with "the sons of Brutus," the Florentine's term for the young nobles whom he insists, on multiple occasions, pose the greatest threat to the stability and liberty of republics. Machiavelli is seldom so adamant as when he insists that proponents and defenders of "a free way of life" must eliminate the sons of Brutus (D III.3).

In the *Discourses*, the sons of Brutus appear, literally, as the sons of Lucius Brutus, Rome's first consul, who led the effort to expel the Tarquin kings and establish the Roman Republic. Brutus oversaw the execution of his sons after they conspired to reinstitute monarchy in Rome (D I.16; D III.1–3). Brutus's sons, and their fellow conspirators among noble youths, conspired to overthrow the Roman Republic because they so deeply resented the common people's newly won liberty. The "sons of Brutus" also appear, euphemistically, as the young Florentine *ottimati* who conspired to overthrow the 1494–1512 Republic, which Machiavelli served so dutifully, and to restore the Medici principality (D III.3). Machiavelli witnessed firsthand and recounted in the *Discourses* how these young nobles conspired to summon a foreign power, the Spanish army, to reinstall the Medici. They did so, Machiavelli suggests, because they could endure neither government by the people collected in the Great Council nor the chief magistracy of Machiavelli's boss, Piero Soderini, whom they considered a traitor to the patrician class.[72] As Machiavelli intimates in the *Discourses*, he urged Soderini to crush these treasonous young Florentine nobles in the manner that Brutus eliminated his insolent sons in ancient Rome. No republic can long endure, and the work of no republican founder or reformer can last, Machiavelli insists, unless he "kills the sons of Brutus" (D III.3).

Such young nobles are well known to students of the history of popular government. They appear in Athens as the young oligarchs who dressed in the Spartan fashion, wielded cudgels to beat their social inferiors in the streets, and who served as the backbone of the two major coups against the democracy. Many of these young Athenian oligarchs were also, perhaps not incidentally, great admirers of Socrates.[73] Brutus's overseeing the executions of his sons and their aristocratic co-conspirators certainly did not prevent the reemergence of this social type in the Roman Republic. Young nobles were, as Machiavelli points out, the major supporters and chief beneficiaries of the Rome's first tyranny, that of Appius Claudius and the Decemvirate (D I.46).[74] Machiavelli, of course, witnessed firsthand on the streets of Florence the insolent behavior of the sword-wielding young aristocrats, the *campagnacci*, who, like their Athenian and Roman predecessors had a propensity to beat commoners in the streets, fancied themselves connoisseurs of Platonic philosophy, and who eventually instigated the coup that re-established the Medici principality.[75]

Yet Strauss is almost completely silent on Machiavelli's recommendation that young elites must be periodically eliminated if popular government is to thrive and republican liberty is to endure; and for the same reasons young *peoples* must be empowered, civically, militarily, and perhaps philosophically. No less than twenty-four references to the young or to youth appear in *Thoughts on Machiavelli*. Yet there is only one passing reference to the sons of Brutus—a reference, moreover, in which Strauss accentuates neither the youth nor the noble status, so important to Machiavelli, of these treasonous young nobles.[76] Strauss does invoke "the sons of Italy," his own term for the young philosophic-political elite, in whom, according to Strauss, Machiavelli placed his hope for a simultaneous revival of ancient Italian virtue and the establishment of his own new modes and orders.[77] It would seem that Strauss wishes to rehabilitate the moral worth of young elites that Machiavelli so often, and so stridently, impugns. Moreover, Strauss apparently wishes to divert the eyes of his own readers and readers of Machiavelli influenced by his work from the extremely harsh treatment of young elites that Machiavelli's democratic republic requires.

Quite tellingly, Strauss focuses on the importance of young nobles who gained reputation and office early in their careers, mentioned in the crucial last chapter of the *Discourses'* first book (D I.60);[78] yet he completely misses the change in meaning that the term "youth" undergoes in that very chapter. Machiavelli intimates that Rome's extensive inclusion of the plebeians in politics was the republic's greatest achievement in the endeavor of enlisting those who are politically "young." In the center of a chapter ostensibly devoted to the young age at which Rome appointed the likes of Scipio and Pompey to magistracies, Machiavelli writes: "It was appropriate that early-on the plebs entertained hopes of attaining the consulship, and that they were given a taste of it without actually gaining it; but when the hope eventually proved insufficient it was appropriate that the expectation be fully realized" (D I.60).

On the contrary, Strauss prefers to emphasize, as representative of Machiavelli's recommended treatment of those who are politically "new" or civically "young," the example of Fabius (D III.49), "who was deservedly called Maximus for having practically disfranchised 'the new people.'"[79] What appears in the *Discourses* to be an endorsement on Machiavelli's part of Fabius's nativist effort to keep newly enfranchised foreigners from corrupting Rome's "civility," Strauss declares to be "praise of an anti-democratic measure."[80] The chapter is largely concerned with forms of corruption—Bacchanalia and mass poisonings of husbands by wives—imported to Rome from the Eastern Mediterranean, so it would seem that Machiavelli here is more concerned with stemming foreign influences than suppressing the plebs. In any case, this does nothing to undermine the following: Strauss sugarcoats Machiavelli's depiction of young nobles—rendering them alluring objects of seduction rather than uncivil targets of periodic execution—and he erases Machiavelli's praise for modes that infuse the polity with a constant source of political youth through empowerment of the plebs.

It could be surmised that the animus expressed by Strauss over the unprecedented positive evaluation and political power that Machiavelli bestows upon the common people may be likened to the envy that Machiavelli attributes to the sons of Brutus and their senatorial fathers (D I.16, D I.40, D I.52): according to Machiavelli, Brutus's sons and their fellow young, aristocratic co-conspirators interpreted Brutus's bestowal of liberty upon the people to be a diminution of their own power and privilege. So too, Strauss seems deeply, even violently, envious of Machiavelli's laudatory words for and his granting of concrete power to the people. So much so, that he then engages in something of a scholarly conspiracy to usurp this prominent position of the people in Machiavelli's writings by rendering it merely apparent, gestural, and exoteric, and by attempting to seize it back from them for the nobles. Strauss, of course, would eventually find no shortage of co-conspirators among Platonically inclined young scholars with a sweet tooth for oligarchy, who largely constitute the Straussian school of Machiavelli studies. Fortunately, these conspirators can be exposed as readily as were the vicious young nobles in post-Tarquin Rome; unfortunately, or so Machiavelli might lament, a commensurately dire punishment cannot be meted out to them.

In short, Strauss dramatically underplays both the dangerous and the salutary prospects that youth offers to republican liberty: often young, insolent nobles must be eliminated for the public good; and, always, young, politically innocent peoples must be empowered, both militarily and civically, for that very same end. Strauss, however, endeavors to make young nobles appear better than they actually do in Machiavelli's writings and to make the common people appear much worse than they actually are in those very same texts.

Conclusion

One who endeavors to strike a mortal blow against a king had better not miss. If this, in fact, had been my intention in undertaking a critique of Strauss's interpretation of Machiavelli, then woe to me. However, my objective in this chapter has been much less ambitious: I have merely sought to open space for challenges to a particularly dominant view of Machiavelli's conception of popular government prevalent in an especially influential literature on the Florentine's political thought. I wish to give those readers who go to the considerable but worthwhile trouble of engaging Strauss's interpretation of Machiavelli sufficient reason to challenge the unassailable aura of infallibility that Strauss himself projects and that he enjoys within the Straussian literature; specifically, the belief that Strauss's logic is wholly incontrovertible and his adducing of evidence always beyond reproach. I have endeavored to show that Strauss, either deliberately or inadvertently, misinterprets the respective roles of the people and elites in Machiavelli's model of democratic republics. To do so, I have taken Strauss on his own terms, reading Machiavelli's texts with careful attention to their surface before speculating over or extrapolating upon whatever true, deeper meaning might obtain on some other level of the text.

In doing so, I have not availed myself of the abundant biographical and historical evidence that a priori would have raised serious questions about Strauss's pronoble, philosenatorial reading of Machiavelli's writings: after all, throughout his public career, Machiavelli exhibited intense hostility toward the Florentine *ottimati* who opposed the democratic republic that he served so faithfully. Indeed, Machiavelli staunchly championed Florence's large citizen assembly, the Great Council, and advocated the creation of a large-scale citizen militia in the city that was obstructed to a serious extent by the republic's nobles.[81] Furthermore, even while living under Medici rule, Machiavelli consistently proved to be a champion of popular empowerment despite the risks that this opinion posed for his personal wellbeing; on notable occasions, he advised the ruling family to shift their base of power from the patricians, who helped reinstate them, to the multitude, whom the family, in collusion with the young Florentine nobles, had stripped of political power.[82] Anyone remotely familiar with Machiavelli's political career would find preposterous the suggestion that his advocacy of popular government in the *Discourses* is strictly cover for his lessons concerning better executed aristocratic rule, or exclusively rhetorical-philosophical preparation for the overthrow of the Classical-Biblical tradition.[83]

Still, we must consider: what could possibly account for the imbalanced treatment of the few and the many in Strauss's engagement with Machiavelli? Why would such a brilliant, meticulous, sensitive reader of political-philosophical texts, one who enjoins us not to stray too far or rapidly from the surface of things, go to such great lengths to demonstrate that Machiavelli did not actually mean what he explicitly declares on the surface? Indeed, why would such a perspicacious reader manipulate the surface of a text in ways that make his object of investigation more amenable to a subsequently revealed, if entirely preformulated, esoteric reading? Throughout his remarkable intellectual career, Strauss equivocates over what he takes to be the actual views of early modern philosophers, like Spinoza and Hobbes, on the intellectual capacities of common people. Nevertheless, two prongs of his assessment may be summed up as follows: Spinoza and Hobbes did not actually mean what they said when elevating the judgment of the masses to the level of—or even to a level beyond—that of the supposedly enlightened few. If they did in fact mean what they said in this regard, then, with all due respect to these authors, they were sorely and fatefully mistaken.

To shorten and simplify a rather long and complicated story, a core component of Strauss's fundamental moral outlook, a moral intuition harbored deep within his heart, is the belief that no genuine philosopher could actually favor in any serious way the judgment of peoples over those of elites.[84] Strauss's fundamental moral motivation from the heart—"a powerful prejudice," to use a phrase that Strauss himself invoked in a different context—in favor of the few over the many seems to have decisively impacted his interpretation of Machiavelli's political thought.

For all his criticisms of Machiavelli, there is no question that Strauss stood in awe of the Florentine's mind. Consequently, it is simply beyond Strauss's comprehension that such a mind could think so favorably of the many, especially in comparison with the few. Thus, I do not necessarily attribute Strauss's misinterpretations of Machiavelli to any duplicity on Strauss's part, but rather to sheer incredulity over what actually obtains at the core of the Florentine's thought. As a result of Strauss's fundamental moral commitments, Strauss casts Machiavelli, in a somewhat anachronistic and revisionist manner, as a thinker who communicates criticisms of democracy to an audience already living in an age of democratic ascendance and not as one who is enduring, as Machiavelli was, an age of democratic-republican decline. Yet, it does Machiavelli a great disservice, and it subjects his writings to a great deal of violence, to refashion him as a Tocqueville, or a Mill—or a Strauss!—warning contemporary elites about the purported excesses of popular government.

On the contrary, Machiavelli attempts to induce an aristocratic audience into accepting and reinvigorating democratic republics as practicable political models. If such elites are not amenable to this advice, then Machiavelli instructs the peoples and the founders and reformers of democratic republics the proper way of dealing with such intransigent elites, especially young, insolent ones. Most succinctly, the fundamental difference between Strauss and Machiavelli resides in the fact that Machiavelli enjoins his young, elite audience to become traitors to the aristocracies of republics, not to become the *grandi*'s philosophical or political partisans.

6

The Cambridge School's
"Guicciardinian Moments" Revisited

I NOW ENGAGE the most influential contemporary approach to the study of classical and early-modern republicanism and Niccolò Machiavelli's supposed place within that tradition—the Cambridge School of intellectual history, most prominently represented by J.G.A. Pocock and Quentin Skinner.[1] I argue that these world-renowned intellectual historians obscure important aspects of both republican and Machiavellian political thought; specifically, they largely ignore the fact that ancient and modern republicanisms secure the privileged position of elites more than they facilitate political participation by citizens.[2] They also underplay the fact that Machiavelli's political prescriptions more substantively empower common people and more actively facilitate popular contestation of elites than did most authors and regimes that typify republicanism.[3] Cambridge scholars obscure the fact that republicanism, both early modern and modern, owes more to Machiavelli's young, aristocratic interlocutor, Francesco Guicciardini, than to Machiavelli himself.[4]

Despite their ostensibly historicist or contextualist orientation,[5] Cambridge-associated scholars of republican political thought, such as Pocock and especially Skinner, often attempt to use insights derived from their historical research in ways intended to inform, enhance, and broaden contemporary political theory and practice. They, in many ways quite admirably, show us what contemporary

liberal democracy, whatever commonalties it shares with republicanism, lacks in contrast with the latter tradition: for example, the expression of nonxenophobic patriotism, attention to the common
good, emphasis on duties as opposed to rights, and commitment to
broader conceptions of liberty.[6] Nevertheless, in what follows I raise
serious questions concerning such endeavors; I challenge these
scholars, and those influenced by them, to reconsider the meaning
and use of the term "republicanism," and, more importantly, to reflect
further upon their attempts to supplement contemporary democracy
with insights derived from that tradition. After all, republicanism, unless substantially qualified or reconstructed almost beyond recognition, tends to reinforce rather than ameliorate the elitist aspects of
contemporary representative democracy; it justifies, explicitly or by
omission, the free hand that wealthy citizens and public officials
enjoy at the expense of the general populace. I ground this challenge
in the writings of an intellectual figure claimed by Cambridge School
republicans as one of their own: Machiavelli himself.[7]

While we owe Cambridge-associated interpreters of Machiavelli
a tremendous debt of gratitude for helping lay to rest interpretations
that too narrowly portray the great Florentine as simply an immoral-
ist or advisor of tyrants, I suggest that their inattention to the inherent oligarchic bias of traditional republicanism and their obfuscation
of Machiavelli's steadfast anti-elitism renders their attempts to improve the contemporary theory and practice of popular government—and, moreover, to enhance our understanding of Machiavelli's political thought—substantively and deleteriously wanting.

Pocock and the Guicciardinian Republican Model

John Pocock, while less prescriptively inclined than Quentin Skinner, nevertheless establishes the framework for interpreting Machiavelli's relationship to republicanism that, in several important respects, many other scholars follow. This interpretative approach
either posits Machiavelli as the principal exemplar of the republican
tradition or largely assimilates his thought to the mainstream of republicanism conceived in a fairly homogeneous way. I will demonstrate how these interpretive moves distort Machiavelli's political

thought, obscure the elitist biases of the republican tradition, and, ultimately, undermine Cambridge attempts to address contemporary political issues, specifically, the deficiencies of liberalism or representative democracy.

For his part, Pocock attempts to show how modern republicanism emerged out of a new concern with temporal finitude corresponding with certain secularization trends in Renaissance thought; specifically, he argues that republicans promoted the mixed regime that came to characterize "the North Atlantic republican tradition" as a viable if not perfect solution to this problem of temporality. However, Pocock much more heavily emphasizes the *temporal* dimension of his narrative than he does the *institutional* model that supposedly emerged in response to a new conception of temporal finitude; in so doing, he winds up accentuating Machiavelli's role in the history of republican political and institutional thought over, for instance, Guicciardini's, in a peculiar and inappropriate way. In short, Machiavellian political existentialism overwhelms Guicciardinian aristocratic republicanism in Pocock's historical account such that Machiavelli appears more conventionally republican, but modern republicanism appears less overtly elitist than, respectively, they actually are.

Pocock's imposing opus, *The Machiavellian Moment*, argues that late medieval and Renaissance polities and intellectuals, especially in the Florentine context, sought to reconcile classical republican texts with a Christian worldview, as well as with the novel historical circumstances that confronted them; specifically, the threat posed to Italian republics by the emergence of Europe's national monarchies. On the first point, Pocock writes: "Civic humanists posed the problem of a society [where] the political nature of man as described by Aristotle was to receive its fulfillment [within] the framework of a Christian time-scheme which denied the possibility of any secular fulfillment."[8] I term the political theory that Pocock extracts from this context "republican existentialism," a political-philosophical orientation that, in Pocock's words, grappled with "the problem of the republic's existence in time."[9] The theorists expounding this view surmised that polities characterized by *governo misto*, regimes that combined monarchical, aristocratic and democratic elements, were best suited to enduring and flourishing in the face of the vagaries posed by temporal contingency.

From the standpoint of Pocock's political existentialism, Machiavelli, the theorist of *fortuna* and *virtù* par excellence, becomes something like the founder of modern republics and their analysis.[10] However, had Pocock as carefully accentuated the social and institutional dimensions of these mixed regimes, and of the theorists espousing them, as he does questions of political temporality and endurance, he might have more accurately titled the book *The Guicciardinian Moment*. After all, the aristocratically inflected model of the mixed regime espoused by Machiavelli's younger patrician contemporary and sometime interlocutor, Francesco Guicciardini, eventually wins out historically. As I have emphasized previously in this book, electoral and senatorial republican models, such as Guicciardini's or Rousseau's, rather than Machiavelli's assembly-based and tribunician one, serve as the constitutional forerunner of modern representative democracies.

In Pocock's work, the theme of a republic's "temporal finitude," the fact that such polities were "finite and located in space and time," overwhelms the author's recognition of a major source of such finitude, class conflict, and prevents him from frankly acknowledging the institutional form most consistently recommended by republican theorists for dealing with it: a republic that circumscribes effective popular participation as much as possible such that these polities closely approximate the model of an aristocratically dominated *governo stretto*.[11] Certainly, it would be inappropriate to underestimate Machiavelli's radically innovative thoughts on political contingency;[12] but when one looks beyond republican existentialism, modern republics simply appear institutionally and socioeconomically much more Guicciardinian than they do Machiavellian. A major subtext of Pocock's book, never made explicit, is the fact that the more egalitarian and popularly empowering political models proposed by, for instance, Girolamo Savonarola, Donato Giannotti and, especially, Machiavelli, lose out in the long run to Guicciardini's aristocratic republican model.

When read from this perspective, *The Machiavellian Moment* is particularly frustrating because it provides ample evidence for such conclusions even if Pocock neglects to draw them himself. After all, Pocock hardly ignores questions concerning the extent to which elites ought to (or ought not to) enjoy prominence within the institutional arrangements of Renaissance republics. For instance, he recounts beautifully Aristotle's theory of aristocracy that pervaded Florentine intellectual circles, a theory that was in principle egalitarian because such an aristocracy could conceivably encompass the entire citizenry of a polity.[13] Of course, in practice Florentine elites sought to make sure that wealth and pedigree largely defined who counted as worthy elites.[14]

Pocock's own account of how elites, the *ottimati*, were selected and identified in Florence bears this out. Pocock correctly notes how wealthy and well-born Florentines distinguished themselves from crudely oppressive and self-aggrandizing oligarchs. They identified the oligarchs with the *magnati*, the ancient nobility, who in earlier centuries attempted to monopolize rule over Florence and forcibly sought to prevent poorer or lower-born citizens from contributing anything at all to its governance. On the contrary, Pocock shows how the *ottimati*—eventually emerging out of the *popolani* concentrated in the upper, wealthier guilds, and marrying with members of *magnati* families—explicitly enlisted the participation of social subordinates to recognize and validate their status: the "inner circle of influential Florentine families who considered themselves an elite and identified themselves with the few in the Aristotelian scheme [could not] exercise their natural function of leadership, or develop the virtues pertaining to it, unless there [was] a participant non-elite or many for them to lead."[15]

With this in mind, Pocock recounts how the *ottimati*, after the flight of the Medici in 1494, initially tolerated the establishment of a more popularly inclusive republic, a *governo largo*; they were willing to allow the citizens collected in the Great Council to determine, via selection for office and approval of policies proposed by members of prominent families, who among the *ottimati* were the truly "best" individuals within the citizenry. Pocock seems to accept at face value what Machiavelli clearly did not; namely, Guicciardini's distinction of justifiable elite rule from unjust oligarchy. According to Pocock, while Guicciardini's "bias in favor of a political elite is always ex-

plicit . . . it is important to note that . . . there is an equally strong rejection, whether implicit or explicit, of formally closed oligarchy . . .
if the foundation of liberty is popular government, at Florence the
foundation of popular government is the distribution of magistracies
and dignities by the *Consiglio Grande*."[16]

In the 1494–1512 republic, both the *popolo* and the *ottimati* agreed
that civic participation was necessary and just; thus Pocock recounts
how the new regime did not "confine citizenship to an exactly defined (*stretto*) group among the inhabitants, [thereby acknowledg-
ing] that civic participation is good, something that men aim at, that
develops men toward goodness, that is desirable to extend to as many
men as possible."[17] However, the *ottimati*'s view, typified by Guicciardini, of how the people should participate differed qualitatively
from the *popolo*'s estimation of their own prospectively proactive
contributions to the regime. In terms that already foreshadow the
principal elements of modern electoral democracy, Pocock describes
how the young Guicciardini, author of the *"Discorso di Logrogno"*
(c.1512)[18] *conceived* of "popular government":

> It seems fairly clear that Guicciardini's theory as regards both elec-
> tion and legislation rests upon an Aristotelian conception of
> decision-making by the many. Though not themselves capable of
> magistracy, they can recognize this capacity in others; though not
> themselves capable of framing or even debating a law, they are
> competent judges of the draft proposals of others.[19]

Guicciardini recommended that the people should merely select
which members of the *ottimati* serve as magistrates and should simply ratify or reject the laws that the latter initiate, and he thought that
the *ottimati* should exclusively hold office as well as propose and deliberate over the laws that the people either acclaim or vote down.

As Pocock forthrightly acknowledges, when common Florentines
expressed their desire to participate beyond the boundaries considered appropriate by the *ottimati*, the latter attempted to steer the republic in an even more elite-dominated direction. Members of prominent patrician families like the Rucellai, Salviati, and Guicciardini,
among others, hoped to establish a senate that would usurp virtually
all of the political functions which at that time were performed by the

people assembled in the Great Council.[20] When the disempower-
ment of the Great Council proved nonviable, many, especially young,
ottimati participated in the restoration of the Medici.

With respect to Guicciardini's older, less privileged but more experienced interlocutor, Machiavelli, Pocock, much like other Cambridge authors, consistently underplays the secretary's profound
anti-elitism and misrepresents the full character of his popular advocacy. For instance, Pocock recounts how the Guicciardinian attempt
to combine patrician supremacy with certain aspects of *governo largo*
pervaded Machiavelli's intellectual milieu.[21] But he does not consider the extent to which Machiavelli, given his class position and
anti-elitist inclinations—fully acknowledged by Pocock—might
have been trying to rearrange the political balance in this context,
especially since he emphatically assigns the "guardianship of liberty"
to the people in the *Discourses* (D I.5). As I have argued elsewhere,
Machiavelli employs a rhetorical strategy through which young patricians like those to whom he dedicates his *Discourses* are persuaded
into accepting more democratic institutions in domestic politics with
the promise of greater glory to be gained through command of a
popular army in the field. In short, the Florentine induces them to
accept enjoyment of less domination at home such that they might
maximize the benefits of domination abroad.[22]

To be sure, Pocock's recognition that the *Discourses* expounds a
"democratic theory" of sorts relies extensively on the role of the citizen soldier in Machiavelli's thought.[23] But Pocock accentuates only
one side of the political-military bargain, which, I suggest, that
Machiavelli is attempting to strike rhetorically between the *ottimati*
and the *popolo*: Pocock's citizen-soldier is much more soldier than
citizen; he almost exclusively emphasizes Machiavelli's prescriptions
for popular inclusion in war making, not policy-making. In particular,
Pocock seriously underplays Machiavelli's defense of the people's excellent cognitive capacities when exercising political judgment in
Rome's domestic politics—judgment deployed far more substantively and expansively than Guicciardini countenances in his endorsement of the popular election of magistrates and acclamation of
laws.[24] Furthermore, the following seems to confirm the impression
that, to Pocock's mind, modern republics most principally inherit

from the Florentine secretary a tendency to enlist the masses in the conduct of war. He instructs us that Guicciardini's *Dialogue on the Government of Florence* (1524) directly responds to Machiavelli by identifying excellence not with the "armed many" but with the prudent and experienced and few—as if military rather than civic virtue, in Pocock's estimation, is all that Machiavelli's people have to offer a republic.[25]

None of this is to suggest that Pocock sympathizes with or somehow attempts to paper over the elitism of Guicciardini's republicanism. Note, in particular, his trenchant criticisms of Guicciardini's mature writings like the *Dialogue*, which express even less confidence in average citizens than did early ones like the *Discorso* mentioned above:

> Once the distinguishing quality of the leader ceases to be *virtù* and becomes *esperienza*, [Guicciardini's] belief [in some popular participation] becomes less plausible, since *esperienza* is an acquired characteristic which can be evaluated only by those who have acquired some of it themselves; and since a republic is not a customary but a policy-making community, there is little opportunity for the many to acquire experience of what governors do—a form of experience whose expression is not custom but prudence.[26]

In moving from virtue, which the people can independently identify and perhaps even exhibit, to experience, which they cannot unless allowed to participate extensively in politics, Pocock shows how Guicciardini further justifies the minimizing of the people's participation in the politics of a republic. Moreover, Pocock points out that Guicciardini, in his later writings, finally concludes that the selection of magistrates by elections as opposed to lottery will favor the *ottimati* and that he emphatically endorses this method on precisely those grounds.[27]

Yet, even in Pocock's analysis of Guicciardini's later, more conspicuously aristocratic writings, he still accepts Guicciardini's distinction between republican elitism and crass oligarchy: Guicciardini's "elitist model of government is at every point in the analysis a competitive meritocracy," although it assuredly favors rich and prominent citizens.[28] Pocock points out that Guicciardini's definition of liberty provides opportunities for "the elite to develop their *virtù* to the full."[29] Conversely, the people's virtue, for Guicciardini, consists not in actively defending the liberty of the regime against its own elite or against foreign enemies, as it does for Machiavelli, but rather in passively confirming the virtue of the elite, or of acknowledging their greater experience in public matters.

Certainly, even in Machiavelli's understanding, the nobility's act of lording their privilege over the people does not fully satisfy them when it is merely exercised by force; in Hegelian terms, the master desires the recognition, and not just the compliance, of the servant. As Pocock observes, "Meritocracy necessitates a measure of democracy. The *libertà* of the few [entails the necessity of having] their *virtù* acknowledged by the *res publica*; the *libertà* of the many is to ensure that this acknowledgement is truly public and the rule of *virtù* and *onore* a true one."[30] In Guicciardini's model, the few express their need to rule, and the many, in a rather passive and mechanical fashion, make sure that such governance primarily functions to provide good ends for the regime.

Pocock's analysis of Guicciardini's later writings makes especially clear the extent to which Guicciardini's republicanism foreshadows the workings of modern electoral democracy. Because Guicciardini assumes that the people assembled in the Great Council were "incapable of initiating legislation,"[31] he excludes them "from all *deliberazione*, all framing and discussing of proposed legislation. The people retain only the bare power of *approvazione*, of accepting or vetoing the proposals laid before them by smaller deliberative bodies."[32] Presaging Madisonian and Schumpeterian government, "the many" themselves are enlisted only to influence elite behavior and not to provide, directly, any insight drawn from their own interests, intuitions and experiences.[33] Unlike Machiavelli, who insists that the people's own particular desire not to be dominated must be expressed directly in assembly and in a class-qualified way through the tribunes, Guicciardini restricts popular participation to such an extent that the common people provide nothing specifically "plebeian" to government. Guicciardini "stressed [the people's] function of universalizing decision, of ensuring that it was free from corrupting particular interests. The role of the many was less to assert the will of the non-elite than to maximize the impersonality of government."[34]

Ultimately, without recognizing it, Pocock quite succinctly draws a conclusion from Guicciardini's later writings that would define the essence of modern democracy more than any conclusion one could legitimately draw from Machiavelli's writings: namely, that Guicciardini undertakes "the identification of aristocratic with popular government."[35] At a later point in *The Machiavellian Moment*, in the midst of a discussion of eighteenth-century debates over republicanism in England, Pocock invokes Guicciardini in a way that presents him for what he is, the godfather of elitist, electoral, and minimalist democracy: "Guicciardini, the most aristocratically minded of Florentine republican theorists, had made it clear that the few needed the many to save them from corruption, and that when the many accepted the few as their natural leaders they did not cease to display critical judgment or active citizenship."[36]

How does this observation concerning Guicciardini's politics and its legacy interact with the overarching theme of Pocock's narrative, that is, "republican existentialism" or "the politics of time"? Pocock concedes that Florence's aristocratic theorists, particularly Guicciardini, did not initially address the problem of temporality or *fortuna* within the context of the 1494–1512 republic, presided over, informally, by Savonarola and then, formally, by Soderini.[37] This observation casts Pocock's general thesis in a perverse light: the Guicciardinian institutional model that prevails long-term is therefore *not* the one that was formulated in light of the novel conception of historical temporality that serves as Pocock's central problem. Apparently, the Guicciardinian republican model was not the institutional model most conducive to the theory of political contingency at the core of Pocock's book, namely, "the politics of time."[38] According to Pocock, only after intellectually engaging Machiavelli does Guicciardini himself take up a form of republican existentialism.[39] The political result turns out to be less, not more, Machiavellian.

Machiavelli, of course, argued that more popularly inclusive and empowered regimes better withstand the political contingencies of fortune than patrician-dominated ones. Yet Pocock intimates that this intellectual exchange encourages the mature Guicciardini to

become even more exclusively elitist and to prescribe even more narrowly oligarchic constitutional arrangements for republics. Therefore, since Machiavelli's model of popular government (1) did not
prevail historically and (2) did not affect the model that actually
did—except to inspire its architect to render it more elitist—one
might ask again, what is so "Machiavellian" about this "moment"?
The exchange between Guicciardini and Machiavelli, which, in an
intellectual sense, constitutes the book's signature "moment," signifies little more than the following: the occasion when the populist,
democratic republican shows the elitist, aristocratic republican how
to think about temporality—in response to which the elitist does not
alter his theory, except to make it less like the one favored by the
populist theorist of political existentialism.

Pocock concludes the first of his two Guicciardini chapters with
remarks on Machiavelli's subordinate class position in Florence. According to Pocock, Machiavelli's non-aristocratic origins and status
purportedly inspire him to launch an "intellectual revolution," but,
counterintuitively, a revolution at best tangentially related to social
class. In Pocock's account, Machiavelli takes a revolutionary approach primarily to the temporality of mixed regimes and only sec-
ondarily to the institutionalization of the common people in such
regimes.[40] Indeed, at the book's conclusion, Pocock identifies Machiavelli's singular contribution to modern political theory as the formulation of a philosophy of history appropriate for modern political
thought; he largely ignores any of Machiavelli's insights into institutional design and class conflict.[41] This silently affirms the fact that the
"North Atlantic republican tradition," as Pocock describes it, adopted
Guicciardini's, not Machiavelli's, prescriptions on such matters.

Though Pocock fails to recognize it,[42] as I argued in chapter 2, according to Machiavelli, elite-generated corruption is the major factor
contributing to the temporal precariousness of republics. Modern
republicanism, by eschewing Machiavellian constitutionalism,
thereby shuns the most promising way of addressing the predica-
ment of republics as they confront their spatio-temporal finitude.
The problem, made patently clear in Machiavelli's theory and by
modern electoral practice, is that Guicciardini's patronizing and exclusionary reduction of citizenries to mere electorates renders sus-

tained popular criticism and engagement very difficult. This makes republics more, not less, susceptible to the vagaries of temporality as identified by Pocock, for this temporal precariousness is exacerbated by the tendency of elites to corrupt such regimes, especially by accelerating socioeconomic inequality. For elites to remain uncorrupt—in Machiavellian terms, if they are to be prevented from inevitably corrupting a regime—the people must engage them in a more active way than traditional republicanism, recast by Guicciardini (and later Rousseau), permits; that is, the people must substantively vie for political power and socioeconomic resources with such elites. In light of both Pocock's presentation of Guicciardini's republican politics and my own account of Machiavelli's populist politics, modern republicanism is neither typified by the kind of *governo largo* favored by Machiavelli, nor is it really characterized by the kind of political response to temporal finitude favored by Pocock himself.

Ultimately, Pocock is most concerned with Machiavelli's efforts to direct populist energies into the realm of international relations— that is, in war, which, at least initially, helps a republic to better grapple with fortune and to situate itself in time. As a result, Pocock, like other scholars associated with the Cambridge School, as we will see, examines in only the most general terms Machiavelli's domestic descriptions of ferocious populism against the nobility and the institutionally democratic channels that the Florentine secretary endorsed to sustain such expressions. As Machiavelli describes it, on the one hand, such expressions are almost invariably appropriate responses on the people's part to the nobility's unquenchable desire to dominate; and, on the other, such institutions and practices include a plebeian tribunate, popularly judged political trials and the people's participation in legislation as initiators, deliberators, and deciders of and over laws.

I conclude that Pocock's thesis on political existentialism misrepresents the oligarchic inheritance bequeathed to modern representative governments by Florentine republicanism. Moreover, Pocock's idiosyncratic historical reading obscures the aspects of Machiavelli's thought that are actually most at odds with traditional republicanism; it ignores what is most promising about his understanding of an eternal problem plaguing popular governments: the problem of elite encroachment and oppression, whether these are understood as issues of liberty and equality or of the temporality of republics.

Skinner's Machiavelli—With or Against Cicero?

For Quentin Skinner, much more so than for Pocock, Machiavelli's political thought and its place in the republican tradition are directly relevant for contemporary political concerns.[43] And whereas Pocock accentuates the sociomilitary role that the people play in Machiavelli's political thought, Skinner devotes more attention to the domestic role that the people serve as citizens. Indeed, participation is central to both Skinner's interpretation of Machiavelli and to his recommendations for improving the deficiencies of contemporary democratic politics. As Skinner, with estimable boldness, puts it: "the government of a free state should ideally be such as to enable each individual citizen to exercise an equal right of participation in the making of the laws."[44] There is, however, considerable ambiguity and more than a little irony in Skinner's emphasis on participation.

For Pocock, Florentine republicanism was essentially Graeco-Aristotelian in origin; accordingly, he suggests that the civic-military participation of citizens in their regime was necessary for the fulfillment of their natures. Alternately, Skinner traces Florentine republicanism to Roman-Ciceronian sources for which, he suggests, participation is instrumental for the realization and preservation of liberty—specifically, a negative form of liberty through which citizens live free from subordination, both actual and potential. Somewhat counterintuitively, then, despite the essential place of participation within Pocock's Aristotelian framework, and its instrumental importance within Skinner's neo-Roman one, the latter scholar actually discusses participation more fully than Pocock does, especially the important place of popular participation in Machiavelli's writings.

I will argue, however, that because Skinner's interpretive efforts fail to isolate and accentuate Machiavelli's serious departures from the aristocratic norms of the neo-Roman republican tradition,[45] the type of participation that he associates with the Florentine offers very little that is novel or constructive for his efforts to improve upon contemporary democratic theory and practice. By focusing on elections, on the neutralization of class conflict, on social and institutional balances of power, among other themes—Skinner's appropriation of Machiavelli very much reaffirms the aspirations of traditional aristocratic republicanism as well as the status quo of contemporary representative democracy.

Skinner famously speaks of "the remarkable extent to which Machiavelli continued to present his defence of republican values in traditional terms."[46] According to Skinner, there are significant "positive resemblances" between Machiavelli's theory and traditional Italian republicanism, both ancient and medieval.[47] In particular, Skinner insists, Machiavelli's thought is almost fully consonant with Cicero's—except for the Florentine's adamant defense of tumults, of social discord.[48] Skinner thereby rightfully acknowledges the originality of Machiavelli's political thought with respect to tumult, social discord, and class conflict.[49] Cicero's political philosophy, like Aristotle's before and Bruni's after him, aspired to civic tranquility and stability, whereas Skinner correctly notes that Machiavelli attributes beneficial political outcomes to civic "disunion." Yet despite his acknowledgement of Machiavelli's repudiation of Cicero's ideal of the *concordia ordinum*, Skinner insists that "the continuities are much more fundamental than has usually been recognized."[50] These continuities between Cicero and Machiavelli include similar views on the common good, mixed government, public over private interest, civic greatness and like matters.[51]

However, one must ask whether the issue of tumult can be so easily relegated to a minor point of divergence in considerations over Machiavelli's place within the republican tradition. After all, it is Machiavelli's praise of Rome's tumults that leads him to endorse practices that were anathema to republicans like Cicero in the past, Guicciardini in his day and, among many others, Rousseau later on.[52] In particular, as both a consequence of initial tumults and as a subsequent instigator of further discord, the plebeian tribunate features centrally in Machiavelli's politics; when he ordains the people as "guardian of liberty," Machiavelli grants them—not nobles, senators or officeholders—the tasks of deciding directly on legislation and political trials, and not simply, as conventional republicans permit, on the appointment of magistrates.

With his emphasis on republican continuity, Skinner subsumes Machiavelli's preference for social conflict and, consequently, advocacy for popular empowerment—the primary points distinguishing him from the main currents of traditional republicanism—into the conventional theory of mixed government that, in Machiavelli's own estimation, ultimately facilitates elite domination of the people.[53] Skinner seriously underplays the political ramifications of Machiavelli's distinction between the appetites of the elite and those of the people, and he obscures the kind of institutions necessary to facilitate control of the elites by the people. I therefore contend that the interpretive move of casting Machiavelli's preference for tumult something like an ultimately inconsequential departure from traditional republican principles enables Skinner to underemphasize its central role in Machiavelli's politics. As a result, Skinner almost wholly reduces republican practice to electoral politics and virtually ignores the popularly participatory and class contestatory elements of Machiavelli's politics, particularly his emphasis on popular judgment and the plebeian tribunate.

Electoral Politics and the "Negative" Conception of Liberty

On these grounds, then, I suggest that Skinner proceeds in an un-Machiavellian fashion when he reduces the domestic politics of republics almost exclusively to elections. For instance, notwithstanding Skinner's noteworthy differences with Hans Baron on the essential characteristics of Florentine republicanism,[54] Skinner fully endorses Baron's confining of "political engagement" within the boundaries of "elective systems of republican rule."[55] Skinner consistently defines "self-governing republicanism" by way of a simple juxtaposition of "elective" versus "monarchical" forms of government, and when he endorses "elective constitutions," Skinner does so in a rather undifferentiated way.[56]

For instance, Skinner never mentions the guild arrangements of Florentine politics that deliberately eschewed general elections and incorporated class specificity and randomization into magistrate appointment procedures.[57] Quite tellingly, when Skinner recounts Machiavelli's discussion of institutions favorable to liberty that the Romans established after the expulsion of the Tarquins (D I.2), he fixates upon the example of the consuls, magistrates who were appointed through general elections; in this context, Skinner altogether neglects to mention the class specific office with which Machiavelli associates Rome's near perfection and its popular guardianship of liberty: the tribunes of the plebs.[58] In his prescriptive writings, as we will observe below, when Skinner invokes the "virtuous" kind of "public service" necessary, albeit instrumentally necessary, to stave off domination and forestall corruption within republics, this virtuous public service never seems to amount to more than participation in conventional electoral politics.[59]

This exclusive focus on electoral politics problematizes the notion of popular participation that Skinner, supposedly inspired by Machiavelli, wishes to revive in contemporary politics. Skinner often seems trapped between endorsing notions of republicanism that call for directly participatory versus representative practices before he embraces the latter. While explaining English republican views on liberty and servitude, Skinner declares both of the following on the very same page: he first writes that "a state or a nation will be deprived of its liberty if it is merely subject or liable to having its actions determined by the will of anyone other than the *representatives* of the body politic as a whole"; however, he then argues that "such a state will nevertheless be counted as living in slavery if its capacity for action is in any way dependent on the will of anyone other than *the body of its own citizens*."[60] Despite this conceptual slippage between the people's representatives and the people themselves as the appropriate agents of republican political will, Skinner makes it clear that he, like the English republicans he discusses, generally favors the elite-centered view.[61] Further problematizing Skinner's attempt to subsume Machiavelli under his conception of republicanism in this context is the fact that, as Skinner himself makes abundantly clear, the other authors whose theories he appropriates—Marchmont Nedham, James Harrington, John Milton, Henry Neville, and Algernon Sydney—all held far more suspicious views of the common people than did Machiavelli.[62]

Moreover, Skinner's emphasis on the negative quality of neo-Roman liberty—i.e., his claim that republicans sought to avoid arbitrary interference, actual and potential, rather than to realize their essential natures through political participation—contributes to the ambiguous quality and indeterminate place of participation in his account.[63] The overly abstract conceptualization that Skinner undertakes in formulating this negative form of liberty leads him to instrumentalize participation such that he waters down participation in ways that undermine Machiavelli's endorsement of popular empowerment and inhibit Skinner's own aspirations for a republican reform of liberal democracy.

Skinner includes Machiavelli among republican writers who value liberty negatively as a principle that prohibits substantive and not merely formal interference in the lives of citizens. Agreeing with scholars such as Marcia Colish and Elena Guarini,[64] Skinner emphasizes passages in which Machiavelli describes the desire of common people to be left free from arbitrary interference in matters pertaining to their persons and property, as well as to live free of the fear that they might be so interfered with.[65] Furthermore, Skinner insists that, for Machiavelli, public service on the part of citizens is "instrumentally necessary to the avoidance of coercion and servitude"; and he suggests that Machiavelli's writings prefigured those of later republicans such as Harrington on this point.[66]

Such claims contain more than a small element of truth. Unfortunately, the fixation on the abstract "concept" of liberty in Machiavelli that substantiates these claims allows Skinner to underestimate, quite dramatically, the specific means that the Florentine deems necessary for the popular attainment, maintenance, and expansion of this liberty. It also allows him to render excessively sharp the distinction between negative and positive facets of Machiavelli's description of liberty in practice. By abstracting so far away from the details of plebeian-noble conflict in Machiavelli's narrations on ancient Rome, Skinner allows himself to waver in the following way: from, on the one hand, rightfully acknowledging the more dangerous appetite for oppression that Machiavelli attributes to the nobles, to, on the other, offering assessments where Skinner relativizes as equally dangerous and pernicious the respective humors of the people and nobles.[67]

Machiavelli prescribes the following forms of popular participation to be necessary for the preservation and extension of liberty within a republic. Certainly, in accord with Skinner's notion of virtuous public service, Machiavelli recommends that common citizens ought to compete directly for offices with the nobles. Far beyond that, however, the Florentine insists that common citizens must hold class-specific offices, such as the plebeian tribunate, and aggressively wield the considerable authority accompanying such offices against elites; they must issue indictments for and level judgment over political crimes in trials that disproportionately target wealthy and prominent citizens; they must freely deliberate and directly decide over legislation in popular assemblies, and not leave these discussions and decisions, as Skinner and his English republicans would, to the people's "representatives"; and, regarding a topic about which Skinner is especially silent, the common people must equitably share in the republic's wealth, which requires redistributing property from the few to the many.[68]

Only by focusing so narrowly on elections, and by ignoring the more extensive (and intensive) array of participatory practices mentioned above, can Skinner render, in a somewhat exaggerated fashion, Machiavelli's notion of liberty as strictly "negative" in quality. Skinner's conceptual commitment to the negative quality of Machiavellian liberty, which serves his argument concerning its fundamentally instrumental character, renders his description of the participation instrumentally necessary to combat coercion and corruption rather passive; it seems to compel him to overlook or underplay how aggressively proactive Machiavellian participation must be to advance and preserve liberty even as an instrumental good. Machiavelli indeed does not describe participation as a practice through which the people realize their political nature in a comprehensively Aristotelian sense; however, for the Florentine, deliberative, assertive, and decisive action on the part of citizens is necessary if the people, collectively, are to be even partially enabled to satisfy their humor not to be dominated, which—as expressive of a collective humor—is indeed natural, if not in an Aristotelian way.

Note how, in the following passage, Skinner's invocation of the humors serves an exclusively individualist rather than a class-collective notion of liberty, one in which Machiavelli's all-important distinction between the popular appetite for nondomination and the aristocratic desire for domination drops out, and within which virtuous public service is denuded of any class-contestatory quality:

> In a theory such as Machiavelli's, the point of departure is not a vision of *eudaimonia* or real human interests, but simply an account of the 'humours' or dispositions that prompt us to choose and pursue our various ends. Machiavelli has no quarrel with the Hobbesian assumption that the capacity to pursue such ends without obstruction is what the term "liberty properly signifieth". He merely argues that the performance of public services, and the cultivation of the virtues needed for performing them, prove upon examination to be instrumentally necessary to the avoidance of coercion and servitude, and thus to be necessary conditions of assuring any degree of personal liberty in the ordinary Hobbesian sense of the term.[69]

To reconcile Hobbes's and Machiavelli's negative conceptions of liberty, Skinner is compelled to apply the Florentine's notion of liberty exclusively to individuals and not at all to social groups, and to transform Machiavellian class conflict—precisely the kind of "intestine discord" that so horrified the Malmesbury philosopher—into an at-best underspecified and at-worst anodyne virtuous public service that functions as the principle means by which citizens oppose domination.

Again, the people, according to Machiavelli, may not need to participate politically to realize their human natures, but they do need to participate class-contentiously to express their collectively manifested humor and achieve its satisfaction. The Florentine often describes popular participation as, in an important sense, positive— that is, as initiative, constructive and proactive—and as generating specifically beneficial results, that is, the diminution and even overcoming (at least temporarily) of aristocratic domination. Machiavelli makes this quite explicit in his endorsement of direct popular judgment over legislation and political trials. Thus, while Machiavelli certainly emphasizes the people's negative goals such as maintaining security and freely enjoying what they materially and affectively possess, he also emphasizes forms of participation that are more positive than merely participating in electoral politics (which, again, is the only form of virtuous public service that Skinner's prescriptions specify) when he describes the people's pursuit of liberty in practice.

Skinner's conceptual approach to liberty, which posits a sharp distinction between negative and positive forms of liberty, clearly prioritizes the principle of liberty over the means to realize it in a way that Machiavelli never does, thus obscuring the close proximity of principle and practice in Machiavelli's theory of liberty within popular government. This stark separation of idea and praxis in large measure highlights a serious shortcoming inherent to all philosophically, as opposed to politically, inclined approaches to Machiavellian liberty. Machiavelli, of course, practiced the pragmatic-rhetorical art of *politique*, not the strictly rationalist one of *philosophie*; consequently, he would have likely considered fairly absurd a predominantly conceptual approach to liberty, one greatly divorced from the empirically bound possibilities and constraints that confront popular liberty in practice. The attempt to draw from Machiavelli a "concept" of liberty—while largely ignoring, as Skinner tends to do, the myriad examples (Roman, Greek, Florentine, Biblical, etc.) that Machiavelli recounts to convey the extent and limits of liberty's possible realization within republics—is quite suspect. As I have demonstrated throughout this study, Machiavelli's rhetoric requires readers to ponder the relationship between his general precepts and the concrete episodes that he employs to expound them, especially the nearly innumerable episodes of conflict between peoples and elites that are almost entirely absent from Skinner's engagement with Machiavelli's works.

Keeping in mind the distinction between philosophy and practice, it is worth noting how Machiavelli rhetorically exposes the profound philosophical naïveté of Polybius's account of the world-famous "cycle of regimes." Rather than endorse as correct all the permutations of the regime cycle which Polybius predicts that each discreet, non-mixed regimes will undergo (as they degenerate from one to

another simple constitutional form), Machiavelli cuts his recapitula-
tion of Polybius short: he rather abruptly interjects the notion that a
neighboring city will invariably conquer such a continually degenerating regime before the ideally theorized regime cycle can ever become an historical, empirical reality (D I.2).[70] Negative liberty, conceived apart from the positive exercise of liberty in practice, is no
more a reality for Machiavelli than is the "cycle of regimes" favored
by Greek or Roman philosophers. Skinner's largely philosophic orientation obfuscates other aspects of the very "republicanism" that he
promotes: he tends to elevate the aristocratic preferences of republican philosopher-statesmen, such as Cicero, to the status of republicanism itself, while ignoring the aspirations of the insurgent-citizen
tradition of plebeian or guild republicanism, thus conflating writing
and politics, ideology and reality.

I have mentioned before the patrician perspective that one ought
to adopt when reading the *Discourses*: Machiavelli makes the case for
democratic republican institutions to a young aristocratic audience,
typified by the book's dedicatees, who harbor strong prejudices for
oligarchic constitutional arrangements reminiscent of ancient Sparta
or modern Venice.[71] Often, to convince this aristocratic audience to
accept institutions that they distrust, such as the plebeian tribunate,
or practices that they fear, such as popular judgment over law-making
and political trials, Machiavelli provides historical examples where
the immediate outcomes prove favorable to the nobility (e.g., D I.78,
D I.47–48). Because Skinner seeks to assimilate Machiavelli's politics
to Cicero's, he tends to overlook other evidence supplied by Machiavelli suggesting that such institutions and practices will not necessarily serve the *grandi* as well as they do the *popolo*. Put simply, Skinner,
like Colish and Guarini, never seriously considers whether Machiavelli ultimately pursues the following rhetorical strategy throughout
the *Discourses*: once members of his aristocratically biased audience
agree to the implementation of popularly empowering institutions,
the outcomes this generates may differ sharply from the examples
that Machiavelli supplies to persuade the *grandi* of the purported
harmlessness of such institutions, or even their apparent usefulness
to the nobles.

Mixed Government and the Humors Relativized

Returning to the issue of tumult, which, Skinner concedes, separates Machiavelli from the republican mainstream: Skinner nevertheless manages to interpret such discord in a way that surreptitiously brings Machiavelli back into line with traditional republicanism. Skinner presents Machiavelli's notion of tumult in terms of an "equilibrium" that balances the supposedly equally dangerous motivations of the nobility and of the people.[72] Skinner often moves from frank recognition of the two different social types that Machiavelli identifies, *popolo* and *grandi*, to a discussion of only one politically relevant type of human beings: selfish individuals who, under proper political arrangements, might become virtuous citizens.[73] Skinner extrapolates a political theory of liberty on the basis of a social type that is characterized by the acquisitive and oppressive qualities that Machiavelli attributes to either the nobles exclusively in the *Discourses*, or mankind generally in *The Prince*; but that Machiavelli himself seldom or never attributes to "the people" as a class.[74] In short, Skinner often transforms Machiavelli's class-based political sociology into a sociologically agnostic one focused on abstract human beings cum citizens.

In the first place, this mode of interpretation equates noble and popular motivations in a manner that Machiavelli explicitly rejects (cf., D I.5, D I.46), and, secondly, it renders closed and docile the open-ended, dynamic, even "wild" quality of social discord described by Machiavelli in the *Discourses* (D I.4). Machiavelli is able to praise conflict in such a radical manner precisely because he separates and privileges the motivations of the Roman plebs over those of the nobility: that is, the *onestà* of the *popolo* over the *insolenzia* of the *grandi*. Machiavelli confidently recommends civic contention because at least one party to the conflict, the people, as the "guardians of liberty," has the honest, decent, even honorable aim of wishing to avoid domination (P 9; D I.5). Had Machiavelli formulated his political sociology in the manner that Skinner suggests—that is, had he argued that the people are essentially just as ambitious and avaricious as the nobles—then the overall result would be the kind of amoral, intransigent, corruption-inducing factional conflict that Machiavelli criticizes elsewhere (e.g., D I.7).[75]

As we observed in both chapters 2 and 3 of this work, throughout the *Discourses* Machiavelli considers expressions of popular "ambition" in Rome to be legitimate responses to the far more excessive and dangerous insolence of the nobles. Skinner too readily likens the purported excesses of the people to those that, in Machiavelli's estimation, are actually attributable to the nobility. In his interpretation of the *Discourses*, Skinner disproportionately and inappropriately equates Machiavelli's evaluations of noble and popular motivations and actions. It would not be until later works, like the *Florentine Histories* and "Discursus on Florentine Affairs," that Machiavelli seems to—and, as I demonstrated in chapter 3, *only* seems to—equate the ambitions of the people and the nobles as casually as Skinner mistakenly insists that the Florentine does in the *Discourses*.[76] Moreover, when Skinner employs the term and concept of equilibrium, he situates himself much more closely to the classical, Ciceronian, and Polybian view of a harmonious relationship among the parts of a mixed regime than to Machiavelli's radicalization of that view which empowers the popular part over and against the aristocratic part.[77] Machiavelli is indeed an advocate of mixed constitutions—a point repeated by Cambridge scholars so often and in such a way as to render it dogma. However, he mixes such regimes in a democratic way, and in neither an aristocratic way nor even in a manner that is equitable to both classes.[78]

Intellectual spokesmen for traditional republicanism generally recommended that the mixing of institutions within mixed regimes favor the nobility; in such schemes members of wealthy and prominent families, usually gathered in senates, almost inevitably wound up with agenda-setting, policy-forming and law-enforcing capacities not available to common citizens. Recall how, on the contrary, Machiavelli lauds efforts by the plebs to gain parity with the nobility, and how Machiavelli's politics transcends a traditional balancing among institutions so as to enable actual rule by the people themselves and to facilitate their containment of Roman elites (e.g., D I.4–7, D I.44, D I.57–58). Also at odds with the traditional republican notion of the people's place in a sociopolitical mixture, as we observed in chapter 2, Machiavelli approves of plebeian attempts to share in the honors and wealth of the nobility (D I.37).

Again, Skinner analyzes Roman constitutional politics from a highly abstract, Polybian perspective rather than by delving into the gritty and roughneck social conflict that Machiavelli recounts once he leaves Polybius's account behind very early in the *Discourses* (D I.2). Skinner does not look too far beyond Machiavelli's summary description of Rome's constitutional arrangement of consuls, senate and—although Skinner affords them rather scant attention—the tribunes at the outset of the *Discourses*; moreover, he largely ignores Machiavelli's subsequent detailed accounts of the way the nobles and plebeians interacted adversarially within and without these institutions in practice (descriptions that often depart dramatically from the accounts of historians of Rome like Livy and Polybius).[79] Even though Skinner acknowledges Machiavelli's praise for the conflict in which Rome's social classes fiercely engaged, because he focuses on the aspects of Machiavelli's account that conform with and are faithful to classical sources rather than those that repudiate and diverge from them, he misses the fully innovative and vitally energetic quality of Machiavelli's conception of sociopolitical contentiousness.[80]

For Machiavelli, noble-popular conflict is not exclusively confined to the Polybianly described formal constitutional structures that serve as Skinner's primary focus. The discords and tumults are far more socially messy and institutionally broad than that. Machiavelli describes how discord plays itself out on the streets of Rome as well as within institutional *fora* and through practices that Skinner largely ignores: the *concilium* of the plebs, *contiones*, public accusations, political trials, attempts by the people to share in the spoils and offices held by the nobility, and so forth. Skinner mentions public accusations as institutional devices that minimize slander and hence inhibit the proliferation of factional strife in republics,[81] but he downplays the extent to which Machiavelli presents them as means by which common citizens chastise, expose, or punish prominent ones (D I.7). Hence, Skinner largely neutralizes the kind of conflict that Machiavelli prefers, conflict often characterized by active, insubordinate, and impudent anti-elitist behavior on the part of the people.

Especially indicative of Skinner's tendency to sterilize Machiavellian politics is his description of the passage of law in Rome. Skinner posits Machiavelli's reconstruction of the legislative process in Rome as follows: a law passes when both of two separate chambers within a "bicameral" institutional structure, senate and assembly, each controlled by a different social class, approves it.[82] This depiction is highly misleading. Machiavelli ascribes to the Roman people, collected in assembly, full legislative sovereignty: the popular assemblies make the laws. To be sure, the senate, as a whole or through the entreaties of individual senators, may initiate or argue for or against a particular law, but the assembled people itself (perhaps, in some cases, excluding the nobility) decides what constitutes law. Moreover, the tribunes, through their veto authority, function such that neither the senate nor the consuls can, unilaterally or in collusion, usurp the people's legislative authority. Clearly, Skinner reads post-eighteenth-century bicameralism into Machiavelli's rendering of the Roman legislative process, a move that makes the republican tradition a less than fertile resource for the improvement of contemporary political theory and practice that Skinner desires. If the republican tradition merely offers institutional options, such as electoral procedures or bicameral legislatures, i.e., options that are virtually identical to those characterizing many contemporary representative governments, then it would seem a fairly feeble resource in endeavors aimed at substantively improving the latter.

Republican Prescriptions for Reforming Liberal Democracy

With that in mind, I will now undertake a closer examination of Skinner's more prescriptive work,[83] in which he draws upon Machiavelli and republicanism to trace the rise and decline of the "neo-roman" notion of liberty in the history of Western political thought.[84] Over time, Skinner begins to employ the term "neo-Roman" rather than "republican" to describe his preferred notion of liberty, in part because the former may be realizable under a monarchy, while the latter, by definition, cannot.[85] As even Machiavelli conceded, the Romans enjoyed certain liberties under particular kings and emperors, and, as Skinner notes, English republicans often made a constitutional place for monarchs alongside institutions belonging to the aristocracy and the bourgeoisie.[86] Again, according to Skinner, neo-Roman liberty, which he explicitly associates with Machiavelli,[87] obtains when either regimes or individuals live free from both actual intervention by another regime or persons and from potential interference, whether or not it actually occurs. In Skinner's account, classical liberalism only defines liberty as the absence of actual interference, and so it ignores the forms of dependence or subordination that living with the *threat* of arbitrary intervention entails for individuals and polities.[88]

Skinner insists that the principle of neo-Roman liberty, as deployed by Machiavelli, applied both to regimes and to individual citizens.[89] But in his account, republican literati almost always focus on the regimes; that is, circumstances in which subject regimes and specific populations are oppressed by, respectively, imperial or absolutist rulers, as well as in circumstances where masters dominate slaves. These categories and examples do not encompass, at least not explicitly, the kinds of infringements on liberty associated with economic inequality and related forms of social subordination. This myopia with respect to broader forms of domination is partly due, perhaps, to the fact that many of the republicans that Skinner cites, especially the English ones, were most concerned with abuses of power on the part of tyrannical rulers and absolute monarchs, whose oppressed subjects they often likened to slaves.[90] But I would venture to suggest that the limited applicability of republican or neo-Roman liberty, in this sense, is due as much to the substance of Skinner's own analysis as to his reliance on these particular historical sources. Skinner's conception of neo-Roman liberty is noticeably weak on social domination for arguably the very same reason that he underestimates, notwithstanding his claims to the contrary, the place of class conflict in Machiavelli's political thought.

In the *Discourses* and the *Florentine Histories*, as we observed in chapters 2 and 3, Machiavelli was concerned with the domination of common people by citizens of great wealth and status, not just by tyrants. Consequently, he theorized remedies to forms of subordination that transcend the examples of enslavement or servitude that preoccupy both Skinner and his other sources.[91] Oligarchic domination of the people, often exercised through debt bondage, withholding of foodstuffs, and monopolizing of public lands, is not identical to that of master over slave, imperial power over subject city, or tyrant over oppressed people—even if Machiavelli sometimes describes it with the same moral disapprobation that he expresses regarding these other forms of oppression. Skinner's use of Machiavelli to define infringements on liberty exclusively in terms of overweening monarchical rule, arbitrary sway over subject cities, and explicit forms of slavery seriously distorts Machiavelli's actual theory of liberty and diminishes the potential efficacy of Skinner's attempt to revive neo-Roman liberty in contemporary political circumstances.

Skinner's neo-Roman conception could be reconstructed and directed against illegitimate social hierarchies that either structurally or directly interfere with people's liberty today.[92] However, Skinner himself does not theorize neo-Roman liberty in such a way except in the context of an ambiguous gesture against Isaiah Berlin at the very conclusion of *Liberty Before Liberalism*.[93] Machiavelli would certainly have applied such a neo-Roman notion of liberty against the aristocratic republicans on whom Skinner relies, theorists such as Milton, Sidney and Neville who would have tolerated or justified arbitrary interference by a republic's best citizens over common ones—writers whose antipopulist leanings Skinner himself makes explicit.[94]

In this light, consider Skinner's exhortation for a revival of republican principles that might transform contemporary political practice and reinvigorate modern citizenries. Skinner audaciously exclaims:

[We] need to have enough prudence and other civic qualities to play *an active and effective role in public life*. To allow the political decisions of a body politic to be determined by anyone other than *the entire membership of the body itself* is, as in the case of a natural body, to run the gratuitous risk that the behavior of the body in question will be directed to the attainment not of its own ends, but merely the ends of *those who have managed to gain control of it*. It follows that, in order to avoid such servitude, and hence to ensure our own individual liberty, we must all cultivate the political virtues and devote ourselves wholeheartedly to a life of public service.[95]

If the elites (whether social, political or both, Skinner is not clear) who have gained control of the polity are not to usurp the will of the entire body politic—and thereby threaten the individuals who constitute it with a denial of their liberty and consequently with a state of servitude—then, Skinner insists, virtuous, active, and efficacious citizen participation is necessary. However, by merging Machiavelli's political thought with the republican tradition that the Florentine so severely criticized—on grounds not dissimilar to those elucidated by Skinner in the quote above—Skinner eliminates the very means that make possible the attainment of his admirable goals. In short, as far as the Florentine was concerned, the citizenry as a whole, "the entire membership" of the body politic, cannot be politically empowered and elites cannot be made accountable and responsive without class conflict, tribunician institutions, and direct popular judgment over political matters besides elections.

Conclusion

I conclude by summarizing the ways in which Cambridge scholars tend to misinterpret Machiavelli by artificially emphasizing his conformity with traditional republicanism: Pocock and Skinner underemphasize class conflict in the Florentine's political thought such that they ignore the institutional means through which Machiavelli empowered the people to render elites responsive and hold them to account; they respectively associate popular agency in Machiavelli's thought primarily with military service and elections as opposed to intensive and extensive participation in domestic politics; they inappropriately equate his criticisms of the nobility with those of the people, thereby undermining the prominent role that Machiavelli assigns to the people as "guardians of liberty"; they fixate on Machiavelli's abstract definitions of liberty at the expense both of his specific policy recommendations for how to achieve and maintain it, and his historical examples of how liberty operates in political practice; they inappropriately use Machiavelli to formulate a definition of liberty that is opposed to political oppression such as monarchical and imperial rule, but that is fairly weak with respect to forms of social domination besides slavery; and they remain largely silent on the kind of domestic domination of the people by elites that was fully congruent with republican theory and very often perpetrated in republican practice.

It bears repeating that their determined focus on the abstract concept of liberty and the purportedly passive or reactive political disposition of the general populace in Machiavelli's theory conforms with the elective, acclamatory, and senatorial quality of modern representative, elite-privileging "democratic" arrangements. This focus compels Cambridge authors to largely overlook the active, ferocious, populist defense of popular liberty that is pursued through directly participatory, extraelectoral devices and practices in Machiavelli's "assembly-based," "tribunician," democratic reconstruction of ancient Rome—a social disposition and a set of political institutions with tantalizingly constructive implications for contemporary theory and practice.[96] More generally, misinterpretations of the kind catalogued above yield two results: Machiavelli's criticisms of social domination go largely overlooked, and republicanism is interpreted too easily as a progressively anti-hierarchical political theory. As such, these interpretations are helpful for neither Machiavelli studies nor for democratic theory today.

In a rousing conclusion to the afterword of the reissue of *The Machiavellian Moment*, with a spirit all too wanting in the body of the book, Pocock denounces the oligarchic tendencies of contemporary representative government. Speaking of the "fictitious" form of representation formulated by the likes of James Madison, Pocock remarks:

> Representation was in fact a fiction, and the creation of an entirely fictive, and fictitious, system of government might prove incompatible with the notion that one acted as a citizen or a being naturally political. . . . It may very well be that we have ourselves reached a condition where the knowledge of fictiveness is unsatisfying to the point of being intolerable; in doubting whether the oligarchy of politicians who oblige us to choose between them

represent us in any way worth speaking of, we doubt whether we have selves left to be represented.[97]

If only Pocock had originally oriented his majestic tome to the task of making the Guicciardinian moment, in which the citizens of representative democracies still live, more genuinely Machiavellian! Perhaps then there would be less cause for his own more recent complaint against the woeful state of popular participation and elite accountability in the republics of our day.

Similarly, we have observed Skinner lament the way that decreased popular participation has encouraged elites to encroach upon the liberty of citizens. It is worth quoting him once again:

> If we wish to maximize our own individual liberty, we must cease to put our trust in princes, and instead take charge of the public arena *ourselves*. . . . There are many areas of public life . . . where increased public participation might well serve to improve the accountability of our *soi disant* representatives. . . . [U]nless we place our duties before our rights, we must expect to find our rights themselves undermined.[98]

As I have demonstrated, Skinner himself eschews direct popular control of politics as a solution to this problem; for him, neo-Roman liberty is decidedly negative, not positive, in essence. Given the strictly electoral quality of his republicanism, exactly what kind of "public participation" does Skinner expect will secure individual liberty and ensure elite accountability? In a similar spirit, overly alarmist responses to "populism" and a persistently expressed mistrust of majoritarianism pervade contemporary democratic theory. Prominent scholars may complain about the threats that wealth inequality and elite prerogative pose to popular liberty in contemporary democracies, and yet they too often devote the full thrust of their critiques to demonstrating how populist movements and popular majorities actually pose a more dangerous threat to liberty than do elites.[99]

Since Pocock and Skinner dramatically underspecify popular participation in Machiavelli's political thought and democratic politics generally, Cambridge accounts bestow on us the vague equation of

popular participation with consent, acclamation, and magistrate selection that already characterized aristocratically enabling forms of
republicanism from Aristotle, Cicero, and Bruni to Guicciardini,
Rousseau, and Madison. Participation on the terms granted by the
republican proponents of *governo stretto*, ancient and modern, subordinates popular participation to elite rule and hence brings us back
to the unsatisfactory square one from which Pocock and Skinner
launch their complaints on behalf of a more robust notion of liberty.
Without the popularly empowered and elite contestatory politics
and institutions of what I have previously called Machiavellian democracy, republicanism facilitates the very corruption of citizenries
and the unfettered behavior of elites that so displease these scholars
associated with the Cambridge School.

Machiavelli rejects the institutional arrangements prescribed by
the other historians and philosophers that Skinner and Pocock associate with republicanism; Machiavelli reminds us that, historically,
the vast majority of citizens within republics deemed as insufficient
merely electoral and senatorial institutions, recognizing them as ve-
hicles of their own domination by socioeconomic and political elites.
To various degrees, Cambridge scholars abandon important characteristics and functions of the Roman institutions—plebeian tribunes,
fully inclusive assemblies, and popularly judged political trials—
through which the people counteracted the privilege of wealthy and
prominent citizens. On the contrary, Machiavelli's reconstruction of
the Roman Republic suggests that if we are to find some semblance
of objectivity and love for the common good in real-world republics,
it will most certainly not reside among a collection of the enlightened
few advocated by the philosophers—not among Plato's philosopher
kings, Cicero's senatorial best men, or Guicciardini's elected magistrates. It will, rather, be found in the body of citizens, institutionally
empowered to deliberate and decide for themselves what constitutes
liberty.

Scandalous Writings, Dubious Readings, and the Virtues of Popular Empowerment

ALLOW ME TO CONCLUDE by summarizing the arguments concerning Machiavelli's political thought set forth in this book. The chapters comprising Part I analyzed a specific theme within each of Machiavelli's three major political works and elucidated how these respective themes exemplify the effectual truth of popular empowerment within Machiavelli's political thought. Chapter 1 traced Biblical resonances within Machiavelli's account of Cesare Borgia in *The Prince*. The Florentine devotes more space to Borgia—or, as both Machiavelli and "the vulgar" prefer to call him, "Duke Valentino"— than to any other figure in the book. I argued that Machiavelli's extensive use of Biblical allegories throughout his painstaking recounting of Borgia's career imparts the following lessons: even within a principality, Machiavelli believed that the common people must serve as the ultimate arbiters of political reality; and, despite sometimes suggesting that princely virtue entails unconstrained autonomy, Machiavelli actually shows through the example of a quasi-Christological Valentino that a prudent prince must foster relations of mutual dependence between himself and his subjects— a relationship consecrated by shedding the blood of mutual adversaries. The chapter therefore problematizes the idea that Machiavelli's goal was to thoroughly de-theologize politics; in fact, my reading suggests that, for the Florentine, the founding of all polities must be sanctified in quasi-religious terms to insure that the people's "spirit" is receptive to the benefits of "good government."

The chapter demonstrated that Machiavelli's intentions are not necessarily so anti-theological, or even so anti-Christian, as interpreters often present the Florentine's views on religion to be. Most fundamentally, perhaps, my interpretation prompts readers to reimagine what, on Machiavelli's view, a genuinely Christian founder of a polity might look like, and what such a founder's relationship with the people—a relationship comprised of both fear and love, but absent of hatred—ought to be. Borgia's greatest strength, Machiavelli shows, was the loyalty he elicited from the people of the Romagna, whom he convinced to recognize that they and the duke shared a common enemy in the rapaciously lawless Romagnol nobility eliminated by Borgia. After the spectacularly bloody execution of Borgia's henchman Remirro d'Orco, the people correctly choose—admittedly with a certain degree of cognitive dissonance—to validate the cruel methods through which Borgia bestowed the benefits of orderly government on the people.

Chapter 2 demonstrated Machiavelli's fundamental commitment, expressed in the *Discourses*, to socioeconomic equality within well-ordered republics; moreover, it explored the extent to which economic egalitarianism is fully entwined with Machiavelli's more famous arguments in favor of armed citizenries. I highlighted a certain rhetorical strategy in the *Discourses* through which Machiavelli endorses, despite apparent statements to the contrary, the redistributive agenda of the Brothers Gracchus, Roman tribunes traditionally blamed for initiating the collapse of the Republic. Many of Machiavelli's republican predecessors and contemporaries criticized the Gracchi for attempting to redistribute land from Rome's wealthy nobles to its vastly poorer plebs (and to prevent future aristocratic appropriation of territories conquered by Rome's plebeian soldiers). Machiavelli, for his part, professes sympathy for the tribunes' aspiration—but discreetly suggests that their methods were deeply flawed. The Florentine subtly intimates that other prospective reformers of corrupt republics beset by economic inequality must employ violent means to succeed where the Gracchi had failed. Machiavelli invokes "prudence" in his passages devoted to the Gracchi; following this lead, I accentuated the form of prudential rhetoric that Machiavelli himself employs in such instances to communicate his advocacy for property redistribution and economic equality; moreover, I pointed toward the prudential form of violence he thought necessary if republics were to, in his words, "keep the public rich, and the citizens poor."

I challenged, in chapter 3, the now hegemonic notion that Machiavelli's later political writings, especially the *Florentine Histories*, express his recently developed social and political conservatism: more specifically, the view that the Florentine had become more critical of the common people and more laudatory of nobles within republics, especially Florence. I argued that the literary-rhetorical method that Machiavelli employs in the *Histories* substantially fortifies, rather than in any way undercuts, Machiavelli's previously expressed democratic proclivities in his later, seemingly more conservative, political writings. The evidence affirming Machiavelli's consistent view of social classes across the span of his political writings, I explained, is deeply embedded within the *Histories'* narrative. It only becomes apparent when one compares Machiavelli's accounts of the people and the nobles in the *Histories* with those set forth in *The Prince* and the *Discourses*.

In three crucial instances of social conflict within the *Histories*, I contrasted Machiavelli's overt criticisms of the Florentine people and plebs—which rehearse well-worn traditional aristocratic calumnies concerning their purported immoderation and irrationality—with his depiction of the people and plebs in action, which connotes behavior entirely consistent with Machiavelli's positive assessments of the common people voiced in earlier works. Contextual constraints, I suggested, explain Machiavelli's apparent reversal of opinion concerning the moderate, rational, and just nature of the people and his resort to dramatic, if implicit, contrasts between words and deeds in these episodes. Because Machiavelli was writing the *Histories* at the behest of the Medici, who had just permitted him re-entry into the Florentine political world, and who were surrounded by aristocratic counselors and a hostile Florentine populace, Machiavelli camouflaged the provocative populism still embedded within the heart of the text with a surface veneer of traditional aristocratic prejudice.

The interpreters of Machiavelli whom I discussed in Part II share a proclivity to distort or overlook the radically democratic character of the Florentine's political thought. While Rousseau's elite-friendly emendations of Machiavelli's republicanism have perhaps garnered less attention than those undertaken by other 18th century authors (such as Harrington, Montesquieu or Madison), it is the Genevan's exalted status as the father of modern democratic theory that motivated my critique of his engagement with Machiavelli's political thought. Rousseau's displacement of Machiavelli's class-conscious populism and class-specific institutional prescriptions, to my mind, marked a wrong turn in the history of democratic principles and practice. Modern democracy, I avow, would have been better served historically, and may be constructively reformed in a more progressive manner presently, had it adopted a Machiavellian and not a Rousseauian spirit, and were it to adopt such a spirit today.

After World War II, Rousseau's still controversial view that Machiavelli was a republican became settled opinion in the English-speaking world. Machiavelli was no longer considered merely the nefarious advisor of tyrants. The notion that the Florentine was an advocate of republics, and of the liberty that they uniquely afford, found powerful voices at the University of Chicago and in Cambridge, England. The two distinct forms of republicanism emanating from Chicago and Cambridge that, respectively, Leo Strauss and the Cambridge School attributed to Machiavelli, shared this quality in common: both interpretations cast Machiavelli as an elitist—either staunchly oligarchic or mildly aristocratic—republican.

In chapter 4, I argued that Rousseau, in the Social Contract, reconstructs the constitution of ancient Rome in deliberate and direct opposition to the more democratic and anti-elitist model of the Roman Republic championed by Machiavelli in the Discourses. In spite of Rousseau's fraternal recognition of Machiavelli as a fellow republican, I demonstrate that the Genevan prescribes, in an entirely anti-Machiavellian manner, institutions that obstruct popular efforts at diminishing the excessive power and influence wielded by wealthy citizens and political magistrates. Silently rebuking Machiavelli in the final and longest (and least read) book of the *Social Contract*, Rousseau eschews the establishment of magistracies, like the plebeian tribunate, reserved exclusively for common citizens, and he endorses assemblies where the wealthy are empowered to outvote the poor in law-making and elections. On the basis of sociologically anonymous principles like generality and popular sovereignty, and by confining elite accountability to general elections, the Genevan's neo-Roman institutional proposals—in direct repudiation of the Florentine's prescriptions—aim to pacify the contestation of class hierarchies and inflate elite prerogative within republics—under the cover of more formal, seemingly more genuine, equality.

Chapter 5 engaged the daunting interpretation of our author's political writings ventured in Strauss's *Thoughts on Machiavelli*. The chapter attempted to upend Strauss's highly influential reading of Machiavelli as a covert critic of popular judgment and of democratic republics as desirable political regimes. Through a close reading of Strauss's book, I indicated a number of inconsistencies and flaws in Strauss's interpretations and conclusions: I argued that Strauss—incapable of accepting the veracity of Machiavelli's surface proclamations about the vital role of the people in any well-ordered regime—rushed to rather forced pronouncements over Machiavelli's allegedly hidden reservations concerning popular judgment and rule. Strauss and his many students, perhaps more than any other school today, are famously enamored with the writings of those ancient philosophers and historians—"the writers"—whom Machiavelli criticized for their ochlophobic and antidemocratic biases. Nevertheless, as I showed, Strauss manages with remarkable confidence to make extensive use of Machiavelli in what turns out to be solely Strauss's own conservative critique of democracy. Machiavelli, Strauss claims, did not really mean everything (if anything) that he wrote when he championed the people against traditional writers. On the contrary, Strauss insists that while Machiavelli broke decisively with the aristocratic classical tradition of moral philosophy, he did not in fact break with the elitist classical tradition of political and constitutional

theory. In fact, Strauss insists, the Florentine actually favored extensive, albeit more secretly wielded, rule by elites—even in regimes
considered to be democracies or democratic republics.

I demonstrated how Strauss takes every opportunity to undermine Machiavelli's self-professed endorsement of popular judgment
by cherry-picking instances of poor popular decisions within Machiavelli's texts, while never examining with commensurate verve or
tenacity the more numerous and often more catastrophic examples
of poor judgment exhibited in his writings by groups of nobles. This
myopia, I argued, reveals something profound about Strauss's insistence that Machiavelli destroyed classical, aristocratic moral-
philosophical standards but nevertheless continued to adhere, fundamentally, to classical, elitist political standards. Put simply, it
reveals how desperately Strauss and Straussians cling to the notion
that Machiavelli shares their own sweet tooth for oligarchy. Their textually unsupported and unsupportable position betrays the fact that,
much more than Straussians admit, politics—a deeply antidemocratic form of politics—rather than philosophical probity chiefly
drives the supposedly antiquarian, dispassionate, and nonpartisan
amalgam upon which Strauss confers the venerated appellation "political philosophy."

In chapter 6, I revealed how scholars affiliated with the Cambridge
School, most notably, J.G.A. Pocock and Quentin Skinner, accentuate the common good, electoral politics, mixed government, class
equilibrium, and republican liberty in Machiavelli's writings; and
how, while doing so, they dramatically underestimate the Florentine's
preference for class conflict and underplay his insistence on popular
empowerment and elite accountability. I argued that they obscure
the full extent of Machiavelli's anti-aristocratic critique of the republican tradition, which, they fail to disclose, is predominantly oligarchic in character. Pocock and Skinner both stress Machiavelli's republican commitments but portray them as largely consistent with,
respectively, Greek and Roman republican traditions. Although they
briefly acknowledge how Machiavelli differed from the republican
tradition in his praise of class conflict, they present this element as
merely one exception to an otherwise lengthy list of common convic-
tions among republicans concerning the common good and civic

virtue. On the contrary, I argued that Machiavelli's praise of class conflict, and the unavoidable populist and democratic implications that follow from this, necessarily and fundamentally separate the Florentine's political thought from the aristocratic and senatorial republican tradition.

The prescriptive lessons that Cambridge scholars draw from republicanism for contemporary politics reinforce rather than reform the senatorial, electorally based, and socioeconomically agnostic republican model (originally devised by Machiavelli's aristocratic interlocutor, Francesco Guicciardini, and later refined by Rousseau and Madison) that permits common citizens to acclaim or reject but never determine public policy. Ultimately, Cambridge School hermeneutic endeavors and political interventions have little connection with Machiavelli's tribunician, class-specific model of popular government elaborated in the *Discourses* and in his constitutional reform proposals—a model that relies on extraelectoral accountability measures and embraces direct popular judgment over law-making and political trials.

To stylize matters, Cambridgeans turn Machiavelli into Cicero, a traditional republican who emphasized social concord, one for whom public spiritedness and rule by the best men conforms with the common good. Straussians, on the contrary, turn Machiavelli into a radically Nietzschean republican. Republics, for Strauss's Machiavelli, provide the space within which voraciously ambitious elites, either individually or collectively as members of the nobility, dominate others out of greed for wealth or in pursuit of glory (Strauss is unsure which they prize more highly). The common good is only achieved in such regimes, according to Strauss, to the extent that rapacious elites check each other by disingenuously exposing the tyrannical motivations and behaviors of their similarly motivated rivals to the inherently gullible judgment of the citizenry—until such time as one of them exploits the opportunity to assume control of the polity for himself. In Part II, I exposed the erroneous nature of these two pervasive interpretations of Machiavelli's republicanism, accentuating, on the contrary, the anti-elitist, class-conflictual, popularly empowering form of democratic republicanism that Machiavelli advocates.

On the basis of my engagement with these interpreters, it is fair to wonder whether Machiavelli would have dismissed Strauss, Pocock, Skinner, and even Rousseau, in much the same manner that he disdained "the writers" who comprised the Western tradition of ancient and medieval political thought—all of whom he considered pusillanimous propagandists for the enduring power of wealthy elites. Machiavelli often exposed the powerful forces operating throughout intellectual history that disparaged the political judgment of the people, hence prompting his own defiant, often uproarious, distancing of himself from that tradition. In this sense, my efforts to contest the influential interpretations of Machiavelli offered by Rousseau, the Straussian school, and the Cambridge School—which portray the Florentine either as amenable to elite-dominated republicanism or as an unqualified critic of popular government—were intended to serve as a Machiavellian critique of Machiavelli scholarship itself.

NOTES

Introduction. Vulgarity and Virtuosity: Machiavelli's Elusive "Effectual Truth"

1. Niccolò Machiavelli, *Il Principe* (*De Principatibus*), composed circa 1513 and published in 1532, G. Inglese, ed. (Turin: Einaudi-Gallimard, 1995), hereafter P; Machiavelli, *Discorsi*, composed circa 1513–18 and published in 1531, C. Vivanti, ed. (Turin: Einaudi-Gallimard, 1997), hereafter D; and Machiavelli, *Istorie Fiorentine*, composed circa 1520–25 and published in 1532, Franco Gaeta, ed. (Milan: Feltrinelli, 1962), hereafter FH.

2. See John P. McCormick, *Machiavellian Democracy* (Cambridge: Cambridge University Press, 2011).

3. As the inimitable Hanna Pitkin, whose interpretation of Machiavelli I greatly admire, put it while describing competing engagements with Machiavelli: "Each reading claims foundation in the texts, yet none has ever succeeded in displacing the others." See Hanna Fenichel Pitkin, *Fortune is a Woman: Gender and Politics in the Thought of Niccolò Machiavelli* (Berkeley: University of California Press, 1984), 3.

4. On the full expanse of the harmonious, consensual, concord-centered Latin and Italian humanist-republican tradition, represented by Cicero, that—*pace* Cambridge scholars—Machiavelli strived to overturn, see Gabriele Pedullà, *Machiavelli in Tumult: The Discourses on Livy and the Origins of Conflictual Politics* (Cambridge University Press, forthcoming 2018).

5. Cambridge scholars, perhaps above all others, repeatedly (one might say repetitively) advance the argument that Machiavelli can neither be deemed a democrat, nor can a democratic politics be attributed to him, for the simple fact that he was a staunch adherent of the traditional republican doctrine of mixed government, associated with Aristotle, Polybius, and Cicero. To be sure, Machiavelli recommends that all well-ordered republics establish senates that provide positions of honor to citizens of wealth and status. However, Machiavelli does so on highly unorthodox grounds: firstly, senates are necessary to at least temporarily placate a republic's most ambitious, domineering citizens (not to accommodate its best, most public spirited ones), such that republics might prove less susceptible to oligarchic coups (D I.29);

secondly, senates are necessary so that all the nobles are conveniently gathered in one place when it becomes necessary to kill them at a stroke, in instances where their oppressive behavior has become unbearable to the common people and dangerous to the city (P 8; D I.16). These are decidedly not Ciceronian or Polybian justifications for mixed government. See John P. McCormick, "Subdue the Senate: Machiavelli's 'Way of Freedom' or Path to Tyranny?" *Political Theory* 40, no. 6 (December 2012), 717–738. Cambridge scholars seldom if ever acknowledge that Machiavelli's criticisms of, in particular, Athens for failing to provide an institutional place for its nobles in D I.2 are significantly qualified in D I.29, D I.58, and D II.2.

6. On the entwinement of virtue, political rhetoric and political action in Machiavelli's writings, see Victoria Kahn, *Machiavellian Rhetoric: From the Counter-Reformation to Milton* (Princeton: Princeton University Press, 1994).

7. See, paradigmatically, Victoria Kahn, "*Virtù* and the Example of Agathocles in Machiavelli's *Prince*," *Representations* 13 (Winter 1986), 63–83.

8. Note how Skinner wishes to have it both ways in the following passage concerning Machiavelli's relationship with Ciceronian humanism: "the most *original and creative* aspects of his political vision are best understood as a series of *polemical—*sometimes even *satirical*—reactions against the humanist assumptions he inherited and basically *continued to endorse*." See Quentin Skinner, *Machiavelli: A Very Short Introduction* (Oxford: Oxford University Press, 2001) (preface, emphases added). See also Skinner, *Machiavelli*, 39–40, 61–62. As we will observe, this hermeneutic tendency is endemic to Cambridge approaches to Machiavelli's political thought: such scholars often concede that Machiavelli's theory indeed deviates in discernible ways from the thinking of classical and traditional republicans, such as Aristotle, Polybius, Cicero, and Bruni; but these deviations, according to the adherents of this approach, ultimately portend no significant consequences for the substance of Machiavelli's thought.

9. Leo Strauss, *Thoughts on Machiavelli* (Glencoe, IL: The Free Press, 1958), 127.

10. Strauss's interpretation of Machiavelli has impacted the work of the following important scholars: Ryan Balot, Paul Carrese, Markus Fischer, Steven Forde, Christopher Lynch, Harvey Mansfield, Waller Newell, Roger Masters, Clifford Orwin, William Parson, Paul Rahe, Kim Sorensen, Nathan Tarcov, Michelle Tolman Clarke, John Scott, Vickie Sullivan, and Catherine Zuckert, among others.

11. The impressive list of scholars who have, to varying degrees, been influenced by Pocock's or Skinner's interpretations of Machiavelli's political thought include, among others: David Armitage, Patrick Baker, Richard Bellamy, Gisela Bock, Annabel Brett, Martin Dzelzainis, Andrew Fitzmaurice, Mark Goldie, Mikael Hörnqvist, Karen Kupperman, Eric Nelson, Markku Peltonen, Martin Ruehl, Alan Ryan, Peter Schröder, Peter Stacey, James Tully, Martin van Gelderen, and Maurizio Viroli.

12. Recent admirable and valuable efforts in an apologetic vein are: Peter Stacey, *Roman Monarchy and the Renaissance Prince* (Cambridge: Cambridge University Press, 2007); and Erica Benner, *Machiavelli's Ethics* (Princeton: Princeton University Press, 2009).

13. Regarding Machiavelli's assault on the political dimensions of traditional Florentine humanism, see: Mark Jurdjevic, "The Guicciardinian Moment: The *Discorsi Palleschi*, Humanism, and Aristocratic Republicanism in Sixteenth-Century Florence," in *Humanism and Creativity in the Italian Renaissance: Essays in Honor of Ronald G. Witt*, C. Celenza and K. Gouwens, eds. (Leiden: Brill, 2006), 111–137; Jurdjevic, "Machiavelli's Hybrid Republicanism," *English Historical Review* 122 (December 2007), 1228–1257; Danielle Charette, "Catilinarian Cadences in Machiavelli's *Florentine Histories*: Ciceronian Humanism, Corrupting Consensus and the Demise of Contentious Liberty," *History of Political Thought* (forthcoming 2018); and Pedullà, *Machiavelli in Tumult*. On the political impact of civic humanism, see: Mikael Hörnqvist, "The Two Myths of Civic Humanism"; John Najemy, "Civic Humanism and Florentine Politics"; James Hankins, "Rhetoric, History, and Ideology: The Civic Panegyrics of Leonardo Bruni," all three of which appear in James Hankins, ed., *Renaissance Civic Humanism: Reappraisals and Reflections* (Cambridge: Cambridge University Press, 2000), 105–178; Mark Jurdjevic, "Civic Humanism and the Rise of the Medici," *Renaissance Quarterly* 52, no. 4 (1999), 994–1020; Anthony Grafton, "Humanism and Political Theory," and Nicolai Rubinstein, "Italian Political Thought, 1450–1530," both of which appear in J. H. Burns and M. Goldie, eds., *The Cambridge History of Political Thought, 1450–1700* (Cambridge: Cambridge University Press, 1991), 9–29 and 30–65, respectively.

14. See Machiavelli, "Ai Palleschi" (1512), in Machiavelli, *Opere I*, 87–89. For an English translation, see Machiavelli, "Memorandum to the Newly Restored Medici," in M. Jurdjevic, N. Piano, and J. P. McCormick, eds., *Florentine Political Writings from Petrarch to Machiavelli* (Philadelphia: University of Pennsylvania Press, forthcoming 2019).

15. See Machiavelli, "Discursus Florentinarum Rerum Post Mortem Iunioris Laurentii Medices" (1520) in Machiavelli, *Opere I*, 733–745. For an English translation, see Machiavelli, "Discursus on Florentine Matters after the Death of Lorenzo de' Medici the Younger," in *Florentine Political Writings*.

16. On the republican aspects of *The Prince*, see Mary G. Dietz, "Trapping the Prince: Machiavelli and the Politics of Deception," *American Political Science Review* 80, no. 3 (September 1986), 777–799.

17. A growing and welcome trend in Machiavelli studies accentuates the egalitarian dimensions of the Florentine's political thought: see Filippo Del Lucchese, *The Political Philosophy of Niccolò Machiavelli* (Edinburgh: Edinburgh University Press, 2015); Christopher Holman, *Machiavelli and the Politics of Democratic Innovation*

(Toronto: University of Toronto Press, forthcoming); and Yves Winter, *Machiavelli and the Orders of Violence* (Cambridge: Cambridge University Press, forthcoming).

18. On the civic ramifications of popular arms in Machiavelli's political thought: see Timothy J. Lukes, "Martialing Machiavelli: Reassessing the Military Reflections," *Journal of Politics* 66, no. 4 (November 2004), 1089–1108; Yves Winter, "The Prince and His Art of War: Machiavelli's Military Populism," *Social Research* 81, no. 1 (Spring 2014), 165–191; Nathan Tarcov, "Arms and Politics in Machiavelli's *Prince*," in *Entre Kant et Kosovo: Etudes offertes á Pierre Hassner*, Anne-Marie Le Gloannec and Aleksander Smolar, eds. (Paris: Presses de Sciences Po, 2003), 109–121; Tarcov, "Freedom, Republics, and Peoples in Machiavelli's *Prince*," in *Freedom and the Human Person*, ed. Richard Velkley (Washington, DC: Catholic University of America Press, 2007), 122–142; and Pedullà, *Machiavelli in Tumult*.

19. I substantiate this claim more elaborately in the book-in-progress "The People's Princes: Machiavelli, Leadership and Liberty."

20. See John P. McCormick, "Faulty Foundings and Failed Reformers in Machiavelli's *Florentine Histories*," *American Political Science Review* 111, no. 1 (February 2017), 204–216.

21. See, among historians, Gene Brucker, "The Ciompi Revolt," in Nicolai Rubinstein, ed., *Florentine Studies: Politics and Society in Renaissance Florence* (London: Faber and Faber, 1968), 314–356; and John Najemy, *Corporatism and Consensus in Florentine Electoral Politics, 1280–1400* (Chapel Hill: University of North Carolina Press, 1982). The significance of the Ciompi Revolt and Machiavelli's analysis of it has been brought into the field of political theory with much spirit and sophistication by Yves Winter: see "Plebeian Politics: Machiavelli and the Ciompi Uprising," *Political Theory* 40, no. 6 (November 2012), 736–766; and *Machiavelli and the Orders of Violence*. I treat Machiavelli's engagement with the revolt in chapter 3 of this book and in McCormick, "Faulty Foundings and Failed Reformers."

22. On the long arc in Machiavelli's narrative of Florentine history from the relative equality of the guild republic that vanquished the ancient nobility to the rampant inequality that facilitated the rise the Medici principate, see Amanda Moure Maher, "The Corrupt Republic: The Contemporary Implications of Machiavelli's Critique of Wealth Inequality and Social Dependence" (PhD Dissertation, University of Chicago, Political Science Department, 2017).

23. See Christopher Lynch, "War and Foreign Affairs in Machiavelli's *Florentine Histories*," *Review of Politics* 74, no. 1 (Winter 2012), 1–26.

24. See John P. McCormick, "Faulty Foundings and Failed Reformers."

25. See Bernard Manin, *The Principles of Representative Government* (Cambridge: Cambridge University Press, 1997); and McCormick, *Machiavellian Democracy*, chapter 7.

26. The term originates with Giovanni Botero, *The Reason of State* [1589], Robert

Bireley, ed. (Cambridge: Cambridge University Press, 2017). On Machiavelli's supposed place in this tradition, see Friedrich Meinecke, *Machiavellism: The Doctrine of Raison d'État and Its Place in Modern History*, trans. Douglas Scott (New York: Praeger, 1962).

27. See Barrington Moore, *Social Origins of Dictatorship and Democracy: Lord and Peasant in the Making of the Modern World* (Boston: Beacon Press, 1966); Perry Anderson, *Lineages of the Absolutist State* (London: Verso, 1979); and Charles Tilly, *Coercion, Capital and European States, A.D. 990–1992* (Oxford: Blackwell, 1992).

Chapter 1. The Passion of Duke Valentino: Cesare
Borgia, Biblical Allegory, and *The Prince*

1. See Maurizio Viroli, *Machiavelli's God*, trans. Antony Shugaar (Princeton University Press, 2010); although the willful (even cynical) quality of the author's naïve posture largely undermines the credibility of his argument. For more sober recent engagements with Machiavelli's views on religion, see Marco Geuna, "Ruolo dei conflitti e ruolo della religione nella riflessione di Machiavelli sulla storia di Roma," in R. Caporali, V. Morfino, and S. Visentin, eds., *Machiavelli: Tempo e Conflitto* (Milan: Mimesis, 2012), 107–140; and Alison McQueen, *Political Realism in Apocalyptic Times* (Cambridge: Cambridge University Press, 2017).

2. See William B. Parson, *Machiavelli's Gospel: The Critique of Christianity in The Prince* (Rochester: University of Rochester Press, 2016), which forcefully complements Vickie B. Sullivan's similarly motivated study of Machiavelli's *Discourses*; see Sullivan, *Machiavelli's Three Romes: Religion, Human Liberty, and Politics Reformed* (DeKalb: Northern Illinois University Press, 1996).

3. Niccolò Machiavelli, *Il Principe (De Principatibus)* [1513/1532], ed. G. Inglese (Turin: Einaudi-Gallimard, 1995), hereafter P. See also Machiavelli, *Discorsi* [1513–17/1531], C. Vivanti, ed. (Turin: Einaudi-Gallimard, 1997), hereafter D.

4. Jean-Jacques Rousseau, "Of the Social Contract, Or Principles of Political Right," in Victor Gourevitch, trans. and ed., *Rousseau: The Social Contract and Other Later Political Writings* (Cambridge: Cambridge University Press, 1997), 39–152, here 95n.

5. See Jacob Burckhardt, *The Civilization of the Renaissance in Italy*, trans. S.G.C. Middlemore (New York: Macmillan, 1904), 113–117. John T. Scott and Vickie B. Sullivan appropriate Burckhardt's thesis for Straussian purposes in "Patricide and the Plot of the *Prince*: Cesare Borgia and Machiavelli's Italy," *American Political Science Review* 88, no. 4 (December 1994), 887–900.

6. Recent interpreters who adhere to the notion that Machiavelli's depiction of Borgia is mostly satiric or ironic include: John M. Najemy, "Machiavelli and Cesare Borgia: A Reconsideration of Chapter 7 of *The Prince*," *Review of Politics* 75, no. 4 (Fall

220 NOTES TO PAGES 22–31

2013), 539–556; and Erica Benner, *Machiavelli's Prince: A New Reading* (Oxford: Oxford University Press, 2014), 94–111.

7. Note that the Florentine patrician Francesco Guicciardini refers to him as Duke Valentino for a more conventional reason: "Cesare Borgia [was] called Valentino because he possessed a state in France by that name." See Guicciardini, *History of Florence*, trans. M. Domandi (New York: Harper, 1970), 177.

8. Machiavelli, "Draft of a Letter to Giovan Battista Soderini (September 13–27, 1506)," in William J. Connell, ed., Machiavelli, *The Prince* (Boston: Bedford, 2005), 127.

9. Dante Alighieri, *Monarchy*, trans. Prue Shaw (Cambridge: Cambridge University Press, 1996), 52.

10. Cf. Matthew 17:1–9, Mark 9:2–8, Luke 9:28–36.

11. Machiavelli, "A Description of the Method Used By Duke Valentino in Killing Vitellozzo Vitelli, Oliverotto da Fermo, and Others," in A. Gilbert, *Machiavelli: The Chief Works and Others, Vol. I* (Durham: Duke University Press, 1965), 163–169.

12. Cf. Acts 9:1–19a, 22:6–11.

13. Cf. 1 Corinthians 11:23–26, Mark 14:20–21, Matthew 26:23–26:25, John 13:26–13:27.

14. Cf. Mark 1:14–15, 1 Corinthians 15:1–9, Justin Martyr 1 Apology.

15. See Max Weber, "The Profession and Vocation of Politics," composed circa 1917, in P. Lassman and R. Speirs, eds., *Max Weber's Political Writings* (Cambridge: Cambridge University Press, 1994).

16. The following article thoughtfully analyzes the relationship between cruelty well used and Christianity in *The Prince*: Clifford Orwin, "Machiavelli's Unchristian Charity," *American Political Science Review* 72, no. 4 (December 1978), 1217–1228. However, Orwin's title could easily be refashioned "Machiavelli's Unconventionally Christian Charity."

17. Cf. 1 Cor. 15: 3–4, 1 Peter 3:18, John 3:16, Hebrews 10:12–14.

18. Sebastian de Grazia offers an alternative, more mundane explanation: see *Machiavelli in Hell* (Princeton: Princeton University Press, 1990), 84, 327.

19. See Luke 2:11.

20. See Genesis 17:23–27. Gentiles and observant Jews might understand the act of circumcision differently: the former could conceivably understand the act of cutting the foreskin to entail a severing of the member as a whole, while the former are likely to distinguish the two such that the cutting of the foreskin leaves the member intact, that is, not severed. On the practice in medieval Europe, see Elisheva Baumgarten, "Circumcision and Baptism: The Development of a Jewish Ritual in Christian Europe," in E. W. Mark, ed., *The Covenant of Circumcision: New Perspectives on an Ancient Jewish Rite* (Waltham, MA: Brandeis University Press, 2003), 114–127.

21. See Guicciardini, *History of Florence*, respectively, 197, 126, and 193–194.

22. See John P. McCormick, "Machiavelli, Weber and Cesare Borgia: The Science of Politics and Exemplary Statebuilding," *Storia e Politica* I, no. 1 (2009), 7–34. However, as chapters 2 and 3 of the present study make plain, Machiavelli's conception of popular legitimacy does not stop there.

23. See John P. McCormick, *Machiavellian Democracy* (Cambridge: Cambridge University Press, 2011).

24. See Dante, *Monarchy*, 58–59.

25. See Machiavelli, *Istorie Fiorentine* [1520–25/1532], Franco Gaeta, ed. (Milan: Feltrinelli, 1962), especially Book I.

26. See Regis Martin, *The Last Things: Death, Judgment, Hell, Heaven* (Charlotte: Saint Benedict Press, 2009).

27. Cf. John 18:36.

28. Cf. Matthew 5:38–42, Luke 6:27–31.

29. See, again, Burckhardt, *The Civilization of the Renaissance in Italy*, 113–117.

30. Cf. Mark 16:1–8, Matthew 28:1–10, Luke 24:1–8, John 20:1.

31. See Isaiah Berlin, "The Question of Machiavelli," *The New York Review of Books* 17, no. 4 (November 4, 1971).

32. See 1 John 2:18, 1 John 2:22, 1 John 4:3, 2 John 1:7.

33. Machiavelli, "First Decennale," in A. Gilbert, ed., *Machiavelli: The Chief Works and Others, Vol. III*, 1444–1457, at 1456.

34. William Parson resoundingly declares "yes": "Machiavelli surely invites a comparison of Christ and Cesare . . . but he does so to emphasize the deleterious effects of Christ's legacy, rather than any potential value Christian teachings might have for a modern founder." Parson, *Machiavelli's Gospel*, 68. For a response to Parson on this score, and for some remarks on Straussian engagements with Machiavelli's treatment of Christianity, see John P. McCormick, "Book Review: Parson, *Machiavelli's Gospel*," *Review of Politics* 79, no. 3 (Summer 2017), 522–524.

35. We must leave aside for now a full examination of Freud's suggestion that the Hebrews actually killed Moses in the desert, effectively turning the prophet's sword against himself, with long-term spiritual-psychological consequences for his people. See Sigmund Freud, *Moses and Monotheism*, trans. Katherine Jones (New York: Vintage, 1955).

Chapter 2. "Keep the Public Rich and the Citizens Poor": Economic Inequality and Political Corruption in the *Discourses*

1. See Charles R. Beitz, *Political Equality: An Essay in Democratic Theory* (Princeton: Princeton University Press, 1979); and Robert Alan Dahl, *On Political Equality* (New Haven: Yale University Press, 2006).

2. See Danielle Allen, "Liberty and Equality Aren't Mutually Exclusive," *Washington Post* (October 17, 2014).

3. See Larry M. Bartels, *Unequal Democracy: The Political Economy of the New Gilded Age* (Princeton: Princeton University Press, 2010); Pablo Beramendi and Christopher J. Anderson, eds., *Democracy, Inequality, and Representation in Comparative Perspective* (New York: Russell Sage Foundation, 2011); Jacob Hacker and Paul Pierson, *Winner-Take-All Politics: How Washington Made the Rich Richer and Turned Its back on the Middle Class* (New York: Simon and Schuster, 2011); Martin Gilens, *Affluence and Influence: Economic Inequality and Political Power in America* (Princeton: Princeton University Press, 2012); Thomas Piketty, *Capital in the Twenty-First Century*, trans. A. Goldhammer (Cambridge, MA: Harvard University Press, 2014); and Steven Fraser, *The Age of Acquiescence: The Life and Death of American Resistance to Organized Wealth and Power* (New York: Little, Brown and Company, 2015).

4. See Robert Alan Dahl, *Democracy and its Critics* (New Haven: Yale University Press, 1989).

5. See Bernard Manin, *The Principles of Representative Government* (Cambridge: Cambridge University Press, 1997).

6. See Jeffrey A. Winters, *Oligarchy* (Cambridge: Cambridge University Press, 2011); and Gordon Arlen, "Aristotle and the Problem of Oligarchic Harm: Insights for Democracy," *European Journal of Political Theory* (published online: August 25, 2016), DOI: 10.1177/1474885116663837.

7. See Niccolò Machiavelli, *Discorsi* [1513–17/1531], in C. Vivanti, ed., *Opere I: I Primi Scritti Politici* (Turin: Einaudi-Gallimard, 1997), hereafter D. See also Machiavelli, *Il Principe* (*De Principatibus*) [1513/1532], ed. G. Inglese (Turin: Einaudi-Gallimard, 1995), hereafter P.

8. Of course, I refer here to the Cambridge and Straussian schools of Machiavelli interpretation, which I discuss at greater length in, respectively, chapters 6 and 5.

9. This is a classic Roman-republican trope accentuated by Eric Nelson in *The Greek Tradition in Republican Thought* (Cambridge: Cambridge University Press, 2004).

10. Recent articles that astutely trace the link that Machiavelli establishes between economic inequality and sociopolitical corruption are: Julie L. Rose, " 'Keep the Citizens Poor': Machiavelli's Prescription for Republican Poverty," *Political Studies* 64, no. 3 (October 1, 2016), 734–747; Amanda Moure Maher, "What Skinner Misses About Machiavelli's Freedom: Inequality, Corruption and the Institutional Origins of Civic Virtue," *Journal of Politics* 78, no. 4 (October 2016), 1003–1015; and Tejas Parasher, "Inequality and *Tumulti* in Machiavelli's Aristocratic Republics," *Polity* 49, no. 1 (January 2017), 42–68.

11. See Josiah Ober, *Mass and Elite in Democratic Athens: Rhetoric, Ideology, and the Power of the People* (Princeton: Princeton University Press, 1991).

12. Demosthenes, quoted in Ober, *Mass and Elite*, 198.

13. For an especially profound reconsideration of forms of inclusion or exclusion in Athenian democracy, with serious implications for democratic citizenship today, see Demetra Kasimis, *The Perpetual Immigrant and the Limits of Athenian Democracy* (Cambridge: Cambridge University Press, forthcoming 2018).

14. See Nelson, *The Greek Tradition in Republican Thought*; and Paul Cartledge, *The Spartans: The World of the Warrior-Heroes of Ancient Greece* (New York: Vintage, 2004).

15. See Melissa Schwartzberg, *Counting the Many: The Origins and Limits of Supermajority Rule* (Cambridge: Cambridge University Press 2013). Matthew Landauer compares political institutions and practices among ancient Greek tyrannies, such as Gelon's Syracuse and oligarchies such as Sparta, to determine exactly what Athenians understood to be the essential qualities of their democracy. See Landauer, "When does the *Demos* Decide? Agenda Control and Free Speech in Ancient Greek Democracies," paper presented at the University of Chicago Political Theory Workshop, Autumn 2016.

16. See, symptomatically, Maurizio Viroli, *Republicanism* (New York: Hill and Wang, 2002). Gordon Arlen analyzes the persistent temptation to employ wealth as a proxy for virtue in "Aristotle and the Problem of Oligarchic Harm." On the place of material equality in republicanism, broadly conceived, see: Nelson, *The Greek Tradition in Republican Thought*; Alex Gourevitch, *From Slavery to the Cooperative Commonwealth: Labor and Republican Liberty in the Nineteenth Century* (Cambridge: Cambridge University Press, 2015); Steven Klein, "Fictitious Freedom: A Polanyian Critique of the Republican Revival," *American Journal of Political Science* 61, no. 4 (October 2017), 852–863; Robert Jubb, "Whose Republicanism, Which Liberty?" (unpublished ms., Reading University); and John P. McCormick, "The New Ochlophobia? Populism, Majority Rule and Prospects for Democratic Republicanism," in Yiftah Elazar and Geneviève Rousselière, eds., *Republican Democracy* (Cambridge: Cambridge University Press, forthcoming 2018).

17. Whether the Roman Republic is best characterized as an oligarchy or a democracy continues to be a contentious issue. Scholars such as Egon Flaig, Andrew Lintott, Fergus Millar, John North, and T. P. Wiseman have argued that institutions such as the plebeian tribunate, popularly judged political trials, and legislation in the more equitably organized of Rome's assemblies made Roman politics more democratic than scholars had traditionally assumed. Alternatively, Karl-Joachim Hölkeskamp, Robert Morstein-Marx, Henrik Mouritsen, and Kurt Raaflaub have revived and refined the arguments famously associated with Arnaldo Momigliano and Ronald Syme, which insisted that the Republic was an oligarchy, pure and simple.

18. See Polybius, *The Rise of the Roman Empire* (London: Penguin, 1980). See also Andrew Lintott, *The Constitution of the Roman Republic* (Oxford: Oxford University Press, 2003).

19. See Fergus Millar, *The Crowd in Rome in the Late Republic* (Ann Arbor: Michigan University Press, 2002); and Millar, *The Roman Republic in Political Thought* (Waltham, MA: Brandeis University Press, 2002).

20. I leave this issue to the experts to debate. Of course, the classic critique of Athenian democracy under duress is Thucydides, *The Peloponnesian War*, trans. M. Hammond (Oxford: Oxford University Press, 2009). For a revisionist analysis of his critique, see Josiah Ober, "Thucydides' Criticism of Democratic Knowledge," in *Nomodeiktes: Greek Studies in Honor of Martin Ostwald*, R. M. Rosen and J. Farrell, eds. (Ann Arbor: Michigan University Press, 1993), 81–98.

21. See Moses I. Finley, *Democracy Ancient and Modern* (New Brunswick: Rutgers University Press, 1985); and I. F. Stone, *The Trial of Socrates* (New York: Little, Brown and Company, 1987).

22. See Michael A. Flower, "The Invention of Tradition in Classical and Hellenistic Sparta," in A. Powell and S. Hodkinson, eds., *Sparta: Beyond the Mirage* (London: Duckworth, 2002), 193–219; and Melissa Lane, "Founding as Legislating: The Figure of the Lawgiver in Plato's *Republic*," in L. Brisson and N. Notomi, eds., *Selected Papers from the Ninth Symposium Platonicum* (St. Augustine: Academia Verlag, 2013), 104–114.

23. On the corrupting influence of empire in a broader context, see Mary G. Dietz, "Between Polis and Empire: Aristotle's Politics," *American Political Science Review* 106, no. 2 (May 2012), 275–293.

24. See McCormick, *Machiavellian Democracy* (Cambridge: Cambridge University Press, 2011).

25. See Robert Black, *Machiavelli* (Abingdon: Routledge, 2013), 36–39, 45–48, 51–67; John Najemy, M., " 'Occupare la tirannide': Machiavelli, the Militia, and Guicciardini's Accusation of Tyranny," in J. Barthas, ed., *Della tirannia: Machiavelli con Bartolo, Quaderni di Rinascimento* 42 (Florence: Leo S. Olschki, 2007), 75–108; Roberto Ridolfi, *The Life of Niccolò Machiavelli* (Chicago: University of Chicago Press, 1963), 130–132; and Sebastian de Grazia, *Machiavelli in Hell* (Princeton: Princeton University Press, 1989), 95–96, 358.

26. See Jérémie Barthas, "Machiavelli, from the Ten to the Nine: A Hypothesis Based on the Financial History of Early Modern Florence," in D. R. Curto, E. Dursteller, J. Kirchner, and F. Trivellato, eds., *From Florence to the Mediterranean and Beyond: Essays in Honour of Anthony Molho*, 2 vols. (Florence: Leo S. Olschki, 2009), 147–166; Barthas, "Machiavelli, Public Debt, and the Origin of Political Economy: An Introduction," in F. del Lucchese, F. Frosini, and V. Morfino, eds., *The Radical Machiavelli: Politics, Philosophy, and Language* (Leiden: Brill, 2015), 273–305; and Barthas, "Machiavelli, the Republic, and the Financial Crisis," in *Machiavelli on Liberty and Conflict*, D. Johnston, N. Urbinati, and C. Vergara, eds. (Chicago: University of Chicago Press, 2017), 257–279.

27. See Jérémie Barthas, *L'argent n'est pas le nerf de la guerre: Essai sur une prétendue erreur de Machiavel* (Rome: École française de Rome, 2011).

28. See also Machiavelli's series of reflections on Swiss and German cities: Machiavelli, "Rapporto Delle Cose Della Magna" (1508), "Discorso Sopra Le Cose Della Magna E Sopra l'Imperatore" (1509), and "Ritratto Delle Cose Della Magna" (1512), in M. Martelli, ed., *Machiavelli: Tutte Le Opere* (Florence: Sansoni, 1971), 63–71.

29. A growing and welcome trend in Machiavelli studies accentuates the egalitarian dimensions of the Florentine's political thought: see Filippo Del Lucchese, *The Political Philosophy of Niccolò Machiavelli* (Edinburgh: Edinburgh University Press, 2015); Christopher Holman, *Machiavelli and the Politics of Democratic Innovation* (Toronto: University of Toronto Press, forthcoming); and Yves Winter, *Machiavelli and the Orders of Violence* (Cambridge: Cambridge University Press, forthcoming).

30. For the definitive examination of this topic, see Gabriele Pedullà, *Machiavelli in Tumult: The Discourses on Livy and the Origins of Conflictual Politics* (Cambridge: Cambridge University Press, forthcoming 2018).

31. The Agrarian Laws accumulated various provisions over the course of Roman republican history: it began with the Licinian-Sextian law (367 BCE), which restricted land ownership and provided the plebs with debt relief; to this were added limits on interest rates (357 BCE); and eventually significant limitations on usury (342 BCE).

32. On the ambiguity of Machiavelli's pronouncements on Roman agrarian reform, see Nelson, *The Greek Tradition in Republican Thought*, 75–86.

33. On the necessity of reading the *Discourses* through the eyes of its young aristocratic dedicatees, Cosimo Rucellai and Zanobi Buondelmonti, see John P. McCormick, "Tempering the *Grandi*'s Appetite to Oppress: The Dedication and Intention of Machiavelli's *Discourses*," in Victoria Kahn et al., eds., *Politics and the Passions, 1500–1789* (Princeton: Princeton University Press, 2006), 7–29; and McCormick, *Machiavellian Democracy*, chapter 2.

34. Vickie Sullivan takes such a view of the chapter devoted to the Agrarian Laws: see Vickie B. Sullivan, *Machiavelli's Three Romes: Religion, Human Liberty, and Politics Reformed* (DeKalb: Northern Illinois University Press, 1996), 69–70; and Sullivan, *Machiavelli, Hobbes, and the Formation of a Liberal Republicanism in England* (Cambridge: Cambridge University Press, 2004), 47–48.

35. See, among historians, Gene Brucker, "The Ciompi Revolution," in Nicolai Rubinstein, ed. *Florentine Studies: Politics and Society in Renaissance Florence* (London: Faber and Faber, 1968), 314–356; and John Najemy, *Corporatism and Consensus in Florentine Electoral Politics, 1280–1400* (Chapel Hill: University of North Carolina Press, 1982). On the significance of the Ciompi Revolt for Machiavelli's political thought, see Yves Winter, "Plebeian Politics: Machiavelli and the Ciompi Uprising,"

Political Theory 40, no. 6 (November 2012), 736–766, and Winter, *Machiavelli and the Orders of Violence*. I treat Machiavelli's engagement with the revolt in chapter 3 of this book, and also in McCormick, "Faulty Foundings and Failed Reformers in Machiavelli's *Florentine Histories*," *American Political Science Review* 111, no. 1 (February 2017), 204–216.

36. See James Hankins, ed., *Renaissance Civic Humanism* (Cambridge: Cambridge University Press, 2000), 75–178.

37. Nelson establishes Cicero as the paradigmatic Roman (as opposed to Greek) republican on the basis of his criticisms of both the Agrarian Laws and the Gracchi. See Nelson, *The Greek Tradition in Republican Thought*, 57–59. On the place of the Gracchi in Roman political thought, see Daniel J. Kapust, *Republicanism, Rhetoric, and Roman Political Thought: Sallust, Livy, and Tacitus* (Cambridge: Cambridge University Press, 2014), 5, 46, 107, 126–129.

38. Strauss, for instance, asserts that Machiavelli ultimately favors the Roman senate's dilatory tactics in forestalling passage of the Agrarian Laws: Machiavelli "praises the patience and industry with which the Roman nobility prevented the enactment of the Agrarian Law." Moreover, Strauss believes that, in the Florentine context, Machiavelli criticizes the Gracchi's policies because Machiavelli purportedly shares Strauss's view that "the preponderance of the great and exalted over the weak and humble is essential to the strength of society." See Leo Strauss, *Thoughts on Machiavelli* (Glencoe, IL: University of Chicago Press, 1958), 103, 206. Coby, however, taking into account the chapter in its entirety, succinctly and accurately summarizes its main point as follows: the Agrarian law chapter "contradicts the proposition it is meant to confirm," namely, the putative limitlessness of the Roman people's ambition and the fact that the people supposedly ought neither to have sought redistribution of the wealth controlled by the nobility nor to have sought to hold offices beyond the plebeian tribunate. See Patrick J. Coby, *Machiavelli's Romans: Liberty and Greatness in the Discourses on Livy* (Lanham: Lexington Books, 1999), 97. A notable exception among Straussian scholars in recognizing Machiavelli's favorable views on the Agrarian Laws is Nathan Tarcov, "Machiavelli's Modern Turn," in *The Modern Turn*, Michael Rohlf, ed. (Washington, DC: Catholic University of America Press, 2017), 36–53, at 49.

39. Straussians are by no means the only scholars who mistakenly read Book I, chapter 37 to stand as an indictment of the Roman plebs, the Gracchi or the Agrarian Laws. For instance, John Pocock incorrectly asserts that Machiavelli was a critic of the Agrarian Laws because inequality, for Machiavelli, "connotes neither inequality of wealth nor inequality of political authority—there is no reason to suppose that Machiavelli objected to either—but a state of affairs in which some individuals look to others . . . when they should be looking to the public good and public authority." See J.G.A. Pocock, *The Machiavellian Moment: Florentine Political Thought and the*

Atlantic Republican Tradition (Princeton: Princeton University Press, 1975), 211, 209. Furthermore, Miguel Vatter argues that chapter 37 demonstrates Machiavelli's conclusion that the Roman people became "enobled" and hence corrupted by seeking to share offices and especially wealth with the nobles. Machiavelli, according to Vatter, explains the events associated with the Agrarian Laws "in terms of the hegemony of the desire for 'all things.' . . . But this desire is not identical to the desire 'not to be dominated' that is ascribed to the people: if the desire for substances explains the conflict out of ambition, then the desire for freedom accounts for the conflict out of necessity. The logic of ambition can explain the events of the civil war only because the people have become 'ennobled.' In this sense, the conflict around the Agrarian Laws is the struggle between nobles and plebeians over property, as opposed to freedom." See Miguel E. Vatter, *Between Form and Event: Machiavelli's Theory of Political Freedom* (Dordrecht: Springer, 2000), 197; see also 229, 231, n. 30.

40. Many scholars take at face value Machiavelli's reference to the "wondrous equality" that characterizes Florentine social conditions at the opening of Book III of the *Florentine Histories*. Few consider the obvious disjuncture between this assessment and the events that Machiavelli describes in the ensuing book: it recounts both the woolworkers' armed insurrection aimed at overcoming socioeconomic inequality within the republic, as well as their defeat, disarming, and intensified subordination at the Ciompi Revolt's conclusion. An equality, "wondrous," indeed. See Machiavelli, *Istorie Fiorentine* [1520–25/1532], Franco Gaeta, ed. (Milan: Feltrinelli, 1962), Book III. I accentuate and analyze such disjunctures between Machiavelli's words and the deeds he recounts in the *Histories* in chapter 3 of this book. It is nevertheless worth remarking here that the entire *Histories* can be read as an account of how a fabulously wealthy banking family and their aristocratic clients gained political supremacy within the republic. See Amanda Moure Maher, "The Power of 'Wealth, Nobility and Men': Inequality and Corruption in Machiavelli's *Florentine Histories*," *European Journal of Political Theory* (published online September 18, 2017), https://doi.org/10.1177/1474885117730673.

41. See Livy, *History of Rome, Books 1–10* (vols. I–IV), trans. B. O. Foster (Cambridge, MA: Loeb, 1919–26), e.g., IV.49, 51, VI.5, 35; cf. also, *Plutarch's Lives* (Vol. X), trans. B. Perrin (Cambridge, MA: Loeb, 1921), 145–241.

42. Strauss, for instance, accentuates neither the Roman nobility's appetite to oppress the people nor their ambition to maximize economic gain—which Machiavelli explicitly emphasizes in conjunction; rather Strauss accentuates the nobility's purportedly more morally palatable desire to attain glory. Machiavelli, according to Strauss, "deliberately . . . makes the Roman ruling class 'better' than it was; he transforms a group whose best members, being perfectly free from all vulgar prejudices, were guided exclusively by Machiavellian prudence that served the insatiable desire of each for eternal glory in this world." See Strauss, *Thoughts on Machiavelli*, 134.

43. Except, of course, for the notable case of the tyrant Appius Claudius, who was indeed elected by "free votes" (D I.35).

44. Here Machiavelli implicitly criticizes Florence as a badly ordered republic for its unwise modes of appointing magistrates. Elsewhere he specifies that Florence waited too long between the initial baggings of the names of candidates and the final drawings of magistrates; by failing to frequently re-evaluate eligibility, newly virtuous candidates were excluded from the baggings and no-longer virtuous ones were actually appointed; see Machiavelli, "Discursus Florentinarum Rerum Post Mortem Iunoris Laurentii Medices," in *Opere I: I Primi Scritti Politici*, 733-745, at 733.

45. See Landauer on the importance of free speech in Athens as a means of providing the demos with a wide policy agenda over which to level judgment: Landauer, "When does the *Demos* Decide?"

46. Although, as I demonstrate elsewhere, Machiavelli precariously blurs the line between reformer and tyrant; see McCormick, "Subdue the Senate: Machiavelli's 'Way of Freedom' or Path to Tyranny?" *Political Theory* 40, no. 6 (December 2012), 717-738; McCormick, "Of Tribunes and Tyrants: Machiavelli's Legal and Extra-Legal Modes for Controlling Elites," *Ratio Juris* 28, no. 2 (June 2015), 252-266; McCormick, "Machiavelli's Greek Tyrant as Republican Reformer," in *The Radical Machiavelli*, 337-348; and McCormick, "The People's Princes: Machiavelli, Leadership and Liberty" (book manuscript in progress).

47. On Agathocles as Machiavelli's exemplar of a potential republican reformer, see: McCormick, "The Enduring Ambiguity of Machiavellian Virtue: Crime, Cruelty and Christianity in *The Prince*," *Social Research* 81, no. 1 (Spring 2014), 133-164; McCormick, "Machiavelli's Inglorious 'Tyrants': On Agathocles, Scipio and Unmerited Glory," *History of Political Thought* 36, no. 1 (2015), 29-52; and McCormick, "Machiavelli's Agathocles: From Criminal Example to Princely Exemplum," in Michèle Lowrie and Susanne Lüdemann, eds., *Between Exemplarity and Singularity: Literature, Philosophy, Law* (Abingdon: Routledge, 2015), 123-139.

Chapter 3. On the Myth of a Conservative Turn in the *Florentine Histories*

1. Niccolò Machiavelli, *Istorie Fiorentine* [1520-25/1532], Franco Gaeta, ed. (Milan: Feltrinelli, 1962), hereafter FH.

2. Niccolò Machiavelli, *Il Principe (De Principatibus)* [1513/1532], G. Inglese, ed. (Torino: Einaudi-Gallimard, 1995), hereafter P; and Machiavelli, *Discorsi* [1513-17/1531], C. Vivanti, ed. (Torino: Einaudi-Gallimard, 1997), hereafter D.

3. Although they differ to varying degrees on how conservative they believe Machiavelli became, the following all agree that his views changed decidedly in that direction: Albert Russell Ascoli, " '*Vox Populi*': Machiavelli, *Opinione*, and the *Popolo*, from the *Principe* to the *Istorie Fiorentine*," *California Italian Studies* 4, no. 2 (2013),

1–23; Francesco Bausi, *Machiavelli* (Rome: Salerno, 2005); Robert Black, *Machiavelli* (Abingdon: Routledge, 2013); Humfrey Butters, "Machiavelli and the Medici," in J. M. Najemy, ed., *The Cambridge Companion to Machiavelli* (Cambridge: Cambridge University Press, 2010), 64–79; Mark Hulliung, *Citizen Machiavelli* (Princeton: Princeton University Press, 1984), 75–78, 86; Mark Jurdjevic, *A Great and Wretched City: Promise and Failure in Machiavelli's Florentine Political Thought* (Cambridge, MA: Harvard University Press, 2014); Mario Martelli, "Machiavelli e Firenze dalla repubblica al principate," in J.-J. Marchand, ed., *Niccolò Machiavelli: politico storico letterato* (Rome: Salerno, 1996), 15–31; David Quint, "Narrative Design and Historical Irony in Machiavelli's *Istorie Fiorentine*," *Rinascimento* 43 (2003), 31–48; Giovanni Silvano, "Florentine Republicanism in the Sixteenth Century," in G. Bock, Q. Skinner, and M. Viroli, eds. *Machiavelli and Republicanism* (Cambridge: Cambridge University Press, 1990), 41–70; Maurizio Viroli, "Machiavelli and the Republican Idea of Liberty," in G. Bock, Q. Skinner, and M. Viroli, eds., *Machiavelli and Republicanism* (Cambridge: Cambridge University Press, 1990), 143–171; and Viroli, *Machiavelli* (Oxford: Oxford University Press, 1998), 126. See also Mario Martelli's introduction to his edition of Machiavelli's *Il Principe* (Roma: Salerno, 2006), 15–31.

4. The following scholars offer important analyses of this passage without necessarily endorsing the "conservative turn" thesis: Anna Maria Cabrini, *Per Una Valuatione delle Istorie Fiorentine del Machiavelli: Note sulle Fonti del Secondo Libro* (Florence: La Nuova Casa Editrice, 1985), 367–370; Gisela Bock, "Civil Discord in Machiavelli's *Istorie Fiorentine*," in Bock, Skinner, and Viroli, eds., *Machiavelli and Republicanism*, 187–189; Gennaro Sasso, *Niccolò Machiavelli: La Storiografia, Vol. II* (Bologna: Il Mulino, 1993), 185–199; Harvey C. Mansfield, "Party and Sect in Machiavelli's *Florentine Histories*," in Mansfield, *Machiavelli's Virtue* (Chicago: University of Chicago Press, 1996), 150–151; and Marina Marietti, *Machiavelli: L'Eccezione Fiorentina* (Florence: Cadmo, 2005). Although see Cabrini, *Interpretazione e Stile in Machiavelli: Il Libro Terzo delle Istorie* (Rome: Bulzoni, 1990), 12–14, 93.

5. The present chapter emphasizes the conciliatory nature of both the Florentine people and plebs—their *onestà*, their affinity for the common good, their willingness to accept peace over justice—until they are pushed too far by oligarchic oppression. However, it must be stated that Machiavelli does not fully intend this to be a compliment. The people—in Rome, Florence, and in all polities—are in some sense too good. The world would be a better place, Machiavelli's intimates, if the people were actually slightly closer to the nobles along on the continuum from *onestà* to oppression; that is, if they were quicker to crush the nobles in efforts to reform republics in more just and stable ways. This is why Machiavelli often demonstrates that populist tyrants are necessary, most of the time, to eliminate the *grandi* of corrupt republics because the people are so seldom inclined to do so themselves. See John P. McCormick, "Machiavelli's Greek Tyrant as Republican Reformer," in F. del Luc-

chese, F. Frosini, and V. Morfino, eds., *The Radical Machiavelli: Politics, Philosophy, and Language* (Leiden: Brill, 2015), 337–348; and McCormick, "The People's Princes: Machiavelli, Leadership and Liberty" (book manuscript in progress).

6. To the extent that Machiavelli may be relying on contemporary chroniclers in conveying this information, there are good reasons to believe that he is mistaken about the precise distribution of seats in *Signoria* among the different sets of guilds. See John M. Najemy, *Corporatism and Consensus in Florentine Electoral Politics, 1280– 1400* (Chapel Hill: University of North Carolina Press, 1982), 141–142.

7. For a serious study that nevertheless takes Machiavelli's assertion here at face value, see David Quint, "Armi e nobiltà: Machiavelli, Guicciardini, e le artistocrazie cittadine," *Studi italiani* 21 (2009), 53–74.

8. See Jurdjevic, *A Great and Wretched City*, 124–127.

9. For compelling, alternative readings of the nameless *ciompo's* speech, see: Cabrini, *Interpretazione e Stile*, 85–98; Gabriele Pedullà, "Il divieto di Platone: Machiavelli e il discorso dell'anonimo plebeo," in Jean-Jacques Marchand and Jean-Claude Zancarini, eds., *Storiografia repubblicana fiorentina (1494–1570)* (Firenze: Cesati, 2003), 209–266; Jeffrey Edward Green, "Learning How Not to Be Good: A Plebeian Perspective," *The Good Society* 20, no. 2 (2011), 184–202; and Yves Winter, "Plebeian Politics: Machiavelli and the Ciompi Uprising," *Political Theory* 40, no. 6 (2012), 736–766.

10. The city's elite had used the circumstances of the Black Death in 1348 to reduce their number of priors by one. See John M. Najemy, *A History of Florence, 1200–1575* (New York: Wiley-Blackwell, 2008), 145.

11. This account of the distribution of seats in the *Signoria* may exaggerate the number allotted to middling and minor guilds: see Najemy, *Corporatism and Consensus*, chapters 5 and 6.

12. See John P. McCormick, "Subdue the Senate: Machiavelli's 'Way of Freedom' or Path to Tyranny?" *Political Theory* 40, no. 6 (2012), 714–735, at 730.

13. See John P. McCormick, *Machiavellian Democracy* (Cambridge: Cambridge University Press, 2011).

14. See Machiavelli, "Ai Palleschi" (1512), in Machiavelli, *Opere I: I Primi Scritti Politici*, C. Vivanti, ed. (Torino: Einaudi-Gallimard, 1997), 87–89. For an English translation, see Machiavelli, "Memorandum to the Newly Restored Medici," in M. Jurdjevic, N. Piano, and J. P. McCormick, eds., *Florentine Political Writings from Petrarch to Machiavelli* (Philadelphia: University of Pennsylvania Press, forthcoming 2019).

15. Roberto Ridolfi, *The Life of Niccolò Machiavelli* (Chicago: University of Chicago Press, 1963), 130–132; Sebastian de Grazia, *Machiavelli in Hell* (Princeton: Princeton University Press, 1989), 34–40; and Robert Black, *Machiavelli* (Abingdon: Routledge, 2013), 75–80.

16. See Machiavelli, "Discursus Florentinarum Rerum Post Mortem Iunioris

Laurentii Medices," in Machiavelli, *Opere I*, 733–745. For an English translation, see Machiavelli, "Discursus on Florentine Matters after the Death of Lorenzo de' Medici the Younger," in *Florentine Political Writings*.

17. See, especially, Silvano, "Florentine Republicanism, 56–61, and Viroli, "Machiavelli and the Republican Idea," 154–155.

18. Although accepting as fact Machiavelli's adoption of a tripartite understanding of social class, Raimondi puts this notion in the service of an interesting reading of Machiavelli's preference for social "mixing": see Fabio Raimondi, *Constituting Freedom: Machiavelli and Florence* (Oxford: Oxford University Press, 2018).

19. On the Florentine's fascination with the various putative Roman founders of their city, and Machiavelli's exploitation of this fascination in his critique of humanism, see Danielle Charette, "Catilinarian Cadences in Machiavelli's *Florentine Histories*: Ciceronian Humanism, Corrupting Consensus and the Demise of Contentious Liberty," *History of Political Thought* (forthcoming 2018).

20. For considerations on the differences between elite-popular social integration in Rome and Florence, see McCormick, *Machiavellian Democracy*, 101–103.

21. Felix Gilbert, "The Venetian Constitution in Florentine Political Thought," in Nicolai Rubinstein ed., *Florentine Studies: Politics and Society in Renaissance Florence* (London: Faber and Faber, 1968), 463–500.

22. See Francesco Guicciardini, "Considerations on the Discourses of Niccolò Machiavelli," in James Atkinson and David Sices, eds., *The Sweetness of Power: Machiavelli's Discourses and Guicciardini's Considerations* (DeKalb: Northern Illinois University Press, 2002), 397.

23. I offer a more elaborate analysis of the "Discursus" in McCormick, *Machiavellian Democracy*, 103–107.

Chapter 4. Rousseau's Repudiation of Machiavelli's Democratic Roman Republic

1. Jean-Jacques Rousseau, "Of the Social Contract, Or Principles of Political Right" (1762/1997), in Victor Gourevitch, trans. and ed., *Rousseau: The Social Contract and Other Later Political Writings* (Cambridge: Cambridge University Press, 1997), 39–152; hereafter SC. I take the liberty of reducing to lowercase many words that the translator capitalizes.

2. See Niccolò Machiavelli, *Discorsi* [1513–17/1531], in C. Vivanti, ed., *Opere I: I Primi Scritti Politici* (Turin: Einaudi-Gallimard, 1997), hereafter D. See also Machiavelli, *Il Principe (De Principatibus)* [1513/1532], G. Inglese, ed. (Turin: Einaudi-Gallimard, 1995), hereafter P; and *Istorie Fiorentine* [1520–25/1532], F. Gaeta, ed. (Milan: Feltrinelli, 1962), henceforth FH.

3. I contribute to the line of interpretation opened by Jean Starobinski, who carefully delineates the oligarchic dimensions of Rousseau's political thought. See Staro-

binski, *Jean-Jacques Rousseau: Transparency and Obstruction*, trans. A. Goldhammer (Chicago: University of Chicago Press, 1990).

4. See Thomas Piketty, *Capital in the Twenty-First Century*, trans. A. Goldhammer (Cambridge, MA: Harvard University Press, 2014); Steven Fraser, *The Age of Acquiescence: the Life and Death of American Resistance to Organized Wealth and Power* (New York: Little, Brown and Company, 2015); Douglas A. Arnold, "Can Inattentive Citizens Control Their Elected Representatives?" in L. Dodd and B. Oppenheimer, eds., *Congress Reconsidered* (Washington, DC: CQ Press, 1993), 401–416; Adam Przeworski, Susan C. Stokes, and Bernard Manin, eds., *Democracy, Accountability, and Representation* (Cambridge: Cambridge University Press, 1999; and Jane Mansbridge, "Rethinking Representation," *American Political Science Review* 97, no. 4 (November 2003), 515–528. Any theory of popular government that takes seriously the republican principle of "nondomination" requires robust institutional means that insure elite accountability. On this principle, if not the institutional apparatus to realize it, see Philip Pettit, *Republicanism: A Theory of Freedom and Government* (Oxford: Oxford University Press, 1999); and Pettit, *On the People's Terms: A Republican Theory and Model of Democracy* (Cambridge: Cambridge University Press, 2013). See John P. McCormick, "The New Ochlophobia?: Populism, Majority Rule and Prospects for Democratic Republicanism," in Yiftah Elazar and Geneviève Rousselière, eds., *Republican Democracy* (Cambridge: Cambridge University Press, forthcoming 2018).

5. On this widespread deficiency of the literature on this score, see David Lay Williams, *Rousseau's Social Contract: An Introduction* (Cambridge: Cambridge University Press, 2014), 171.

6. Important exceptions regarding Book IV within the literature—even if these engagements do not alter the substantively egalitarian or democratic interpretations of Rousseau proffered by such scholars—include: Ethan Putterman, *Rousseau, Law and the Sovereignty of the People* (Cambridge: Cambridge University Press, 2010); Williams, *Rousseau's Social Contract: An Introduction*; Chiara Destri, "Rousseau's (Not So) Oligarchic Republicanism," *Critical Review of International Social and Political Philosophy* 19, no. 2 (2016), 206–216; and Geneviève Rousselière, "On the Possibility of a Modern Republic: Rousseau and the Puzzle of the Roman Republic," in D. L. Williams and M. W. Maguire, eds., *Cambridge Companion to Rousseau's Social Contract* (Cambridge: Cambridge University Press, forthcoming). The overwhelming number of scholars engage Book IV only to examine Rousseau's general considerations on sovereignty set forth the book's first three chapters, or to analyze his conception of civil religion elaborated in chapter 8—it would be only a slight exaggeration to declare that, as far as the vast secondary literature is concerned, chapters 4 through 7 of Book IV might just as well not exist.

7. Formidable efforts to apply Rousseau's political thought to contemporary democratic theory include: Benjamin Barber, *Strong Democracy: Participatory Politics*

for a New Age (Berkeley: University of California Press, 1984); James Miller, *Rousseau: Dreamer of Democracy* (New Haven: Yale University Press, 1984); Joshua Cohen, *Rousseau: A Free Community of Equals* (Oxford: Oxford University Press, 2010); Céline Spector, *Au Prisme de Rousseau: Usages Politiques Contemporains* (Oxford: Voltaire Foundation, 2011); Melissa Schwartzberg, *Counting the Many: The Origins and Limits of Supermajority Rule* (Cambridge: Cambridge University Press, 2013); and Eoin Daly, *Rousseau's Constitutionalism: Austerity and Republican Freedom* (London: Bloomsbury, 2017). See also the following exchange: Ethan Putterman, "Rousseau on Agenda-Setting and Majority Will," *American Political Science Review* 97, no. 3 (August 2003), 459–469; John T. Scott, "Rousseau's Anti-Agenda-Setting Agenda and Contemporary Democratic Theory," *American Political Science Review* 99, no. 1 (February 2005), 137–144; and Putterman, "Rousseau on the People as Legislative Gatekeepers, Not Framers," *American Political Science Review* 99, no. 1 (February 2005), 145–151. Unfortunately, none of these otherwise thoughtful efforts consider, at any length or in any depth, the counter-majoritarian institutional prescriptions that Rousseau sets forth for large republics in the chapters of his *Social Contract* devoted to the Roman Republic.

8. Rousseau asserts: "I believe I can posit as a principle that when the functions of government are divided among several tribunals the least numerous will sooner or later acquire the greatest authority; if only because of the ease in dispatching business, which naturally leads them to acquire it" (SC III 4, 91). Machiavelli suggests something quite similar, but in a more nuanced manner: when he pronounces that "the few always behave in the mode of the few," Machiavelli argues that small political bodies are much more inclined than large ones (preferably ones comprising the whole citizenry) to act in a biased fashion when passing judgment on prominent citizens accused of threatening liberty (D I.7; see also I.49). After all, in most cases, the wealthy and prominent citizens who tend to sit on such committees share the political proclivities of the accused. But, unlike Rousseau, Machiavelli also leaves open the possibility that members of smaller tribunals may be more susceptible to intimidation and, so, such bodies can actually be deemed weaker than large bodies.

9. In *The Prince*, Machiavelli suggests that a republic is any regime where more than one person rules, as opposed to a principality where only one rules (P 1). To formulize this insight in a manner that might have pleased Rousseau: in a principality, rule = 1; in a republic, rule = 1 + n.

10. See Rousseau, *Discourse on the Origin and Foundations of Inequality Among Men* (1754–55), in *Rousseau: The Discourses and Other Early Political Writings*, 111–223. See also Rousseau, "Letters Written from the Mountain," in Rousseau, *Collected Writings of Jean-Jacques Rousseau, Vol. 9*, C. Kelly and E. Grace, eds. (Hanover: Dartmouth College Press, 2001), 134–306. Important engagements with Rousseau's egalitarianism include: Judith N. Shklar, *Men and Citizens: A Study of Rousseau's Social Theory* (Cambridge: Cambridge University Press, 1965); Alberto Burgio,

234 NOTES TO PAGES 113-115

Eguaglianza, Interesse, Unanimità: La politica di Rousseau (Napoli: Bibliopolis, 1989); Karma Nabulsi, *Traditions of War: Occupation, Resistance and the Law* (Oxford: Oxford University Press, 2000), 70–78, 177–240; Timothy O'Hagan, ed., *Jean-Jacques Rousseau; International Library of Essays in the History of Social and Political Thought* (Abingdon: Routledge, 2007); Frederick Neuhouser, *Rousseau's Theodicy of Self-Love: Evil, Rationality, and the Drive for Recognition* (Oxford: Oxford University Press, 2008); Robert Wokler, *Rousseau, the Age of Enlightenment, and Their Legacies*, Bryan Garsten and Christopher Brooke, eds. (Princeton: Princeton University Press, 2012); Neuhouser, "Rousseau's Critique of Economic Inequality," *Philosophy & Public Affairs* 41 (2013), 193–225; Mark Hulliung, ed., *Rousseau and the Dilemmas of Modernity* (Abingdon: Routledge, 2015); Avi Lifschitz, ed., *Engaging with Rousseau: Reaction and Interpretation from the Eighteenth Century to the Present* (Cambridge: Cambridge University Press 2016); Céline Spector, *Rousseau et la Critique de L'économie Politique* (Bordeaux: Presses Universitaires de Bordeaux, 2017); Helena Rosenblatt and Paul Schweigert, eds., *Thinking with Rousseau: From Machiavelli to Schmitt* (Cambridge: Cambridge University Press, 2017); James Lindley Wilson, *Democratic Equality* (book manuscript, University of Chicago, 2017); and David Lay Williams, "Forestalling 'the ever-widening inequality of fortunes': Jean-Jacques Rousseau on Economic Inequality and the General Will," in Williams, *The Greatest of All Plagues: Economic Inequality in Western Political Thought* (Princeton: Princeton University Press, forthcoming).

11. See Patrick Riley, "Rousseau's General Will," in Riley, ed., *The Cambridge Companion to Rousseau* (Cambridge: Cambridge University Press, 2001), 124–153; Tracy B. Strong, *Jean-Jacques Rousseau: The Politics of the Ordinary* (Lanham: Rowman and Littlefield, 2002), 67–103; Gabriella Silvestrini, *Diritto naturale e volontà generale: Il contrattualismo repubblicano di Jean-Jacques Rousseau* (Turin: Claudiana, 2010); Putterman, *Rousseau, Law and the Sovereignty of the People*; Williams, *Rousseau's Social Contract: An Introduction*; James Farr and David Lay Williams, eds., *The General Will: The Evolution of a Concept* (Cambridge: Cambridge University Press, 2015) (see the essays comprising part III by Williams, Richard Boyd, Sankar Muthu and Tracy Strong, as well as the contribution by Christopher Brooke); and Joel I. Colón-Ríos, "Rousseau, Theorist of Constituent Power," *Oxford Journal of Legal Studies* 36, no. 4 (June 2016), 885–908.

12. See Lily Ross Taylor, *Roman Voting Assemblies* (Ann Arbor: University of Michigan Press, 1990).

13. Rousseau famously remarks: "if there were a people of Gods, it would govern itself democratically. Such a government is not suited for men" (SC III 4, 92). Explaining this statement, Manin remarks that for Rousseau the ability to act generally in one instance and concretely in the next "is beyond human capacity." See Bernard Manin, *Principles of Representative Government* (Cambridge: Cambridge University

Press, 1997), 75–76. As we will see, the differences between the people assembled in, respectively, Athenian and Roman fashions, enables Rousseau to attribute this rare, indeed divine, ability to decide both general and particular tasks to the Roman "people" when gathered in the centuriate assembly.

14. Rousseau also provides a foreign policy rationale for preferring elective aristocracy to assembly democracy: "the state's prestige is better upheld abroad by venerable senators than by an unknown and despised multitude" (SC III 5, 93).

15. Manin, *Principles of Representative Government*, 42–93, 132–160.

16. John P. McCormick, "Contain the Wealthy and Patrol the Magistrates: Restoring Elite Accountability to Popular Government," *American Political Science Review* 100, no. 2 (May 2006), 147–163.

17. See Gordon Arlen, "Aristotle and the Problem of Oligarchic Harm: Insights for Democracy," *European Journal of Political Theory* (published online: August 25, 2016), DOI: 10.1177/1474885116663837.

18. For a more generous interpretation of Rousseau on this score, see Dana Villa, *Teachers of the People: Political Education in Rousseau, Hegel, Tocqueville, and Mill* (Chicago: University of Chicago Press, 2017).

19. Destri argues that however much Rousseau intended the Roman Republic to serve an exemplary constitutional role in the *Social Contract*, he thoroughly changed his mind by the time he wrote "The Letters Written from the Mountain." See Destri, "Rousseau's (Not So) Oligarchic Republicanism."

20. Other important differences that, for Rousseau, condition the possibility of popular government in Greece and Italy are the place of slavery within Athens and Italy as well as their respective climates. The Roman people, for instance, could not constantly assemble because slaves were not responsible for most material reproduction as in Greece, and, unlike in Hellas, the seasons varied widely from temperate to intemperate weather in Italy (SC III 15, 115).

21. On the full ramifications of Rousseau's enmity toward representation, see Richard Fralin, *Rousseau and Representation: A Study of the Development of His Concept of Political Institutions* (New York: Columbia University Press, 1978); and Nadia Urbinati, *The Principles of Representative Democracy* (Chicago: University of Chicago Press, 2006), 60–100.

22. For more details of Roman political institutions, see Claude Nicolet, *The World of the Citizen in Republican Rome*, trans. P. S. Falla (Berkeley: University of California Press, 1980); and Andrew Lintott, *The Constitution of the Roman Republic* (Oxford: Oxford University Press, 1999).

23. To be generous, this remark may not reflect overt class elitism so much as a stark fear of political corruption: Rousseau might not be outraged here at the prospect of former slaves holding office per se, but merely anxiously aware of the fact that in Rome such men were notoriously dependent on their former masters, who

remained their patrons. As we will see, Rousseau does not mind that wealthy nobles served as patrons to poor plebeians—in fact, he recommends the practice. However, he cannot abide the idea that magistrates should serve as clients to a wealthy patron. In his estimation, it would seem, personal dependence is compatible with the practice of Roman citizenship but not with the exercise of Roman imperium.

24. See Fergus Millar, *The Roman Republic in Political Thought* (Waltham: Brandeis University Press, 2002), 28, 20–21.

25. Nancy Rosenblum situates Rousseau's "republican holism" within the context of various lineages of antiparty, antipluralist and, hence, antipolitical thought. See Nancy L. Rosenblum, *On the Side of the Angels: An Appreciation of Parties and Partisanship* (Princeton: Princeton University Press, 2008), 32–34. I would supplement this account with the argument that Rousseau's holism is actually the most systematically developed version of an aristocratic republicanism that emphasizes the "common good," political generality, and social homogeneity, while actually elevating some particular, materially advantaged sub-set of the citizenry to political preeminence.

26. For a detailed account of the prevalence of clientelism in Roman and Florentine republicanism, and of Machiavelli's severe criticisms of it, see Amanda Moure Maher, "The Corrupt Republic: The Contemporary Relevance of Machiavelli's Critique of Wealth Inequality and Social Dependence" (PhD Dissertation, Political Science Department, University of Chicago, 2017). On the problem of philanthropy as a form of patron-client domination in contemporary democracies, readers should consult, in addition to Maher, the scholarship of Chiara Cordelli, Ryan Pevnick, Rob Reich, and Emma Saunders-Hastings.

27. Rousseau suggests that lottery is used in a democracy because magistracy is a burden (presumably because even the poor must assume office), not necessarily due to anti-oligarchic motivations (SC IV 3, 125).

28. See Mogens Herman Hansen, *The Athenian Democracy in the Age of Demosthenes* (Oxford: Oxford University Press, 1991), 230–231.

29. In fact, the lottery determining which particular century would enjoy the "prerogative" of voting first was confined to only the wealthier census classes. See Nicolet, *The World of the Citizen in Republican Rome*, 257, and Taylor, *Roman Voting Assemblies*, 70–74.

30. In his discussion of Rousseau's account of the lottery by which the Romans determined the "prerogative century," Williams overlooks the vast statistical advantages enjoyed by the wealthier voting classes. See Williams, *Rousseau's Social Contract: An Introduction*, 174.

31. On the democratic possibilities of sociopolitical arrangements that permit common citizens who do not rule to surveille elites who actually do, see Jeffrey

Edward Green, *The Eyes of the People: Democracy in an Age of Spectatorship* (Oxford: Oxford University Press, 2011).

32. In this sense, Rousseau's endorsement of the Roman centuriate assembly can be said to facilitate "domination" of the many by the few, according to the definition of domination formulated by Philip Pettit (even if Pettit himself is often more concerned with domination by the many): see Philip Pettit, *Republicanism*; and Pettit, *On the People's Terms*. See McCormick, *Machiavellian Democracy*, chapter 6.

33. While I agree that Machiavelli could be more precise in his discussion of the Roman assemblies, Millar goes too far in his criticisms of the institutional deficiencies of the Florentine's *Discourses*—especially given his quasi-democratic reading of Rousseau on Rome's assemblies. See Millar, *The Roman Republic in Political Thought*, 71, 75, 113. On Machiavelli's use of Roman history, class relations, and political institutions, see J. Patrick Coby, *Machiavelli's Romans: Liberty and Greatness in the Discourses on Livy* (Lanham: Lexington, 1999).

34. Machiavelli's aristocratic interlocutor, Francesco Guicciardini, promoted general election—open eligibility and wide suffrage—on precisely these grounds: Francesco Guicciardini, *Dialogue on the Government of Florence*, trans. Alison Brown (Cambridge: Cambridge University Press, 1994); and Guicciardini, "Considerations of the *Discourses* of Niccolò Machiavelli," in *The Sweetness of Power: Machiavelli's Discourses and Guicciardini's Considerations*, James B. Atkinson and David Sices, eds. and trans. (DeKalb: Northern Illinois University Press, 2002), 381–438.

35. The historical *concilium* almost certainly excluded patricians. While Lintott cannot say so definitively, he muses that "it would surely have been improper, even repugnant, to include patrician votes in a decision which would be described as 'X . . . plebem rogavit plebesque iure scivit' "; that is, a law made by and for the plebeians. See Lintott, *The Constitution of the Roman Republic*, 54. He adds a footnote of citations supporting the fact that patricians did not attend the *concilium* until late in the republic (54, n. 67), which Taylor, *Roman Voting Assemblies*, 60–64, corroborates.

36. Urbinati grasps the singular novelty of this aspect of Machiavelli's political thought within the republican tradition: see Nadia Urbinati, *Mill on Democracy: From the Athenian Assembly to Representative Government* (Chicago: University of Chicago Press, 2002), 65.

37. See e.g., Cicero, *On the Commonwealth and On the Laws*, James Zetzel, ed. (Cambridge: Cambridge University Press, 1999), 164–167; and C.B.S. de Montesquieu, *Considerations on the Causes of the Greatness of the Romans and their Decline*, trans. D. Lowenthal (London: Hackett, 1999), 84.

38. See S. E. Finer, *The History of Government from the Earliest Times, Vol. I: Ancient Monarchies and Empires* (Oxford: Oxford University Press, 1997), 316–369.

39. See Finer, *The History of Government from the Earliest Times, Vol. I*, 385–410; and Finer, *The History of Government from the Earliest Times, Vol. 2: The Intermediate Ages* (Oxford: Oxford University Press, 1999), 950–985.

40. See Machiavelli, "Discursus Florentinarum Rerum Post Mortem Iunioris Laurentii Medices," in Machiavelli, *Opere I*, 733–745.

41. See Plutarch, *Makers of Rome*, trans. Ian Scott-Kilvert (New York: Penguin, 1965), 153–194.

42. Sallust, *The Jugurthine War and the Conspiracy of Catiline*, trans. S. A. Handford (New York: Penguin, 1963), 78–79; Appian, *The Civil Wars*, trans. J. Carter (New York: Penguin, 1996), 5–8; and Plutarch, *Makers of Rome*.

43. In a note, Rousseau, quite curiously, seems to contradict himself: he depicts Rome as "a genuine democracy" whose transformation into the tyranny of the emperors was generated by aristocratic corruption (SC III 10, 107, n). On the "Machiavellian" possibilities pregnant in this contradiction, see Miller, *Rousseau: Dreamer of Democracy*, 68–69. Nevertheless, Rousseau still manages to criticize the tribunes rather than, like Machiavelli, exonerate them in this analysis.

44. See Lintott, *The Constitution of the Roman Republic*, 120.

45. See, e.g., Richard Tuck's *The Sleeping Sovereign: The Invention of Modern Democracy* (Cambridge: Cambridge University Press, 2016), in which Rousseau is cast as a decisive, perhaps the decisive figure, in the development of modern democratic politics.

46. The literature tends to emphasize the commonalities between the two thinkers, highlighting only the most superficial differences: see, e.g., Maurizio Viroli, *Jean-Jacques Rousseau and the "Well-Ordered Society"* (Cambridge: Cambridge University Press, 1988); and Viroli, "Republic and Politics in Machiavelli and Rousseau," *History of Political Thought* 10, no. 3 (Autumn 1989), 405–420. Much better in this respect are: Marco Geuna, "Rousseau interprete di Machiavelli," *Storia del pensiero politico* 2, no. 1 (2013), 61–87; and Annelien de Dijn, "Rousseau and Republicanism," *Political Theory* (October 2015), 1–22.

Chapter 5. Leo Strauss's Machiavelli and the *Querelle* between the Few and the Many

1. See Machiavelli, *Discorsi* [1513–17/1531], C. Vivanti, ed. (Turin: Einaudi-Gallimard, 1997), henceforth D; *Il Principe (De Principatibus)* [1513/1532], G. Inglese, ed. (Turin: Einaudi-Gallimard, 1995), henceforth P; and *Istorie Fiorentine* [1520–25/1532], F. Gaeta, ed. (Milan: Feltrinelli, 1962), henceforth FH.

2. See Leo Strauss, *Thoughts on Machiavelli* (Glencoe, IL: Free Press, 1958).

3. Strauss, *Thoughts on Machiavelli*, 132.

4. Strauss, *Spinoza's Critique of Religion* [1930] (New York: Schocken, 1965), 108;

and Strauss, *The Political Philosophy of Thomas Hobbes* [1936] (Chicago: University of Chicago Press, 1952), 130, 170.

5. However, in his post-emigration career, as Strauss launched an ostensible critique of "historicism," and, not unrelatedly, established an interpretive-political school, he, at least overtly, disavowed efforts to understand authors better than they did themselves. As Strauss declared in 1959: "an adequate interpretation is such an interpretation as understands the thought of a philosopher exactly as he understood it himself." See Strauss, "Political Philosophy and History," in Strauss, *What is Political Philosophy? and Other Studies* (Chicago: University of Chicago Press, 1988), 56–77, at 66. Note that Strauss here regards this to be the requirement of an adequate but not necessarily a valid, correct, or true interpretation. Strauss is more adamant in *Thoughts on Machiavelli* when he declares, regarding early modern authors, such as Machiavelli, that we must "learn again to understand those thinkers as they understood themselves." Strauss, *Thoughts on Machiavelli*, 231.

6. See Strauss, "Preface to the American Edition," in *The Political Philosophy of Thomas Hobbes*, xv–xvi; and Strauss, *Thoughts on Machiavelli*, 173.

7. Strauss, *Thoughts on Machiavelli*, 13 (emphasis added). While most commentators emphasize the Platonic character of Strauss's methodology, this quote also exhibits a decidedly modern phenomenological disposition. On the idea of Strauss as a political phenomenologist, albeit a less than fully successful one, see Stanley Rosen, "Leo Strauss and the Problem of the Modern," in *The Cambridge Companion to Leo Strauss*, S. B. Smith, ed. (Cambridge: Cambridge University Press, 2009), 119–136.

8. Strauss, *Thoughts on Machiavelli*, 321, n. 118.

9. See John P. McCormick, "Subdue the Senate: Machiavelli's 'Way of Freedom' or Path to Tyranny?" *Political Theory* 40, no. 6 (November 2012), 714–735, at 732, n. 8; and 734–735, n. 16.

10. Strauss, *Thoughts on Machiavelli*, 127.

11. Strauss, *Thoughts on Machiavelli*, 128.

12. Strauss, *Thoughts on Machiavelli*, 131.

13. Strauss, *Thoughts on Machiavelli*, 294.

14. Strauss, *Thoughts on Machiavelli*, 127–128, 134, 137, 173.

15. Strauss, *Thoughts on Machiavelli*, 127.

16. Strauss, *Thoughts on Machiavelli*, 260.

17. Strauss, *Thoughts on Machiavelli*, 271.

18. Strauss, *Thoughts on Machiavelli*, 130.

19. Strauss, *Thoughts on Machiavelli*, 271.

20. Strauss, *Thoughts on Machiavelli*, 263.

21. Strauss, *Thoughts on Machiavelli*, 263. While Strauss fails to substantiate this claim here, he does, however, append a note to the very next sentence—a sentence

that concerns not necessarily the atrociousness of the plebs' behavior, but rather plebeian credulity regarding the "goodness and liberality" of elites (*Thoughts*, 263). Nevertheless, in that endnote (*Thoughts*, 343, n185), Strauss provides six citations from the *Florentine Histories* that appear to serve Strauss's effort to corroborate his claim, expressed in the previous sentence of the main text, that Machiavelli considers the behavior of the Florentine plebs "atrocious." Yet, when one examines these examples in detail, Strauss's evidence proves rather weak as substantiation of his claim: FH II.34 "beginning" references Machiavelli's claim that the plebs "reveled" at the Duke of Athens's "evil" in executing prominent *popolani* who had supervised the failed military campaign at Lucca; FH II.41 "end" provides an account of the people's looting, pillaging, and burning of the Bardi's houses after prevailing over the ancient nobility in a bitter civil war (that the latter actually started); FH III.17 describes the plebs' armed protest against Michele di Lando for showing excessive favor to the popular nobles (a protest that erupts into civil war only after Michele physically assaults the *ciompi*'s representatives); FH III.18 "beginning" recounts how the popular nobles disenfranchised the plebs at the conclusion of the Ciompi Revolt; FH III.20 invokes the favor that Giorgio Scali and Tommaso Strozzi, who exerted excessive authority in the city, enjoyed with the plebs; and FH VI.24 recounts the violent insurrection of starving plebs in Milan during Francesco Sforza's efforts to take the city. Not all of these episodes (two of which I discussed in chapter 3) concern the behavior of the Florentine plebs; neither are they all Florentine examples. In any case, the only action, either plebeian or popular, that remotely approximates an atrocity is the Milanese example in which the plebs commit deadly violence against the city's magistrates (and against the Venetian ambassador who had falsely promised them relief). The extremity of this violence may be mitigated, for Machiavelli, by the fact that, as he recounts explicitly, the Milanese plebs were "starving to death in the streets"; clearly, this is not a mitigating factor for Strauss.

22. Strauss, *Thoughts on Machiavelli*, 263, emphasis added.

23. Strauss, *Thoughts on Machiavelli*, 235, emphasis added.

24. Machiavelli refers to the temporary insolence of the plebs at D I.55 and to their apparent insolence at FH III.17. He invokes the insolence of a particular set of plebeian tribunes at D III.33.

25. This is not numerology, it is basic arithmetic: see P 7; P 19 twice; D I.2; D I.3; D I.16; D I.18; FH I.16; FH II.11; FH II.12; FH II.22; FH II.39 twice; FH III.9; FH III.20; and FH IV.9.

26. Strauss, *Thoughts on Machiavelli*, 128.

27. Strauss, *Thoughts on Machiavelli*, 263, emphasis added.

28. Strauss, *Thoughts on Machiavelli*, 128–129.

29. Strauss, *Thoughts on Machiavelli*, 182.

30. Strauss, *Thoughts on Machiavelli*, 217.

31. Strauss, *Thoughts on Machiavelli*, 260.

32. Strauss, *Thoughts on Machiavelli*, 171.

33. Strauss, *Thoughts on Machiavelli*, 260.

34. Strauss, *Thoughts on Machiavelli*, 127.

35. Strauss, *Thoughts on Machiavelli*, 128.

36. Strauss, *Thoughts on Machiavelli*, 128.

37. Strauss, *Thoughts on Machiavelli*, 128, 129, emphases added.

38. Strauss is not quite so succinct here, but it is worth observing how he applies a Husserlian-Heideggerian hermeneutic method, in this case, to a political-philosophical issue: "Machiavelli had contended that the opinion of the people is likely to be right regarding particulars, whereas it is likely to be wrong regarding generalities; hence even if not only writers but the peoples themselves were to deny wisdom to the peoples, this verdict, being a judgment on something general, may well be wrong and yet the people may be wise in particular matters; in the very 58th chapter Machiavelli does not go beyond contending that the multitude or the people is marvelous in foreseeing its own evil and its own good, i.e., its particular good or evil here and now. Yet in the earlier discussion he had shown how easy it was for the Roman senate to deceive the people or the plebs in regard to particulars. Granted that the multitude possesses sound judgment on particulars, such judgment is of little value if the context within which the particular comes to sight is beyond the ken of the multitude: by changing the context one will change the meaning of the particular. And the generalities regarding which the people is admittedly incompetent are an important part of that context: sound judgment regarding particulars is impossible if it is not protected by true opinion about generalities." Strauss, *Thoughts on Machiavelli*, 128–129. The method employed here may be more Husserlian than Heideggerian: see Pierpaolo Ciccarelli, "Leo Strauss nell' 'aporia teologica-politica': Religione e politica in prospettiva fenomenologica," in G. Baptist, ed., *Sui presupposti di un nuovo umanesimo: Tra ragione, scienza e religione* (Milan: Mimesis, 2015), 241–258; Ciccarelli, "Politische Philosophie versus Geschichtsphilosophie: Leo Strauss' Interpretation von Husserls 'Philosophie als strenge Wissenschaft,'" in von V. Gerhardt, C. Kauffmann, H.-C. Kraus, F.-L. Kroll, P. Nitschke, H. Ottmann, M. P. Thompson, eds., *Jahrbuch Politisches Denken* 26 (Berlin: Duncker and Humblot, 2016), 1–20; and Ciccarelli, "Hobbes schmittiano o Schmitt hobbessiano? Sul 'cambio di orientamento' nelle 'Note a Carl Schmitt' di Leo Strauss," *Bollettino telematico di filosofia politica* (2017), 1–20. Whether the political motivations are in fact more Heideggerian than Husserlian remains an open question.

39. See Patrick J. Coby, *Machiavelli's Romans: Liberty and Greatness in the Discourses on Livy* (Lanham: Lexington Books, 1999), 81.

40. See Timothy J. Lukes, "Descending to the Particulars: The Palazzo, The Pi-

azza, and Machiavelli's Republican Modes and Orders," *Journal of Politics* 71, no. 2 (April 2009), 520–532.

41. Since three of Machiavelli's four examples on this issue involve a highly particular sphere of judgment—election of magistrates—Strauss can be said to denigrate particularity by extrapolating so far away from this specific particularity into the realm of generalities. Just as Strauss accused the people of being entirely incapable of judging particulars because they could not see how generalities frame the manner in which the particular "comes to sight," Strauss himself may be accused of misunderstanding Machiavelli's generalities because he does not consider how the very particular particulars in these circumstances inform the presentation of the general generality.

42. See, e.g., Strauss, *Thoughts on Machiavelli*, 13, 20, 30, 31, 36, 43, 47, 60, 79, 95, 104, 107, 108, 115, 117, 157, 137, 138, 158, 163, 221, 231, 236, 305, 307, 245.

43. Strauss, *Thoughts on Machiavelli*, 137.

44. Most Straussian accounts of Machiavelli's *Discourses*, and his political writings generally, tend to read his accounts of the few in an unwarrantedly favorable light. See, for example: Harvey C. Mansfield, *Machiavelli's Virtue* (Chicago: University of Chicago Press, 1996); Vickie B. Sullivan, *Machiavelli, Hobbes, and the Formation of a Liberal Republicanism in England* (Cambridge: Cambridge University Press, 2004); and Paul Anthony Rahe, *Against Throne and Altar: Machiavelli and Political Theory Under the English Republic* (Cambridge: Cambridge University Press, 2008). All gesture toward populist strains in the Florentine's writings; but all ultimately conclude that, for Machiavelli, it is the few or princes who do (or should) rule, even, or especially, in republics.

45. Strauss, *Thoughts on Machiavelli*, 190, 130, 132, 134. Strauss is unable to give a clear account of his own understanding of Machiavelli's nobility.

46. Strauss, *Thoughts on Machiavelli*, 129.

47. Strauss, *Thoughts on Machiavelli*, 259.

48. See John P. McCormick, *Machiavellian Democracy* (Cambridge: Cambridge University Press, 2011), 202, n. 31.

49. For example, while Machiavelli declares explicitly that, in all polities, the *grandi* are motivated by the insatiable desire to oppress (D I.4–5)—a fact which he demonstrates, time and again, through examples drawn from the actions of the Roman nobility (e.g., D I.6, I.39, I.44)—Strauss, again, transforms this motivation into the morally more palatable desire to attain glory: Machiavelli, according to Strauss, "deliberately ... makes the Roman ruling class 'better' than it was; he transforms a group whose best members, being perfectly free from all vulgar prejudices, were guided exclusively by Machiavellian prudence that served the insatiable desire of each for eternal glory in this world." See Strauss, *Thoughts on Machiavelli*, 134.

50. Strauss, *Thoughts on Machiavelli*, 129.

51. Strauss, *Thoughts on Machiavelli*, 129.

52. Strauss, *Thoughts on Machiavelli*, 47.

53. See McCormick, *Machiavellian Democracy*, 45, 79.

54. Strauss, *Thoughts on Machiavelli*, 127.

55. Mansfield avers that Machiavelli offers a far less "prosy" version of the "elite" theory of democracy that others would later conceptualize as the iron law of oligarchy. See Mansfield, *Machiavelli's Virtue*, 94. Whether or not this characterization actually applies to Machiavelli, on the basis of the above-cited remarks, it is fair to say that the elitism that Strauss himself attributes to the Florentine is more than slightly prosaic. Modern elite theorists of democracy, in any case, may not be as elitist as Mansfield thinks, or as Strauss reveals himself to be: see Natasha Piano, "Revisiting Democratic Elitism: Classical Elite Theory, Robert Dahl, and the Problem of Plutocracy," *Journal of Politics* (forthcoming 2018).

56. Strauss, *Thoughts on Machiavelli*, 127, 131.

57. Strauss, *Thoughts on Machiavelli*, 132.

58. Strauss, *Thoughts on Machiavelli*, 263.

59. Miguel E. Vatter effectively criticizes Straussian inattention to examples of collective popular action in Machiavelli's writings: see Vatter, *Between Form and Event: Machiavelli's Theory of Political Freedom* (London: Kluwer, 2000), 209, 221.

60. Strauss, *Thoughts on Machiavelli*, 206.

61. Strauss remarks on Virginius: "as long as Rome remained incorrupt, men like Virginius could never play the role which Savonarola played in Florence; the senate was there to undeceive the people." Strauss, *Thoughts on Machiavelli*, 206. But this assessment does not conform to Machiavelli's accounts of either Savonarola's or Virginius's demise in the *Discourses*. Neither was undone by a senate, but rather by popular defection prompted by their own actions: according to Machiavelli, both Savonarola and Virginius abrogated laws that they strenuously advocated through which the people, not leaders like Savonarola or Virginius, would decide the fate of citizens charged with capital crimes. Hence, they lost the confidence of the multitude (D I.45).

62. Although Machiavelli deems it better to have a virtuous commander than a virtuous army (in cases where a republic must do without one or the other), he does observe that a virtuous army can compensate for the poor leadership of an unworthy commander, because such an army is composed "of so many good heads" (D III.13).

63. Strauss, *Thoughts on Machiavelli*, 130.

64. Strauss, *Thoughts on Machiavelli*, 129–130, emphasis added.

65. Strauss, *Thoughts on Machiavelli*, 130.

66. Strauss considers the famous Machiavellian adage—princes found republics and peoples maintain them (D I.19, D I.58)—to be an exoteric, vulgar exposition and not Machiavelli's esoterically conveyed, more wise, considered view on the matter:

"The vulgar delusions regarding glory find their most important expressions in the vulgar reverence for the single founder, i.e., in the vulgar blindness to the fact that in every flourishing society foundation is so to speak continuous. The highest glory goes to men of the remote past who are vulgarly thought to be the greatest benefactors of mankind." Strauss, *Thoughts on Machiavelli*, 287–288; see also 168.

67. Strauss, *Thoughts on Machiavelli*, 32, 78, 166, 212, 216–217, 219.

68. Strauss, *Thoughts on Machiavelli*, 130.

69. Strauss, *Thoughts on Machiavelli*, 50.

70. Strauss, *Thoughts on Machiavelli*, 168.

71. Strauss, *Thoughts on Machiavelli*, 105, 170.

72. See H. C. Butters, *Governors and Government in Early Sixteenth-century Florence, 1502–1519* (Oxford: Oxford University Press, 1985), 163–164; and Melissa Meriam Bullard, *Filippo Strozzi and the Medici: Favor and Finance in Sixteenth-Century Florence and Rome* (Cambridge: Cambridge University Press, 2008), 64–65.

73. See I. F. Stone, *The Trial of Socrates* (New York: Little, Brown and Company, 1988), 121–123, 143–146.

74. The paradigmatic "sons of Brutus" in Livy and Machiavelli are perhaps, respectively, Caeso Qunictius and Corso Donati. See Livy, *History of Rome, II: Books 3–4* (Loeb Classical Library), trans. B. O. Foster (Cambridge, MA: Harvard University Press, 1922), III.11–15; Machiavelli, FH II.13–22.

75. See Lorenzo Violi, *Le Giornate*, G. C. Garfagnini, ed. (Florence: Olschki, 1986), 73–74; Pasquale Villari, *The Life and Times of Niccolò Machiavelli, Volume 1*, trans. L. Villari (Honolulu: University Press of the Pacific, 2004), 224–225; Michael Rocke, *Forbidden Friendships: Homosexuality and Male Culture in Renaissance Florence* (Oxford: Oxford University Press, 1996), 220–222.

76. Strauss, *Thoughts on Machiavelli*, 258.

77. Strauss, *Thoughts on Machiavelli*, 81.

78. Strauss, *Thoughts on Machiavelli*, 236.

79. Strauss, *Thoughts on Machiavelli*, 118.

80. Strauss, *Thoughts on Machiavelli*, 321, n. 108.

81. See McCormick, *Machiavellian Democracy*, 3–8, 26–28, 36–41.

82. See "Ai Palleschi" (1512), and "Discursus Florentinarum rerum post mortem iunioris Laurentii Medicis" (1519–20), in Machiavelli, *Opere I: I Primi Scritti Politici*, C. Vivanti, ed. (Turin: Einaudi-Gallimard, 1997), respectively, 87–89 and 733–745. English translations appear in M. Jurdjevic, N. Piano and J. P. McCormick, eds., *Florentine Political Writings from Petrarch to Machiavelli* (Philadelphia: University of Pennsylvania Press, forthcoming 2019).

83. Straussian scholars are notoriously skeptical of invocations of biographical and historical context as means of understanding texts of political philosophy. This would be a more acceptable methodological stance if they adhered to it consistently in their own hermeneutic endeavors; Straussians do, after all, draw upon biographi-

cal and historical context when it is convenient for their arguments. See, in the context of Florentine geopolitical affairs, Roger D. Masters, *Machiavelli, Leonardo, and the Science of Power* (South Bend: Notre Dame University Press, 1996). Straussian scholars engaging with Machiavelli's literary works also often invoke the Florentine historical context as it suits them. But overall such scholars never refer to the anti-aristocratic disposition and behavior that Machiavelli exhibited in Florentine domestic politics during the 1494–1512 republic. More reliable guides in this regard are: Jérémie Barthas, Robert Black, William Connell, Sebastian de Grazia, Felix Gilbert, Mark Hulliung, Mark Jurdjevic, Gabriele Pedullà, Fabio Raimondi, and especially John Najemy.

84. This is readily apparent in Strauss's elevation of medieval Jewish and Islamic engagements with Aristotle and, especially, Plato over Christian and Enlightenment ones: see Strauss, *Philosophy and Law: Contributions to the Understanding of Maimonides and His Predecessors* (1935), trans. E. Adler (Albany: SUNY Press, 2002), 57, 63–64, 85, 102–105, 119, 127.

Chapter 6. The Cambridge School's "Guicciardinian Moments" Revisited

1. See Pocock, *The Machiavellian Moment: Florentine Political Thought and the Atlantic Political Tradition* (Princeton: Princeton University Press 1975); and Skinner, *Liberty Before Liberalism* (Cambridge: Cambridge University Press 1998).

2. See Wilfried Nippel, *Mischverfassungstheorie und Verfassungsrealität in Antike and früher Neuzeit* (Stuttgart: Klett-Cotta, 1980) and Nippel, "Ancient and Modern Republicanism," in *The Invention of the Modern Republic*, Biancamaria Fontana, ed. (Cambridge: Cambridge University Press 1994), 6–26; as well as the essays in Anthony Molho, Kurt Raaflaub and Julia Emlen, eds., *City-States in Classical Antiquity and Medieval Italy* (Ann Arbor: University of Michigan Press, 1991).

3. For trenchant alternative critiques of Skinner's and Pocock's interpretations of Machiavelli: see Nicholas Buttle, "Republican Constitutionalism: A Roman Ideal," *Journal of Political Philosophy* 9, no. 3 (2001), 331–349; Daniel Kapust, "Skinner, Pettit, and Livy: The Conflict of the Orders and the Ambiguity of Republican Liberty," *History of Political Thought* 25, no. 3 (2004), 377–401; Mark Jurdjevic, "Machiavelli's Hybrid Republicanism," *The English Historical Review* 122, no. 499 (December 2007), 1228–1257; Marco Geuna, "Quentin Skinner e Machiavelli," in A. Arienzo and G. Borrelli, eds., *Anglo-American Faces of Machiavelli: Machiavelli e machiavellismi nella cultura anglo-americana*, vols. XVI–XX (Monza: Polimetrica 2009), 579–624; and Amanda Moure Maher, "What Skinner Misses About Machiavelli's Freedom: Inequality, Corruption and the Institutional Origins of Civic Virtue," *Journal of Politics* 78, no. 4 (October 2016), 1003–1015.

4. In this and other respects, the present chapter serves as a refinement and

elaboration of specific sections of McCormick, "Machiavelli Against 'Republican-ism': On the Cambridge School's 'Guicciardinian Moments,'" *Political Theory* 31, no. 5 (October 2003), 615–643.

5. On the methodological controversies generated by Pocock and Skinner, see: *The Languages of Political Theory in Early-Modern Europe*, Anthony Pagden, ed. (Cambridge: Cambridge University Press, 1987); *Meaning and Context: Quentin Skinner and His Critics*, James Tully, ed. (Princeton: Princeton University Press, 1989); *The Political Imagination in History: Essays Concerning J.G.A. Pocock*, D. N. DeLuna, ed. (Baltimore: Owlworks, 2006); and *Rethinking The Foundations of Modern Political Thought*, A. Brett, J. Tully and H. Hamilton-Bleakley, eds. (Cambridge: Cambridge University Press, 2007).

6. See Maurizio Viroli, *For Love of Country: An Essay on Patriotism and Nationalism* (Oxford: Oxford University Press. 1997); Quentin Skinner, *The Foundations of Modern Political Thought, Vol. 1: The Renaissance* (Cambridge: Cambridge University Press, 1978); J.G.A. Pocock, *Virtue, Commerce and History: Essays on Political Thought and History, Chiefly in the Eighteenth Century* (Cambridge: Cambridge University Press, 1985).

7. See Machiavelli, *Discorsi* [1513–17/1531], C. Vivanti, ed. (Turin: Einaudi-Gallimard, 1997), henceforth D; *Il Principe* (*De Principatibus*) [1513/1532], G. Inglese, ed. (Turin: Einaudi-Gallimard, 1995), henceforth P; and *Istorie Fiorentine* [1525], F. Gaeta, ed. (Milan: Feltrinelli, 1962), henceforth FH.

8. Pocock, *The Machiavellian Moment*, vii.

9. Pocock, *The Machiavellian Moment*, vii.

10. I am not the first to note the strongly existential aspect of Pocock's book. See Kari Palonen, *Das 'Webersche Moment' " Zur Kontingenz des Politischen* (Heidelberg: Springer, 1998).

11. Pocock, *The Machiavellian Moment*, 3.

12. See John P. McCormick, "Addressing the Political Exception: Machiavelli's 'Accidents' and the Mixed Regime," *American Political Science Review* 87, no. 4 (1993), 888–900; and McCormick, "Pocock, Machiavelli and Political Contingency in Foreign Affairs: Republican Existentialism Outside (and Within) the City," *History of European Ideas* 43, no. 2 (online June 2016).

13. Pocock, *The Machiavellian Moment*, 69, 73.

14. See Gene Brucker, *Florentine Politics and Society, 1343–1378* (Princeton: Princeton University Press, 1962); and John M. Najemy, *A History of Florence: 1200–1575* (Oxford: Blackwell, 2006).

15. Pocock, *The Machiavellian Moment*, 118–119.

16. Pocock, *The Machiavellian Moment*, 127.

17. Pocock, *The Machiavellian Moment*, 118.

18. Also known as *"Del Modo Di Ordinare Il Governo Popolare."* See Francesco

Guicciardini, *Dialogo e Discorsi del Reggimento di Firenze* (Bari: Laterza, 1931), R. Palmarocchi, ed., 218–259. An English translation appears in M. Jurdjevic, N. Piano, and J. P. McCormick, eds., *Florentine Political Writings from Petrarch to Machiavelli* (Philadelphia: University of Pennsylvania Press, forthcoming 2019).

19. Pocock, *The Machiavellian Moment*, 129.

20. Pocock, *The Machiavellian Moment*, 122, cf. 257.

21. Pocock, *The Machiavellian Moment*, 185–186.

22. McCormick, *Machiavellian Democracy*, chapter 2.

23. Pocock, *The Machiavellian Moment*, 212.

24. Pocock, *The Machiavellian Moment*, 212.

25. Pocock, *The Machiavellian Moment*, 232. See Francesco Guicciardini, *Dialogue on the Government of Florence* [1524], Alison Brown, ed. (Cambridge: Cambridge University Press, 1994).

26. Pocock, *The Machiavellian Moment*, 234.

27. Pocock, *The Machiavellian Moment*, 234.

28. Pocock, *The Machiavellian Moment*, 248.

29. Pocock, *The Machiavellian Moment*, 235.

30. Pocock, *The Machiavellian Moment*, 253.

31. Pocock, *The Machiavellian Moment*, 255.

32. Pocock, *The Machiavellian Moment*, 255.

33. Although this may be a much too hasty assessment of Schumpeter: see Natasha Piano, "'Schumpeterianism' Revised: The Critique of Elites in *Capitalism, Socialism and Democracy*," *Critical Review* (forthcoming 2018).

34. Pocock, *The Machiavellian Moment*, 255.

35. Pocock, *The Machiavellian Moment*, 253.

36. Pocock, *The Machiavellian Moment*, 485.

37. Pocock, *The Machiavellian Moment*, 156.

38. Pocock, *The Machiavellian Moment*, 183.

39. Pocock, *The Machiavellian Moment*, e.g., 237, 251.

40. Pocock, *The Machiavellian Moment*, 155.

41. Pocock, *The Machiavellian Moment*, 503.

42. Pocock, *The Machiavellian Moment*, 207–211.

43. Skinner authored one of the most trenchant criticisms of postwar democratic theory, one that seeks to mediate between empirical and normative, elitist and substantive approaches: see Skinner, "The Empirical Theorists of Democracy and Their Critics: A Plague on Both Their Houses," *Political Theory* 1, no. 3 (1973), 287–305.

44. Skinner, *Liberty Before Liberalism*, 32.

45. Skinner attributes the neo-Roman conception of liberty to both Machiavelli and his Florentine antecedents and contemporaries in a rather unqualified way: Roman liberty, according to Skinner, was revived "by the defenders of republican

libertà in the Italian Renaissance, above all by Machiavelli in his *Discorsi* on Livy's history of Rome." Skinner, *Liberty Before Liberalism*, 10.

46. Skinner, "Machiavelli's *Discorsi* and the Pre-Humanist Origins of Republican Ideas," in *Machiavelli and Republicanism*, Gisela Bock, Quentin Skinner and Maurizio Viroli, eds. (Cambridge: Cambridge University Press 1990), 121–141, at 123.

47. Skinner, "Machiavelli's *Discorsi*," 137.

48. Skinner, "Machiavelli's *Discorsi*," 136. I have found the following critical engagements with Cicero's political thought to have been especially helpful and enlightening for thinking about neo-Roman republicanism and Skinner's efforts to affiliate Machiavelli with that tradition: Marcia L. Colish, "Cicero's *De officiis* and Machiavelli's *Prince*," *Sixteenth Century Journal* 9 (1978), 81–93; Michelle Zerba "The Frauds of Humanism: Cicero, Machiavelli, and the Rhetoric of Imposture," *Rhetorica* 22, no. 3 (2004), 215–240; Joy Connolly, *The State of Speech: Rhetoric and Political Thought in Ancient Rome* (Princeton: Princeton University Press, 2007); Daniel J. Kapust, *Republicanism, Rhetoric, and Roman Political Thought: Sallust, Livy, and Tacitus* (Cambridge: Cambridge University Press, 2014); and Gary A. Remer, *Ethics and the Orator: The Ciceronian Tradition of Political Morality* (Chicago: University Of Chicago Press, 2017).

49. Skinner, *Past Masters: Machiavelli* (New York: Hill and Wang, 1981), 65–66; Skinner, "Machiavelli's *Discorsi*," 130, 136.

50. Skinner, "Machiavelli's *Discorsi*," 137. See also Skinner, *Past Masters: Machiavelli*, 25, 36, 64; and Skinner, *Visions of Politics, Vol. II: Renaissance Virtues* (Cambridge: Cambridge University Press 2002), 207–209.

51. Skinner, "Machiavelli's *Discorsi*," 140. Skinner's less influential but not inconsequential protégé Maurizio Viroli concurs with his teacher's claim that Machiavelli's political thought ultimately accords with the principles and practices of "humanist and Ciceronian" republicanism. See Viroli, "Machiavelli and the Republican Idea of Politics," in *Machiavelli and Republicanism*, 143–171, at 157 and 154.

52. Pocock concedes that Skinner is correct in charging that he overemphasizes Aristotle at the expense of Cicero in his discussion of Florentine political thought; but he also observes that Machiavelli's thought cannot be assimilated to Cicero's as easily as Skinner insists: see Pocock, "Afterword," in *The Machiavellian Moment*, 2nd ed. (Princeton: Princeton University Press, 2003), 553–584, at 558. Richard Tuck recognizes that Machiavelli jettisoned many important strains of Cicero's thought, especially those that overlapped with Seneca's stoicism. However, he insists that the Florentine's political thought still retained important Ciceronian elements, particularly those pertaining to the security of the republic and the not exclusively moral character of virtue. See Tuck, *Philosophy and Government, 1572–1651* (Cambridge: Cambridge University Press, 1993), 20–21.

53. See Danielle Charette, "Catilinarian Cadences in Machiavelli's *Florentine His-*

tories: Ciceronian Humanism, Corrupting Consensus and the Demise of Contentious Liberty," *History of Political Thought* (forthcoming 2018).

54. Skinner, *The Foundations of Modern Political Thought*, 69–84.

55. Skinner, "Machiavelli's *Discorsi*," 122.

56. Skinner, "Machiavelli's *Discorsi*," 125, 132–133, 140. Viroli, faithfully following Skinner, emphasizes the primary roles that elections and mixed government played in traditional republicanism: Italian republics were characterized, in Viroli's words, by "the rule of *elective magistrates* with limited tenure appointed by the sovereign body of the citizens"; and such republics were instantiated in an institutional paradigm that "wisely combines the virtues of *monarchy, aristocracy and popular government*." On these issues, Viroli asserts, Machiavelli was, again, "in full agreement with the tradition." See Viroli, *Founders: Machiavelli* (Oxford: Oxford University Press, 1998), 117 and 121, emphases added.

57. See John M. Najemy, *Corporatism and Consensus in Florentine Electoral Politics, 1280–1400* (Chapel Hill: University of North Carolina Press, 1982).

58. Skinner, "Machiavelli's *Discorsi*," 141. Viroli also largely ignores Machiavelli's unqualified endorsement of the plebeian tribunate, mentioning the institution only in passing: see Viroli, "Machiavelli and the Republican Idea," 167. Instead, Viroli, recounts how, like Cicero, Machiavelli preferred the best and most virtuous citizens to hold magistracies, writing out of Machiavelli's analysis the crucial distinction between consular and tribunician, patrician and plebeian offices. See Viroli, "Machiavelli and the Republican Idea," 155.

59. Skinner, *Visions of Politics, Vol. II*, 210–211.

60. Skinner, *Liberty Before Liberalism*, 49, emphases added.

61. Skinner, *Liberty Before Liberalism*, 32.

62. Skinner, *Liberty Before Liberalism*, 31–32.

63. See Skinner, *Visions of Politics, Vol. II*, 197–198.

64. See Marcia L. Colish, "The Idea of Liberty in Machiavelli," *Journal of the History of Ideas* 32 (1971), 323–350; and Elena Fasano Guarini, "Machiavelli and the Crisis of the Italian Republics," in *Machiavelli and Republicanism*, 17–40.

65. Skinner, *Visions of Politics, Vol. II*, 198. More broadly, this account of liberty is congruent with Philip Pettit's "republican" theory of "freedom as non-domination." See Pettit, *Republicanism: A Theory of Freedom and Government* (Oxford: Oxford University Press, 1999); and Pettit, *On the People's Terms: A Republican Theory and Model of Democracy* (Cambridge: Cambridge University Press, 2013).

66. Skinner, *Visions of Politics, Vol. II*, 211, 196.

67. For instance, Skinner sometimes accurately conveys Machiavelli's view that the people generally are inclined to enjoy and protect civic liberty while the nobles are mostly inclined to undermine or destroy it (see Skinner, *Visions, Vol. II*, 162); while he usually insists that Machiavelli views the two humors or "outlooks" as

equally threatening to liberty: the people and the nobles, Skinner writes, "will *at all times* seek to promote its own advantage unless restrained," since they are each merely "factions" inclined toward governing "purely in its own interests" (Skinner, *Visions, Vol. II*, 156–157, emphasis added).

68. See John P. McCormick, *Machiavellian Democracy* (Cambridge: Cambridge University Press, 2011), chapters 3, 4 and 5; as well as chapter 2 of the present study.

69. Skinner, *Visions of Politics, Vol. II*, 210–211.

70. See Polybius, *The Histories* (London: Penguin, 1979), VI. 5–9. See also Harvey C. Mansfield, *Machiavelli's New Modes and Orders: A Study of the Discourses on Livy* (Ithaca: Cornell University Press, 1979), 33–40.

71. See chapter 2 above, as well as McCormick, "Tempering the *Grandi's* Appetite to Oppress: The Dedication and Intention of Machiavelli's *Discourses*," in Victoria Kahn et al., eds., *Politics and the Passions, 1500–1789* (Princeton: Princeton University Press, 2006), 7–29.

72. For an intriguing interpretation of Machiavellian equilibrium that distinguishes a "mixing" from a "balancing" of social classes within his political thought, see Fabio Raimondi, *Constituting Freedom: Machiavelli and Florence* (Oxford: Oxford University Press, 2018).

73. Skinner, "Machiavelli and the Maintenance of Liberty," *Politics* 18, no. 2 (1983), 3–15, at 10–13. See Maher, "What Skinner Misses About Machiavelli's Freedom."

74. Compare Machiavelli on "mankind generally" and "the people generally" in *The Prince* (P 17 versus P 9 and P 19).

75. See Machiavelli, "Proemio," in *Istorie Fiorentine* [1520–25/1532], Franco Gaeta, ed. (Milan: Feltrinelli, 1962); and Gisela Bock, "Civil Discord in Machiavelli's *Istorie Fiorentine*," in *Machiavelli and Republicanism*, 181–201.

76. Skinner, *Past Masters: Machiavelli*, 66. However, no Cambridge School scholar goes to greater lengths than Maurizio Viroli to make the people seem worse and the nobles seem better than they are actually presented in Machiavelli's writings. In chapter 3, I listed Viroli among the many interpreters who inappropriately insist that Machiavelli, in his historical and constitutional writings on Florence, blames the people as much as he does the nobles for behavior that threatens and undermines liberty. See, for instance, Viroli, *Founders*, 125–126. Yet, Viroli goes even further in distorting Machiavelli's texts to make the nobles seem less inclined toward oppression than Machiavelli himself declares. For instance, in the "Discursus on Florentine Affairs," Machiavelli recommends the establishment of a life-tenured "signorial" class of *ottimati*, who would rotate terms as priors in Florence's *Signoria*. Viroli asserts that Machiavelli's recommendation here is intended, in good Ciceronian fashion, to rightfully accommodate Florence's "wisest and most honoured citizens." See Viroli, "Machiavelli and the Republican Idea," 155. In fact, Machiavelli proposes this institution, he insists, due to the necessity of mollifying Florence's most ambitious, prideful

and condescending citizens: as Machiavelli identifies them explicitly, men of "haughty spirit" (*animo elevato*), powerful citizens who "think they deserve precedence before all others" (*pare loro meritare di procedere agli altri*). See Machiavelli, "Discursus," 738. Viroli ignores this passage, instead focusing on one where Machiavelli mentions "grave and reputed men" (*uomini gravi e di reputazione*), which Viroli conveniently mistranslates as "wisest and most honoured citizens," and which he glosses extravagantly as Machiavelli's invocation of the republic's "best men." See Viroli, "Machiavelli and the Republican Idea," 155.

77. See Cicero, *On the Commonwealth and On the Laws*, ed. James Zetzel (Cambridge: Cambridge University Press, 1999), 19–23; Polybius, *Histories*, 317–318.

78. Michael Hörnqvist sets forth an especially inflexible Cambridge-inspired reading of Machiavelli's model of mixed government in *Machiavelli and Empire* (Cambridge: Cambridge University Press, 2004). For a reliable corrective of Hörnqvist's excesses on political matters both domestic and external, see Alissa M. Ardito, *Machiavelli and the Modern State: The Prince, the Discourses on Livy, and the Extended Territorial Republic* (Cambridge: Cambridge University Press, 2015). Viroli also severely understates Machiavelli's novelty when he expressly assimilates the Florentine's idea of "well-ordered popular government" to Cicero's conception of the mixed regime, according to which "each component of the city has its proper place." Viroli, *Founders*, 125. As I have argued, Cicero and Machiavelli differ dramatically on what constitutes the people's "proper place" in their respective models of a well-ordered regime. See also Viroli, "Machiavelli and the Republican Idea," 154–155.

79. For examples of many of Machiavelli's departures from Livy, see Mansfield, *Machiavelli's New Modes and Orders*.

80. For a comprehensive critique of Skinner's treatment of Machiavelli's theory of class conflict, see Gabriele Pedullà, *Machiavelli in Tumult: The Discourses on Livy and the Origins of Conflictual Politics* (Cambridge University Press, forthcoming 2018).

81. Skinner, *Past Masters: Machiavelli*, 71–72.

82. See Skinner, *Visions, Vol. II*, 156. According to Skinner, Machiavelli argues "that, under their republican constitution, [the Romans] had one assembly controlled by the nobility, another by the common people, with the consent of each being required for any proposal to become law. Each group admittedly tended to produce proposals designed merely to further its own interests. But each was prevented by the other from imposing them as laws. The result was that only such proposals as favoured no faction could ever hope to succeed. The laws relating to the constitution thus served to ensure that the common good was promoted at all times." Skinner, "The Republican Ideal of Political Liberty," in *Machiavelli and Republicanism*, 293–309, at 306.

83. Skinner declares, in partial repudiation of his earlier methodological work, that "intellectual historians can hope to produce something of far more than antiquarian interest" for contemporary politics when conducting their scholarly endeavors. Skinner, *Liberty Before Liberalism*, 118.

84. Skinner, *Liberty Before Liberalism*, especially 108, 110–112.

85. Skinner, *Liberty Before Liberalism*, 11, n. 31; 55, n. 174; 56, n. 176.

86. Skinner, *Liberty Before Liberalism*, 54.

87. Skinner, "Machiavelli and the Maintenance of Liberty," *Politics* 18, no. 2 (1983), 3–15, at 13, n. 9.

88. Skinner, *Liberty Before Liberalism*, ix–x. Judith Shklar's "liberalism of fear" would seem to be an obvious example of a liberal theory not concerned narrowly with injustices associated with direct interference, as such: see Shklar, "The Liberalism of Fear," in Nancy L. Rosenblum, ed., *Liberalism and the Moral Life* (Cambridge, MA: Harvard University Press, 1989), 21–38.

89. Skinner writes: "It remains to ask what Machiavelli means by speaking not merely of individuals but of communities as living, or not living, a free way of life. The short answer is that he means the same in both cases." Skinner, *Visions of Politics, Vol. II*, 198.

90. Skinner, *Liberty Before Liberalism*, 17.

91. Skinner, *Liberty Before Liberalism*, 37.

92. In an intriguing footnote, Skinner notes how "strikingly prominent" is the language of Roman liberty in Marx's analysis of capitalist sociopolitical relations. Skinner, *Liberty Before Liberalism*, x, n. 3. This insight has subsequently been taken up by scholars such as: William Clare Roberts, *Marx's Inferno: The Political Theory of Capital* (Princeton: Princeton University Press, 2016); and Bruno Leipold, "Citizen Marx: The Relationship Between Karl Marx and Republicanism" (PhD Dissertation, Politics Department, Oxford University, October 2017).

93. When speaking about "a conflict within our inherited traditions of thought about the character of the liberal state," Skinner observes: "Both parties to the dispute agree that one of the primary aims of the state should be to respect and preserve the liberty of its individual citizens. One side argues that the state can hope to redeem this pledge simply by ensuring that its citizens do not suffer any unjust or unnecessary interference in the pursuit of their chosen goals. But the other side maintains that this can never be sufficient, since it will always be necessary for the state to ensure at the same time that its citizens do not fall into a condition of avoidable dependence on the goodwill of others." See Skinner, *Liberty Before Liberalism*, 119. Machiavelli is even more partial to the latter view than Skinner seems aware or willing to countenance.

94. Skinner summarizes, on the basis of his authors' deep distrust of the people, their constitutional prescription in this way: "The right solution, they generally

agree, is for the mass of the people to be represented by a national assembly of the more virtuous and considering, an assembly chosen by the people to legislate on their behalf." Skinner, *Liberty Before Liberalism*, 32.

95. Skinner, "The Republican Ideal of Political Liberty," 293–309, at 303–304, emphases added.

96. See McCormick, *Machiavellian Democracy*, chapter 7.

97. Pocock, "Afterword," 582.

98. Skinner, "The Republican Ideal of Political Liberty," 308–309.

99. See John P. McCormick, "The New Ochlophobia? Populism, Majority Rule and Prospects for Democratic Republicanism," in Yiftah Elazar and Geneviève Rousselière, eds., *Republican Democracy* (Cambridge: Cambridge University Press, forthcoming 2018).

ACKNOWLEDGMENTS

MY DEEPEST SCHOLARLY DEBT is owed to the following individuals who carefully read the entire manuscript, generously provided me with detailed criticisms of each chapter, and perspicaciously indicated ways to integrate them into a more cohesive book: Dan Kapust, Steven Klein, Yves Winter, and, most especially, Mark Jurdjevic and Natasha Piano. Insights offered by the following scholars, colleagues, friends, and students greatly improved one or more of the book's chapters: Jordan Appel, Gordon Arlen, David Armitage, Jérémie Barthas, Richard Bellamy, Yuna Blajer de la Garza, Danielle Charette, Julie Cooper, Chiara Destri, Mary Dietz, Marco Geuna, Robert Gooding-Williams, Alex Gourevitch, Kinch Hoekstra, Vicky Kahn, Deme Kasimis, Melissa Lane, Nomi Claire Lazar, Christopher Lynch, Amanda Moure Maher, Chris Meckstroth, Thomas Meyer, Sankar Muthu, Karma Nabulsi, John Najemy, Gabriele Pedullà, Philip Pettit, Jennifer Pitts, Ellen Rabin, Fabio Raimondi, Geneviève Rousselière, Giorgio Scichilone, Melissa Schwartzberg, Jake Soll, Jason Swadley, Nathan Tarcov, Camila Vergara, Stefano Visentin, David Lay Williams, and James Wilson. For over fifteen years, Quentin Skinner has entertained our differences of opinion, both privately and in public, with characteristic poise and magnanimity.

Much earlier and less refined versions of sections and chapters of the book previously appeared in the journals *Political Theory* (2003), *Critical Review of International Social and Political Philosophy* (2007), *Global Crime* (2009), *Representations* (2011), the *Cardozo Law Review* (2013), and *Social Research* (2014); moreover, an abridged version of chapter 3 appeared in *Liberty and Conflict*, N. Urbinati, D. Johnston, and C. Vergara, eds. (2017). I gratefully acknowledge the publishers of these journals (Sage Publications, Taylor and Francis, the University of California Press, Yeshiva University, and Johns Hopkins University Press) as well as the edited volume (University of Chicago Press). Research for this project was supported by the Rockefeller Foundation, which sponsored a pleasurable and productive residence at the Bellagio Center in Italy, April 2013, and the National Endowment for the Humanities, which generously awarded me a grant for the 2017–18 academic year, enabling me to complete the book.

Britnei Clarke, Zully Bosques, and Rebecca Zellelew provided indispensably reliable, expert, and affectionate childcare, for which I am exceedingly grateful.

After many years of discussing, over drinks at various locations across North America, other people's book projects with Rob Tempio of Princeton University Press, I am delighted to finally benefit, myself, from his astute and erudite editorial stewardship. I am deeply indebted to Rob for his painstaking efforts on behalf of this project; as I am to Matt Rohal and Jill Harris for attentive and skillful editorial assistance and to Lynn Worth for copyediting work of astonishing quality.

The book is dedicated to Alyssa Anne Qualls, who did more than anyone else to make it possible, as she makes possible nearly everything worthwhile in my life. Alyssa would be embarrassed, out of modesty (although not nearly as embarrassed as I'd be, out of shame), were I to list the many sacrifices that she graciously made in tending to our children, caring for me, and generally keeping our family going during the book's composition and completion—while still, astoundingly, maintaining her own high-powered career. All I can say is thank you for your continued, inexhaustible support, patience, and love.

Chicago
May 2018

INDEX

A NOTE ON THE TYPE

This book has been composed in Arno, an Old-style serif typeface in the classic Venetian tradition, designed by Robert Slimbach at Adobe.